OUT OF EDEN

OUT OF EDEN

Adam and Eve and the Problem of Evil

■ ■ ■ ■

Paul W. Kahn

PRINCETON UNIVERSITY PRESS

Princeton and Oxford

Copyright © 2007 by Princeton University Press
Published by Princeton University Press,
41 William Street, Princeton, New Jersey 08540
In the United Kingdom: Princeton University Press,
3 Market Place, Woodstock, Oxfordshire OX20 1SY
All Rights Reserved

Kahn, Paul W., 1952–
Out of Eden : Adam and Eve and the problem of evil / Paul W. Kahn.
p.   cm.
ISBN-13: 978-0-691-12693-7 (hardcover : alk. paper)
ISBN-10: 0-691-12693-3 (hardcover : alk. paper)
1. Good and evil. I. Title.
BJ1401.K34   2007
170—dc22   2006015864

British Library Cataloging-in-Publication Data is available

This book has been composed in Sabon and Copperplate display

Printed on acid-free paper. ∞

pup.princeton.edu

Printed in the United States of America

1   3   5   7   9   10   8   6   4   2

CONTENTS

ACKNOWLEDGMENTS

It is difficult to thank people for teaching me about evil. In this book, however, I argue that evil and love are bound to each other, and that we find evil where we find love. To learn about evil, I have studied the pathology of love. I hope that this has not made me bad company to family and friends. I am fortunate in knowing that no amount of interest in evil could threaten the love that sustains my world. For that, I am most grateful.

Of course, I have also had help with theory and text. My first ideas about evil were formed in a seminar I taught at the Yale Law School in 2000. To the diverse group of students in that class, I owe a special debt. In the summer of 2005, the entire manuscript was critiqued by a powerful group of young scholars in an interdisciplinary seminar on law, politics, and theology sponsored by the National Humanities Center and the Berlin Wissenschaftskolleg. These two seminars represented the beginning and end of the process of writing this book, and I owe much to all who were involved. Several friends and colleagues reviewed the entire manuscript, providing many valuable suggestions. In particular, I thank David Luban, Bruce Ackerman, Benjamin Berger, Tico Taussig, Max Kohn, and Ulrich Haltern. Adam Romero helped to get the manuscript in final shape. As with each of my books, Barbara Mianzo kept the whole process moving smoothly. Finally, I acknowledge the institutional support of the Yale Law School, which has made it possible for me to pursue my ideas wherever they may lead me.

OUT OF EDEN

■　　■　　■　　■

THE STUDY OF EVIL

Evil makes us human. We learn this early in *Genesis*, when Adam and Eve are cast out of Eden because they chose to do wrong. *Genesis* tells us that not only ourselves but our world is a consequence of evil: "Cursed be the ground because of you." Finding ourselves fallen, we cannot be at ease: "For dust you are, and to dust you shall return." Nor can we be satisfied with our achievements, for labor is our punishment. If evil brought us to where we are, then the Western religious tradition tells us that our essential task as individuals and communities is to overcome the evil in our nature. We want to return to that "image of God" that we were at creation. We must recover Eden.

Fall and redemption have offered more than a religious frame of reference. These concepts shaped the Western imagination. They offered the frame through which philosophers, theologians, and political leaders, as well ordinary people, understood themselves, their communities, and their relationship to the larger world.[1] Evil and redemption gave meaning to life and death. Without the concept of evil, individuals would not have approached themselves with the same sense of urgency, a sense that their lives are the scene of a great moral battle in which literally everything is at stake.

Today, all this may be changing. Outside of fundamentalist religious groups, there is a reluctance to appeal to the idea of evil. In place of evil, contemporary human sciences examine the social causes of pathology, while postmodernists speak of a need to respect cultural differences. In place of redemption, we are counseled by experts on the need for therapeutic interventions in the lives of individuals and

---

[1] For example, Susan Nieman recently argued that the history of modern philosophy can best be understood as an inquiry into theodicy—the problem of understanding why an omnipotent God allows evil to inhabit our world. S. Nieman, *Evil in Modern Thought: An Alternative History of Philosophy* (2002).

societies. If such remedies fail, there is a turn to law enforcement.[2] But even here there is a fear that the language of evil is more likely to lead to abuse of authority than to efficient and humane policing.

The turn away from the category of evil is a part of the "disenchanted" character of the contemporary world. This has nothing to do with a change in behavior. Man's capacity for atrocious behavior—including hatred, murder, genocide, and torture—continues. Nor have we become blind to the terrible things that individuals and societies do to each other. We continue to distinguish good behavior from bad; we theorize about the nature of justice and injustice. But the distinction between good and bad acts is not the same as that between good and evil. We can identify plenty of injustices in our own political order, but it does not follow that we consider our society evil. Similarly, for the individual, bad choices and bad behavior are not necessarily evil. An evil person is not simply one with a propensity for bad acts; nor is everyone who has committed many bad acts evil. One can be self-destructive without being evil; one can be deficient in one's moral obligations toward others without being evil. Certainly, one can lack civility and yet not be evil.

Of course, evil individuals or societies usually exhibit bad and unjust behavior, but their character as evil is not reducible to these acts or to the propensity to perform them. Something broader and deeper is at stake in the concept of evil—not just a category of behavior, a personality defect, or a political practice but rather a way of being in the world. My aim in this book is first to inquire into what was at stake in the religious conception of evil within the Western tradition, and then to offer a secular interpretation of this conception. I hope to make evil available as a compelling category for contemporary thought. To do so requires an exploration of the genealogy of the concept. While bad or even terrible actions are universal, not every culture has available to it a conception of evil. More is at stake than the form

---

[2] Karl Rove, President George W. Bush's political adviser, deftly captured this set of attitudes—and turned it to partisan political purposes—in his widely reported comment: "Conservatives saw the savagery of 9/11 . . . and prepared for war; liberals saw the savagery of the 9/11 attack and wanted to prepare indictments and offer therapy and understanding for our attackers." See P. Healy, "Rove Criticizes Liberals on 9/11," *N.Y. Times*, June 23, 2005, at A13.

of explanation of bad actions. The absence of the category signifies not just a difference in the understanding of the relationship of man to the world but also a difference in the relationship itself. Who we are is inevitably a function of who we think we are.

The classical Greeks did not have the concept of evil; for Christians, evil is the central category of human existence. In chapter 1, I explore this difference. In chapter 2, I trace the evolving character of the conception of evil in the Judeo-Christian tradition. In the remaining chapters I argue that the conception of evil that emerges from this religious tradition remains critically important to understanding the secular world of family, group, and polity within which we live our lives.

My central argument is that evil does not appear in classical thought because the Greeks lacked a conception of the will. The Judeo-Christian tradition, on the other hand, puts the will at the center of its idea of the human. Where the Greeks saw the problem of man's relationship to the world and to each other as one of meeting—or failing to meet—the demands of reason, once a conception of the will emerges, that relationship is reconceived as one of love. God and men now exist in reciprocal relationships of love. Evil, I argue, is the pathology of the will; it is love gone wrong. Contemporary theory fails to grasp evil, because it measures behavior against the standards of reason, not will. To understand ourselves and the problems we confront, we must stop thinking only of good and bad—or, even worse, of same and different—and recover again an understanding of love and evil. In *Putting Liberalism in Its Place*, I offered an account of politics that put love and sacrifice at its center. Here I am completing the inquiry into the contemporary character of a will that is bound by love and evil. Together these two volumes offer a political theology of modernity.[3]

Confronting the problem of evil, early modern thinkers such as Pierre Bayle, questioned the idea of an omnipotent creator, God. If this world is the product of divine creation, then either God is not omnipotent or He is not good. There is too much evil in the world to reach any other conclusion. Bayle's answer was to turn to Manichae-

---

[3] The need for a modern political theology was noted by Clifford Geertz some time ago. C. Geertz, *Local Knowledge: Further Essays in Interpretive Anthropology* 121, 143 (1983).

ism—the doctrine that the principles of good and evil are coequal sources of the world—as "the most reasonable response to experience."[4] Manichaeism captures the sense that evil is so basic to our experience that it must itself be a first principle. It is the practical output of a failure of metaphysical dimensions.

Bayle's quandary shows us that evil will not appear if the categories we deploy are one-dimensional—whether that single dimension is the goodness of God or the modern liberal's appeal to reason. For example, evil makes no appearance in science, because scientific explanations aim to give causal accounts of phenomena. That the sun will die and the earth is doomed is not evil if it is simply the consequence of a causal chain that marks the birth and death of stars. Similarly, in the biblical account, as long as creation is the product of God's effort alone, evil makes no appearance. God's judgment that creation is "good" is not a contingent judgment expressing the success of his world-making technique. Rather, being and goodness are one and the same in a world that expresses nothing other than the godhead itself. Evil appears in the biblical account when humans act. To explain that action, we need to appeal to something other than the goodness of creation. We need the faculty of the will.

Will is distinct from reason or desire. In Jewish thought it is the faculty that corresponds to the possibility of the covenant. In Christian thought it is the faculty that corresponds to—and receives—divine grace. In both cases, will's domain is that of faith. For moderns, it is the faculty of the soul that has the capacity for love. After all, we cannot reason ourselves to love, and surely we distinguish love from mere desire.[5] Evil, western religious tradition tells us, is a problem of the will. But we go wrong if we think that the problem is that of a will not shaped by reason. Rather, the pathologies of the will begin with the loss or misdirection of faith.

Faith connects will to a source of ultimate meaning outside the self: covenant, grace, beloved. The problem of evil arises when the will insists that it is the source of its own meaning. Adam and Eve would

---

[4] Nieman, *Evil in Modern Thought* 21.

[5] On the faculty of will and its relationship to love, see P. Kahn, *Putting Liberalism in Its Place* 222–27 (2005).

be "like divine beings": that is, they would be dependent upon nothing outside themselves. In the mythical frame, such a being is one that never dies. The Serpent assures Eve, "You are not going to die." With recognition of dependence comes the imagining of one's own death. Having eaten, Adam and Eve learn that they will indeed die. The locus of evil, I argue, is in the refusal to recognize the possibility of one's own death.

Evil shows itself in different acts—political and individual—but their common source is the flight from recognition of mortality. Refusing to recognize one's own finitude, death is projected on to an other. Thus the paradigm of evil is the murderer who claims the power of life and death: he will live, and the other will die. Denying his own death, the evil actor denies that he is a part of nature or, at least, that part of nature occupied by fallen man. In the language of the Genesis myth, he is "ashamed" of his nature.[6] The victim, the slave, the tortured are all identified with what I call the "shame of nature."

Evil is at the center of Judeo-Christian thought, because will, not reason, is at the center of Judeo-Christian metaphysics. Focusing on the will, however, is not a direction in which our modern liberal culture cares to go.[7] When we do see recourse to an idea of the will, it is in the form of "willfulness," meaning a certain recalcitrance toward the demands of reason. Willfulness is a problem to be met by education: the willful child needs the reasonable guidance of a parent or teacher. A politics of willfulness requires that institutional structures cultivating social habits of moderation be built into the constitutional order. Because modern thought is committed to the idea that reason can structure political order and discern personal moral obligation, it must conceive of the will in a way that makes it fully subordinate to reason. A will cured of willfulness has nothing to say. Or, more accurately, it says only what reason tells it to say. This is the language of the will behind the Rawlsian veil of ignorance: it lacks any particularity, speaking only in the universal idiom of reason.[8]

---

[6] As I explain, the Adam and Eve myth is actually two distinct myths with two distinct representations of man's nature. One I refer to as the "image of God" and the other as the "shame of nature."

[7] The failure of liberalism to develop an adequate conception of the will is at the center of my critique in *Putting Liberalism in Its Place*.

[8] See J. Rawls, *A Theory of Justice* 136–42 (1971).

In the Judeo-Christian tradition, knowledge is the problem from which the human condition begins: it was eating of the tree of knowledge that condemned man to a life of labor outside the Garden. Knowledge is not the answer but rather the source of the problem of human existence. The object of reason may be truth, but truth without faith will not redeem man. For the Greeks, on the other hand, knowledge is the goal to be obtained. Even for Plato, who developed a myth of perfect knowledge prior to birth, the mythical idea of recovery grounds a forward-looking process of rational inquiry. In Aristotle's thought, too, that state in which knowledge and being are one and the same is the final cause or end of all existence.

The secularization of modern experience reflects a similar turn to knowledge and reason. The consequence is that our ways of thinking are not adequate to our experience of evil. Economics is the paradigm of contemporary forms of explanation, and there is no evil in economics; there are only differences in tastes. Classical thought and modern liberalism share a common orientation to justice. For both, this is a product of a deep commitment to reason. Both traditions believe that philosophical inquiry is an extension of those everyday discursive practices that should control and structure political and psychological order. This was given visible form in the agora—Socrates' domain. It is expressed as a methodological principle in Rawls's pursuit of a "reflective equilibrium"—testing philosophical principle against practical intuition and vice versa.[9] There is a seamless movement from pedagogy to psychology to politics to philosophy. Evil does not appear in that process. The problem of evil is displaced by the problem of political and social formation, on the one hand, and individual formation, on the other.

For contemporary liberal thought, political and moral failure should be addressed by reform, which is always a matter of identifying and correcting points of irrationality.[10] Those who do wrong are like

---

[9] *Id.* 48–51.

[10] On reason and reform, see P. Kahn, *The Cultural Study of Law* 8 (1999). Early in American political life, George Washington writes of the fortuity that our history begins in an age in which political science has been fully developed: "The foundation of our Empire was not laid in the gloomy age of Ignorance and Superstition, but at an Epocha when the rights of mankind were better understood and more clearly defined . . . the researches of the human mind, after social happiness, have been carried to a great extent, the Treasures of knowledge . . . may be happily applied in the Establishment of our forms of Government." Circular Letter of Farewell to the Army, June 8, 1783. Similarly, the rise of the administra-

children who do not listen to their teachers or like those who fail to apply moral lessons to themselves. They lack self-control; they allow their desires to get the better of their long-term interests; they are mistaken in their beliefs about right and wrong. Nowhere do we encounter evil as an equal and opposite force in the world. Instead, in the liberal polity we encounter an endless concern with the processes required for reason to rule and with pedagogy. These come together in that modern genre of work that focuses on democratic education, on the one hand, and understands democratic politics as educational, on the other.[11]

Even the most well-known account of evil under the conditions of modernity, Hannah Arendt's report on the Eichmann trial, shares this general outlook.[12] Like her teacher, Heidegger, Arendt lacks the general faith in reason characteristic of liberal political and moral theory. Indeed, her account of the possibility of the evil of the German state relies in part on the rise of a bureaucratic, administrative rationality. That rationality is not evil in itself, but it makes Eichmann possible. Arendt's particular contribution was to identify the "banality of evil" in the character of Eichmann. He could manage the Final Solution, she claimed, because he had stopped thinking. Administrative rationality did not itself require thought. Thinking for Arendt has a special quality of recognizing and engaging the other: less pure reason, more dialogical engagement. Eichmann could not imagine the world from the point of view of another subject. Instead of thinking, he relied on clichés.

Thus Arendt shares the view that psychology, politics, and philosophy all work in the same dimension. But, for her, politics must be modeled on the person-to-person dialogical engagement of Socrates in the agora. Much of my argument is directed against this view. If Eichmann is banal, so, too, is every soldier who expresses himself through the clichés of patriotism. It will hardly do to dismiss the political psychology of the modern state as merely "banal." To understand

tive agency, in the early twentieth century, reflects the response of political institutions to the rise of scientific expertise in the form of the empirical social sciences. See P. Kahn, *Legitimacy and History: Self-Government in American Constitutional Theory* 126–27 (1992).

[11] See, e.g., J. Dewey, *Democracy and Education* (1916); A. Gutman, *Democratic Education* (1987); A. Gutman & D. Thompson, *Democracy and Disagreement* (1997).

[12] H. Arendt, *Eichmann in Jerusalam: A Report on the Banality of Evil* (1964).

evil, we must stop measuring action against the standards of reason—as justice or as dialogue—and instead turn to the dynamics of will and faith for a subject who is aware that he is finite and will die.

More common than Arendt's view of the banality of evil as the failure of thought is the view that evil is located in the *wrong* thoughts. Evil, then, is a matter of choosing on the basis of the wrong principles—for example, principles of superiority or subordination. A person who believes that she need not extend equal recognition and dignity to others is not a liberal, but is she evil? We cannot cast the entire prehistory of liberalism as evil. Or is it somehow the case that "now we should know better" and so are no longer excused? Should all hierarchies of caste, or of social and political class, be treated in the same way as slavery—a paradigm of evil? Surely we remain attached to some hierarchies: age, education, professional competence, and political or corporate role. Other societies are attached to hierarchies of gender or religion. We have disagreements across all these lines of division, but we do not think that those who believe in positions other than our own are evil. We do not want to label every illiberal society—past or present—as evil. We may want to reform them, to make them more egalitarian, but we do not condemn them as evil.[13]

The modern clash of ideologies might suggest that there is something to this view that the source of evil is the adoption of the wrong principles as the ground of one's actions. Yet there was no necessary reason that the clash of capitalism and socialism should have been seen as a clash of good versus evil. Principles alone will not explain why we would or should invest so much of ourselves in the question of the ownership of the means of production. We carry on a national debate over the extent of government regulation of markets without suggesting that this is anything other than disagreement in good faith. Even if the principle we erect is the interest of every individual in his or her own happiness, we have not yet entered the domain of evil. Those who pursue success in free markets are not evil; nor are those who advance modern social choice theory.

---

[13] John Rawls confronts this problem of recognizing societies that are neither liberal nor evil, classifying them as "decent hierarchical peoples." J. Rawls, *The Law of Peoples* 62–67 (1999).

If evil were simply an epithet we use against those who appear different from ourselves, it would not be so problematic a concept. But to explain the perception of evil as a reaction to difference is far too easy. On this view, evil, once again, literally slips away. The Jew, for example, was long a symbol of evil for Europeans, but today we are more likely to locate evil in anti-Semitism than in Semitism. We often look back at the history of our hatreds and think that the problem was in ourselves, not in the objects of our hatred. If we think that the perception of evil is only the consequence of our own emotional pathology, then we will be tempted by explanations that point to moral relativism. We will respond with an appeal to the liberal norm of respecting difference. If only we would all appreciate difference, we think there would be no evil. The conflict between religious principles, for example, need not appear as a clash between good and evil. We can celebrate the diversity of faiths and the multiple ways in which individuals realize the sacred. Religious conflict, like political conflict, is often the locus of the perception of evil, but that does not in itself explain why we perceive evil there or anywhere else.

We cannot be satisfied with such suggestions that evil arises out of misperceptions of difference, because we are inheritors of a culture in which evil is understood to arise from within. That, after all, is the point of the myth of the Fall. Evil is not just something that comes to us from without but is something we find at the core of our own experience of the self. We cannot dismiss this as simply a matter of one's point of view; we cannot accept appeals to difference as the explanation. We feel that evil is deeply a part of our world and yet does not belong there. To locate evil in the misperception of difference is simply to ignore one of the key insights of the myth of the Fall—that the problem of evil is intimately related to, and indeed begins with, the acquisition of knowledge. In particular, it begins with knowledge of the finite character of the self.

The problem of evil is much more than a sense that we might judge ourselves or others to be failures when measured against the norms we articulate. Evil is more than merely a point of view; it is not "cured" by adopting new, more forgiving, norms. Evil is not just a contingent aspect of our circumstances—our lingering youth as a community or as individuals—as if we could eliminate evil were we to try harder.

Yet outside the religious tradition of the Fall, how can we understand something to be both essential and wrong? To understand evil requires that we take up this sense of "not belonging" to our own world.

The disappearance of evil from Enlightenment thought was just as critical a development as the introduction of evil in the post-classical world. For much of contemporary thought, the very term "evil" suggests something archaic and suspiciously religious, something that belongs to the pre-Enlightenment character of man. A disenchanted world, a world transparent to reason, is one in which evil has disappeared, along with Satan, witches, spells, and miracles. Nevertheless, the sense of many people that modern philosophical discourses—particularly liberal theories—miss something essential is related to this failure to engage the problem of evil. Evil is deeper than self-regard, deeper than a weakness of the will, and deeper than error.

The absence of evil from the contemporary worldview rests on a failure to grasp what, borrowing from Hannah Arendt, we can call the human condition.[14] Subjecting evil to the same unidimensional scheme of explanation as everything else misses the phenomenon entirely. It is as if we were to read an economist's account of love. Worse, it is as if the lovers themselves had only the language of economics to describe their own experience. That account might afford reasonably accurate predictions of future behavior, but it would not have touched upon the meaning of the experience to the lovers.

Although we may have lost the capacity to speak of evil, the persistence of evil may be the most pressing problem faced by contemporary Western thought. For the moral and political history of the twentieth century is a history of evil, from the slaughter in the European trenches to the torture chambers of authoritarian regimes to the repeated episodes of genocide.[15] Modern liberalism would meet contemporary expressions of evil with the institutions of legality: human rights law and effective criminal prosecutions. Yet there always appears to be an incongruity between the scope of the problem of evil and this remedial response. One measure of that incongruity may be the one hundred thousand Rwandans accused of genocidal behavior and kept in jail

---

[14] See H. Arendt, *The Human Condition* (1958).
[15] See J. Glover, *Humanity: A Moral History of the Twentieth Century* (1999).

for years awaiting a formal judicial process that has barely begun to function.[16] Another would be the International Criminal Tribunal for the Former Yugoslavia, which has had some success applying international criminal law to participants in the former Serbian regime but has left untouched the vast majority of ordinary citizens who supported Slobodan Milosevic and participated in the ethnic cleansing for the sake of a greater Serbia.

There is surely nothing objectionable about punishing the perpetrators of the evils of genocide or ethnic cleansing by applying to them the framework of criminal justice. Punishment and deterrence—the goals of criminal justice—are worthwhile ambitions. Nevertheless there remains an incommensurability, a misunderstanding of the dimensions of the phenomenon, if we are satisfied with the identification of evil as crime.[17] Some evil is not criminal at all, for example, the evil of hatred or jealousy. Some evil overwhelms criminal law, such as genocide. The break between evil and criminality is sometimes noted by speaking of "radical evil."[18] I have no objection to the term, except that today it tends to focus our attention on political manifestations of evil. Its use may keep us from exploring the continuity between the personal and the political in the dimension of evil.

Evil is not an aberration—a failure—in a world otherwise ordered by reason. Rather, it is an effort to make the world anew, to create meaning on a new basis. That new world—the world of evil—is one in which death is projected onto the other. Aristotle wrote that every human action is motivated by a perception of the good. Perhaps we can say, equally, that every human action contains the germ of evil. If we expand our understanding of evil to include hatred, as I do in chapter 3, then none of us is all that far from evil.

---

[16] The figure of one hundred thousand was widely reported in the fall of 2002. Substantial releases occurred in 2003 and 2005, leaving still about forty thousand genocide suspects in prison. See "Rwanda Starts Prisoner Releases," *BBC News*, July 29, 2005, *available at* http://news.bbc.co.uk/Z/hi/africa/4726969.stm (last visited Sept. 30, 2005).

[17] The turn toward truth commissions, and away from formal adjudication, represents more than a search for institutional efficiency. It responds to a felt need to provide a new foundation for the polity through a more general confrontation with the phenomenon of evil. See M. Minnow, *Between Vengeance and Forgiveness: Facing History after Genocide and Mass Violence* (1998); *Truth v. Justice: The Morality of Truth Commissions* (R. Rotberg & D. Thompson, eds. 2000).

[18] See Arendt, *Eichmann* 241; C. Nino, *Radical Evil on Trial* (1996).

The dispute with evil is a kind of metaphysical war; it is a clash all the way down to the very basis of our understanding of the meaning of our lives and our world. For this reason, today's terrorists, who appear to us as the paradigm of political evil, are often spoken of as "nihilists," as if they wanted nothing positive but only to destroy all that is of value. The terrorist, of course, is unlikely to regard himself as a nihilist. He acts for reasons of his own. We speak of nihilism, however, not merely to excuse our own failures of comprehension but to express something essential to our perception of evil. The identification of evil always includes this effort at negation. Evil persons are accused of worshiping false gods, which means that at the basis of their belief is nothing at all. The oldest accusation of evil is that of idolatry. The idol may promise redemption but leaves us with only meaninglessness and death.

If evil is to be a useful concept, rather than a political epithet, we need a new understanding of the phenomenon. For this purpose, I propose a return to origins, to the myth of Adam and Eve. My purpose in turning to *Genesis* is not to establish the true meaning of the myth as either a matter of biblical exegesis or historical inquiry. Rather, I propose a series of interpretive exercises that draw on historical expressions of the myth but press toward an understanding of contemporary forms of evil. I want to use the myth—or actually myths, since there are two versions offered in *Genesis*—to meditate upon the forms of evil that continue to characterize Western experience. Idolatry, for example, may no longer be the compelling form of evil for us that it was in the Old Testament, but hatred, subordination, and torture continue to shape our understanding and experience of evil. The myth allows access to contemporary forms of evil, because it offers a point for reflection upon the problem of the will for a subject who self-consciously confronts the fact of his own death. More than that, the myth puts evil within a matrix of freedom, knowledge, love, and death. This is just where we must go if we are to see evil clearly. Each chapter that follows takes up anew the Genesis myth, emphasizing different points in order to press the inquiry in new directions as I consider evil within family, society, and polity. The common point of origin in *Genesis* for each chapter's interpretive inquiry emphasizes an underlying unity within the different forms of evil. That unity should not, however, be pushed too far. Each chapter is meant to stand on its own as well as to illuminate a common core.

One of the first lessons of *Genesis* is that we can speak coherently of evil only where we can speak of subjects who are free. If we reduce action to events that are to be explained by tracing patterns of cause and effect, then we lose sight of evil. Only the free actor brings evil into the world. Just as evil is related to freedom, it is also related to death. In *Genesis*, death is a consequence of the free act. We will have reason to question the order: the free act that is evil may be a consequence of our awareness of death. Were we immortal, we would have nothing upon which to fix the label of evil. Mortality raises the stakes. Immortal, we might be mischievous, but not evil. Indeed, evil disappears from view for those who believe themselves immortal. Curiously, both classical thought and liberal thought understand the subject from a perspective that would push death out of sight. A subject who identifies the truth of the self with reason does not worry about death, for reason is timeless.

Death, like freedom, sets the conditions within which evil is possible. It is not the thing itself. We need to understand what configuration of self, freedom, knowledge, and death is at work in the experience of evil. The argument I pursue is that evil arises out of the way the free subject responds to the awareness of his own death. Evil forms at the intersection of freedom and death. Some of our oldest images of evil represent it as a personification of death. They suggest that evil is an inversion: an acting on the principle of death rather than life. Today the terrorist—particularly the suicide bomber—is assimilated to these images. He is the literal personification of death. He brings death as a shock into our ordinary lives, appearing as if from nowhere. Thus terrorism brings into the heart of our contemporary political debates a deep and difficult philosophical problem.

Separating, as an analytic matter, evil from death is at the heart of the problem of developing an adequate conception of evil. After all, nature may terrorize us with disease, disability, and death. Death terrorizes a free being, because death is a scandal to the thinking subject. Thinking has no natural end. The modern world is also quite familiar with the experience of angst, that sickness unto death. But angst and evil are not the same, although both are related to death. Angst is passive; evil is active. When death becomes a subject of the free will, we approach the domain of evil. In myth, evil is often represented as the search for immortality gone wrong. We can bring some philosophical clarity to this idea. The problem of evil begins in the flight from death: not the putting off of death, which is characteristic of modernity's culture of entertainment, but a kind of practical metaphysics of overcoming death. The contemporary products of that metaphysics are hatred, murder, slavery, torture, and genocide. These are the subjects of the inquiries that follow.

The locus of evil is not a function of theory or of abstract rationality but of what we actually find in ourselves and in those with whom we interact. For contemporary citizens of the modern Western nation-state, evil is more likely to take familial and political forms than religious forms, because these are the communities that constitute our sense of identity. In truth, we find evil where we find love: in families and in those communities that matter most to us. Both love and evil characterize a free subject who knows he will die. Love would transcend death; evil would conquer death. The modern subject is asked to assume the burden of his or her own contingency. This is an intolerable burden to many—perhaps intolerable to everyone at some point or in some forms. Not every response to this burden is evil, but it may well be that every response has the potential for evil.

If our forms of explanation cannot acknowledge and understand evil, then we will remain opaque to ourselves morally and politically. Here, the philosophical inquiry intersects with practical issues of what to do about the problems of evil that are so pressing in contemporary politics. Philosophy cannot, however, give prescriptions for political or individual action. Philosophers have no particular political expertise, because politics remains an art, a matter of judging the possible within multiple intersecting contexts. This is especially true today, when governments must act simultaneously before domestic and international audiences. Nor can philosophers reach the level of particularity that characterizes the life choices of an individual. Philosophy may help us to understand love and evil, but it cannot tell us whom we should love or whether we should hate.

Philosophers can, however, bring contemporary problems into contact with the larger traditions within which our thinking operates.

They can help to explain why we see our problems and possibilities as we do. Our perceptions of self and world, of meaning and value, are deeply embedded in the history of Western understandings. We do not make the world anew; we inherit it. This is no less true of our conceptual world than our material world. We perceive meaning in certain ways because we perceive the world to be of a certain character. The philosopher's role is to clarify this structure of thought.

The inquiry into evil, as with every philosophical inquiry, is not so much an inquiry into the objects of our judgments as an inquiry into ourselves. What use we make of self-knowledge is a problem beyond philosophy. Philosophy begins and ends with the injunction: "Know thyself." When Socrates took up that task, he did not discover evil embedded in the soul of man. We do. This fundamental change in the character of the human soul is the place to begin.

■   ■   ■   ■

A PRELIMINARY MEDITATION

ON OEDIPUS AND ADAM

Evil terrorizes, but not all that terrorizes is evil. We may be terrorized by illness, but we do not describe it as evil. Evil characterizes an actor, a group, or a regime; it is not simply a bad or frightful experience. Without a perception of agency, there can be terror but not evil. When the collapse of the sun replaced the Last Judgment in our imaginations, cosmology replaced eschatology. Imagining the end of the universe, we lose our moral bearings. We may feel terror, but there is no one to blame—whether ourselves or others—and so there is no demand that we do anything. With that, a subject of intense moral significance was replaced by one of scientific interest.

Evil is connected to death but not just as an expression of the scale of injury. The morally bad actor does not become evil when he moves from maiming to killing. Moreover, whatever the connection of evil and death not all that is evil arises out of a literal killing. Conversely, not every killing—not even large-scale death—has its origin in evil. Both the Final Solution and the National Highway Traffic Safety Administration embody administrative rationality, but even if both envision large-scale death, only one is evil. A world without evil would be one in which we would still have to worry about bad actors, just as we would still have to worry about accidents. While all that is evil may be unjust and harmful, not every injustice and harm is evil.

Part of the problem of evil lies in its attraction. We see something of ourselves in evil; we are not always repulsed by what we see. We imagine ourselves as both terrorized and terrorizing. To grasp this double character of evil, we need to understand the nature of sin and not just bad events, of which unjust human action might be one source. After the Fall, the evil Adam confronts is not a threat from outside himself but one that arises from within. Evil, I argue, is not sin but a response to the condition of sin in which man finds himself. Stripped of the language of myth, we can say that evil is a response to the self-consciousness of death. The account of original sin is an effort to make comprehensible the terror in the face of our universal fate. Evil arises when and where man finds his own finitude an intolerable burden. Enlightenment promised to relieve man of the burdens of the sacred and the polluted, by putting reason in the place of faith. But enlightenment had no answer to the crisis of consciousness that arises with the awareness of death. Accordingly, enlightenment left open the space for evil but left us without the conceptual tools to understand the character of evil.

The terror of death is linked to the terrorizing of evil. Joseph Conrad vividly portrays this link in *The Heart of Darkness*. The protagonist, Kurtz simultaneously perceives the terror of existence—"the horror"—and expresses evil in his own life. Terror arises from an experience of powerlessness. The inevitability of death does not merely represent man's powerlessness; it is, rather, the very substance of that powerlessness. A world characterized by death—and Kurtz lives in a world surfeit with death—is one in which we all are susceptible to the perception of horror. Kurtz's evil is an assertion of power in the face of this horror. Formally, he occupies the ambiguous moral position of colonial commerce, which had the double mission of advancing one civilization and destroying another. Kurtz, however, turns on the intended beneficiaries—the natives—of this cultural gift. He becomes a kind of god to them because he has power—indeed, the power over life itself. He is, we might say, demonic.

Kurtz has become ineffective—powerless—from the perspective of his Western employers, but he is an image of power to those he lives among. Evil is at home in this simultaneous experience of powerlessness—the horror—and of power—the terrorizing. Because power and powerlessness can coexist in the same person, one can be evil and yet see oneself as a victim. Suffering from the terror of powerlessness, the subject asserts a power to master death.

Just here the inquiry into evil is as much metaphysical as it is psychological. We are asking how a finite being overcomes the experience of his or her own finitude. This question points to the intimate connection between love and evil: Kurtz is simultaneously an object of love and an expression of evil. The juxtaposition of love and evil was at the center of Freud's later work, in which he saw eros and thanatos as equiprimordial forces shaping the individual and civilization.[1] It is hard not to see this antinomy when one looks at the dual, Western inheritance of "carnage and culture."[2] Yet love and evil are not simply forces set in opposition to each other. Rather, they express ways of understanding the self in the world, ways that have an intimate and complex relationship to each other.

Already the story of Cain and Abel, the children of Adam and Eve, presents an image of this relationship. The children go before God once they have mastered the culture of the earth in agriculture and husbandry—the labor to which Adam's sin condemned all his descendants. Abel finds favor with God; Cain does not. We are not told what God's acceptance means, but there is a suggestion that Abel is recovering some of what his parents lost, whereas Cain remains condemned to a life of labor and death. When God rejects Cain's offering but takes Abel's, He says to Cain, "If you do well, will you not be accepted?" Cain, however, turns on Abel. He could have embraced Abel's good fortune in an expression of fraternal love; instead, he kills Abel. Cain's power to kill is matched with God's power to protect. Thus, after killing Abel and suffering exposure of his crime, Cain cries to God, "Whoever finds me will slay me." But God marks Cain "lest any who came upon him should kill him." Although the text turns quickly to a generational account, marking births and deaths, there is no mention of Cain's death. This is not to suggest that the evil do not die. We know that Cain dies, but his death is pushed off into an indefinite future that remains out of sight. This is an apt characterization of the power of evil over death: a pushing off, a delay of recognition, a flight.

The biblical story goes further. Cain does not exactly wander the earth. Instead, he founds a city, Enoch. The biblical narrative turns from Cain's generational and political accomplishments to the geneal-

---

[1] S. Freud, *Civilization and Its Discontents* 65–69 (J. Strachey, trans. & ed. 1961).

[2] The expression comes from V. Hanson, *Carnage and Culture: Landmark Battles in the Rise of Western Power* (2001).

ogy of Seth, the child Adam and Eve had in place of Abel. But in a textual confusion, the genealogy of Seth merges with that of Cain, leading to Enoch and finally to Noah. This confused history suggests a deeper point. Love and evil are not just equiprimordial, and they are not just in opposition. They are equally productive in the same dimension of human activity. The men of Noah's time are all judged by God to be evil—they are the descendants of Cain. But they are also the descendants of Seth, so there is among them love as well—Noah and his family. To eliminate evil requires a second, divine intervention: the flood. Neither love nor evil can do away with the other.

Here, then, in archetypal form, is an account of evil. Cain experiences again the terror of Adam's condemnation. Without God's acceptance, Cain remains destined to a life of labor and then death. He is condemned to this life for no apparent reason: like his brother, he, too, made an offering, but it was not accepted. Every person's death appears undeserved and irrational in just this way. Failing to receive divine acceptance, Cain asserts his own power over life and death: he kills his brother. The power of evil, moreover, is genuine: he does avoid his own death at the hands of others. Death is put off. But the power of evil is never separate from the experience of terror. His punishment is worse than the one for Adam's sin: "When you till the ground, it shall no longer yield to you its strength." Cain declares, "My punishment is greater than I can bear." But bear it he does, for man's capacity for suffering is virtually endless. His suffering is matched by his power over other men: he builds a city and founds a line. Men would kill him if they could, just as they would kill countless, later rulers. They do not, and we cannot help but suspect that it is not the mark, but love, that saves him. For founders are loved even as they are feared.[3]

Together Cain and Abel tell us that we cannot identify evil with man's fallen state, not if we want the concept to do any work for us. After the Fall, all have the potential for evil; there is nothing special about Cain. It could have been Abel who killed Cain. Evil is not the condition in which we find ourselves but a form of response to that

---

[3] For a recent reflection on this double quality—hated and loved—of the founder, see I. Buruma, "The Indiscreet Charm of Tyranny," *New York Review of Books*, vol. 52, no. 8 (May 12, 2005).

condition. For that reason, evil is deeply intertwined with that which is creative or constructive in our nature. Satan is often represented as possessing knowledge and culture.[4] Again, consider Kurtz, the agent of European civilization. Seeking to overcome death, we are never far from evil even as we build those deathless products of human creativity: culture, polity, family. Evil is disturbingly close to love.

Evil seems to threaten from without—to terrorize—but to come from within. Focusing on either the inward or the outward aspect alone misses the phenomenon. Viewed from the outside, evil becomes just another source of terror, that is, a part of the horror of it all. Among the horrors of the world are evil men: Abel is killed by his brother. Viewed from the inside, evil becomes just another form of psychological pathology. Evil is to be explained by jealousy, ambition, or rage: Cain is jealous of Abel. Both these accounts appeal to the logic of causal representation. Evil is categorized alongside other phenomena, whether internal or external. Implicit in these accounts is the assumption that we can master evil once we understand it, which means to assign it a cause. Either we can avoid it through oppression and containment—the outside perspective—or we can treat it—the inside perspective. Avoidance and treatment characterize our attitudes toward disease. Not surprisingly, some theories of evil speak of it quite openly as a kind of disease.[5]

But evil is not a disease; it is not even analogous to a disease. Every effort to treat evil as if it were a disease fails, because it is not possible to identify the cause or set of causes that leads to evil. Where and when evil will appear is always unpredictable. There is no constellation of factors, whether psychological or sociological, from which we can confidently predict the appearance of evil. We cannot say that the well-off are less likely to be evil than the poor or that culture and education protect us against evil. There is an implicit acknowledgment of this when people warn, "If the Holocaust could happen in Germany, the center of European culture, then it could happen anywhere." We see the phenomenon of Cain and Abel repeated endlessly within families:

---

[4] For example, Goethe's *Faust* or Stephen Benét's *The Devil and Daniel Webster*.

[5] See, e.g., A. Heller, "The Natural Limits of Natural Law and the Paradox of Evil," in *On Human Rights* 149, 156–57, 170–71 (S. Shute & S. Hurley, eds. 1993).

children raised by the same parents turn out to have completely different moral characters. Again the analogy to love is exact: we cannot identify the conditions in which individuals will realize a love of others, whether individuals or communities. This is not to say that we cannot offer an explanation, point to patterns of causation in particular individuals or groups. But we cannot generalize from any such narrative of an individual or a community. Christianity, with its faith in love, arose within conditions of misery and destitution. That hardly means that we should pursue suffering to find love, although certainly some Christians have done just that.

THE TERROR OF OEDIPUS

We can get a better sense of evil by looking first in a direction from which evil does not appear. The Greeks had myths of terror and powerlessness. They, too, thought about the possibility that man's labor could fail, that it could produce the opposite of its intended aim. Nevertheless, theirs were not myths of evil. Oedipus's experience terrifies; he, too, can speak of the horror. Even blind and old, he terrorizes others. He is polluted, but he is not evil. He only becomes evil on a modern rereading. To make him evil, we have to replace the Greek idea of pollution with a Judeo-Christian idea of sin. We have to assign Oedipus an agency that he lacks in Sophocles' account. Indeed, the very point of Sophocles' play is to say that Oedipus is incapable of such agency. To make Oedipus evil, we first have to kill the Olympian gods and then invest Oedipus with a subconscious.

What terrorized the Greeks was the world, not the inner life. When the Greeks thought about the terror of human existence, they produced tragedy. Tragedy gives the audience just what subjects lack in their ordinary lives: knowledge of the reality that is creating the appearance on the stage. The audience sees what the actor cannot see. Seeing both the actor and the context, the audience understands the drama to represent a gap in knowledge. The play's action is the overcoming of that gap—a direction and goal that the audience perceives as necessary from the moment the play begins.[6] In this sense, the audi-

---

[6] See Aristotle, *Poetics* 1449b(24–28) (I. Bywater, trans.) in *Basic Works of Aristotle* (R. McKeon, ed. 1941) (referring to tragedy as an "imitation of an action that is . . . complete in itself," but also "with incidents arousing fear and pity").

ence knows the whole from the beginning, and experiences a reduction in tension as the perceptions of actor and audience converge at the end. To the extent that the audience identifies with Oedipus onstage, it shares in his experience of terror. But to the extent that the spectator reminds himself that he is not onstage, that he has a comprehensive view of both the stage appearance and its cause, he has some control over that terror. Oedipus may blind himself, but the audience is never blind.[7] The audience can thereby experience a kind of catharsis that is not available to the actor, whether on the stage or in real life. Greek tragedy reveals the terror of life itself—a terror rooted in what we cannot know—but does so in a context within which it is cabined, allowing some temporary relief from the horror of it all.

To see the causes of appearances—to see what men literally cannot see—is to be beyond terror. For this reason, there is nothing of terror in Greek philosophy, which strives to penetrate appearances and to see the real. Plato's cave—the most famous metaphor in all classical philosophy—is all about shifting positions such that one sees fully the context within which the human drama is set. Still today, this is the ambition of reason. If reason can grasp the real, it can provide a firm ground for practical action, whether of social construction or individual therapy. The philosopher turned therapist takes up the position of the classical playwright who brings together, if only temporarily, appearance and reality at the play's conclusion. Psychoanalysis is the construction of just such a drama in which the patient becomes the audience to his own performance. Plato, who would banish the poets from his ideal city, is only the first of a long line of philosophers, psychoanalysts, economists, and others who would drive illusion from the society: they rally to the cry, "To the facts themselves."

Plato's *Republic*, for example, is a profound psychological work, but the psychological problems with which it deals are political problems with political solutions: how to educate a military class, how to produce leaders who will not abuse public power for private ends,

---

[7] If we compare Oedipus to Lear, we see that Shakespeare inverts the position of audience and actor. Lear's madness creates an access to truth not available to the audience. Lear knows more than the audience because he can see beyond the mere appearances to which the audience is bound. See P. Kahn, *Law and Love: The Trials of King Lear* 134 (2000).

how to produce a stable relationship between feelings of familial love and feelings of political identity. Even when the psychological concerns advance beyond the possibilities of ordinary politics, the goal remains pedagogic: how to train philosophers who can see the ultimate unity of being and the good. This is a world in which mistakes will be made, in which there are plenty of human deficiencies to be overcome, but not a world in which terror makes any appearance.[8]

To the degree that concerns with death do appear in the *Republic*, they are met by myths designed to meet the same pedagogic goals. Within the city, death is, first of all, a problem of courage: one must hold to politically appropriate beliefs even under the stress of battle. Elsewhere the message of Plato's dialogues broadens to the relationship of death to other virtues: given what we know about justice and the good, it is irrational to fear death. Indeed, in the *Phaedo*, Socrates goes so far as to say that philosophy itself is a practice of dying, by which he means that the philosopher takes no notice of death.[9] He takes no notice, because he has already withdrawn from that special concern for the self that others associate with dying. To the thinking mind, death makes no appearance because death, in and of itself, has no meaning. Meaning is located in the objects of reason, which are quite independent of any individual's existence or nonexistence. Plato's point is clearer to us if we consider a discipline like mathematics. Death makes no appearance in mathematics because the individual makes no appearance. Only in such disciplines of pure reason does the thinking soul truly find itself, for it overcomes the separation between thought and the object of thought.[10] The terror of Oedipus, Plato suggests, rests upon a gap between appearance and reality. The philosopher forsakes appearances; his truth is not of this world.[11] With that, the gap is to disappear.

---

[8] In the *Republic*, the ultimate recalcitrance of the world to philosophical reconstruction is blamed on an inevitable failure of the cosmic cycles. Thus a cosmological rather than a moral myth is deployed to explain the source of inevitable failure. See Book VII, 546a–d.

[9] Plato, *Phaedo* 63e–65a.

[10] For an alternative view of mathematics, see E. B. Davies, *Science in the Looking Glass: What Do Scientists Really Know?* (2003).

[11] Similarly, there is no terror before death in Aristotle. For him, the philosopher is a man at home in the world because world and mind realize the same principles of reason. Whatever mysteries exist, they do not terrify. The world provides all the resources the philosopher

Yet Plato is hardly representative of a Greek absence of terror in the face of death. Plato's view that philosophy is a practice of dying was not exactly designed to attract a large following. Such a claim was more likely to be the object of derision in comedy than of popular belief.[12] In Plato's *Apology*, Socrates speaks of the contrast between his own calmness before the threat of death and the terrified reactions ordinarily characteristic of those accused of capital offenses. Plato is himself responding to Homer's description of Odysseus's visit to Hades, where Achilles proclaims: "Better, I say, to break sod as a farmhand / for some poor country man, on iron rations, than lord it over all the exhausted dead."[13] The Athenians were no more likely to be Stoics than the rest of us. The Platonic denial of the reality of the mortal body does have a profound impact on the development of Christianity but not as a form of general prescription. A sanctified elite—whether philosophical or religious—might pursue this denial, but the Church had to support a larger community organized in the traditional patterns of familial and political life.[14] The same can be said of the belief in a fully knowable universe. This ideal of the philosopher founds the Western belief in the universal reach of science. The modern man of science is the direct descendent of the Greek philosopher. Again, however, only a few can adopt a comprehensive scientific attitude toward the terrors of lived experience.

The classical philosopher could not conceive of the limits of reason; he could not believe that experience might be impenetrable to discursive inquiry. In Plato's *Apology*, Socrates imagines life after death as a kind of uninterrupted pursuit of the kind of conversations he enjoyed in life. But terror is beyond discourse, just as death is the point at which speech runs out. If people do experience terror, if they seek a practical orientation in the face of terror, the philosopher's answers are not responsive to the conditions within which individuals find

---

needs to achieve the best of ends: happiness. The practical problem for philosophy is to establish the conditions under which the good man can be the good citizen, that is, the point at which there is a reciprocal relationship between the happiness of the individual and the well-being of the community.

[12] Aristophanes' *Clouds* portrays just such a comic Socrates.

[13] Homer, *The Odyssey*, XI, 579–81 (R. Fitzgerald, trans. 1998).

[14] See P. Brown, *The Body and Society: Men, Women, and Sexual Renunciation in Early Christianity* (1988); E. Pagels, *Adam, Eve, and the Serpent* (1988).

themselves. The terrifying world was not the world of the philosophers. This impenetrable domain of terror was, however, the subject of tragedy. *Oedipus the King* may be the most effective presentation of the classical response to the impenetrable character of existence. That response shows us terror but not evil.

The experience of the play is terrifying in a double sense. Oedipus is terrified by what he comes to learn of himself: he is terrified to learn of the gap between appearance and reality. The audience is equally terrified not just for him but along with him, as it is drawn into the play and sees the world from his perspective. Strikingly, neither our terror nor his rests on a misuse of freedom. The horror of the play is metaphysical, not ethical: free, deliberate action, we learn, may be nothing other than a play of appearance. The failures of action represented in the play do not have their source in any failure of Oedipus's soul—for example, lack of reason, weakness of the will, overbearing desire, or absence of sympathy. We cannot speak of a failure of forethought, a failure of courage, or a failure to control desire. Oedipus seeks to act virtuously despite the ill prophesies. He exercises reason in all the choices he makes. He does show himself to have a temper, but the source of the tragedy is hardly that. The disaster comes not from his emotional reactions but from his measured, deliberate actions. The problem is in the world, not in himself.

Oedipus tries to escape the fate that was prophesied for him as a youth at Corinth: that he would kill his father and marry his mother. He flees home and city. It cannot be a fault to try to escape such a horrible fate, especially when it means death and destruction for those one loves. Whatever we think about the inevitability of fate, we cannot think it appropriate to do nothing but watch the tale unfold. When told of the immeasurable tragedy that will be the tale of his life, Oedipus must do something. If we speculate about what he "should have done," we are engaging in the same battle with fate that Oedipus chooses. The ethical choice in his situation is hardly not to deliberate any more than it is not to act. To think otherwise is to confuse the idea of fate with a prediction of a causal sequence. Our fate does not appear to us as the end of a scientific experiment that happens to be our lives.

Measured against the ordinary norms that govern choice, Oedipus is faultless. He saves Thebes from the Sphinx and then rules well. His ambitions are not for personal power but for the realization of justice in his community. Similarly, he loves well. His attachments to family are genuine. His concern is not for himself but for the well-being of his loved ones. He has virtues of character and of reason; he pursues justice with genuine sympathy for others. He achieves all those virtues that are within the power of the individual and the community. He deploys those virtues for admirable ends—to save family and city. When he has to choose between self-interest and the interest of others, he chooses the latter. Although he has fled his fate, there is not some dark secret brooding about his heart. He is not using others for private, undisclosed ends; he is not hiding his true interests from others. His actions are not what they seem, but not because he is in some way a hypocrite, a pretender, or a subject with a deep break between an inner and outer self. The break is in the order of reality, not in his soul. Nothing Oedipus believes to be true is true: his parents are not really his parents, his wife is his mother, his children are his siblings. Reality is not what it seems, despite his best efforts to understand.

Oedipus appears in the play's opening as the good man and the good citizen. He is shocked beyond horror—terrorized—to discover that all these virtues are mere appearances, that at the center of his existence is a violation of the order of the universe. He is not in control of what he does, even as he thinks of himself as virtuous. He is not in control because that which he thinks he knows, he does not know. The problem is one of knowledge, but the problem is incurable. Thus his wife, Jocasta, tells him: "Why should man fear since chance is all in all / for him, and he can clearly foreknow nothing? / Best to live lightly, as one can, unthinkingly." He is not himself a riddle to be solved like the problem of the sphinx. Again Jocasta: "God keep you from the knowledge of who you are!"[15]

Reading more Plato or Aristotle would not help Oedipus. He lives in a world impenetrable to human reason: a world in which signs and omens are more truthful than one's own eyes, more reliable than

[15] *Oedipus*, in *The Complete Greek Tragedies*, vol. 2, 977–79, 1068 (D. Greene & R. Lattimore, eds. 1960).

rationality and deliberation. He is not forced to kill his father when he would rather not. He kills his father, thinking that in his flight he has protected his father. He marries his mother, thinking that he is maintaining the royal order of Thebes. In a world in which things are not what they seem, deliberation is not a trustworthy guide to action. Yet reason is the only guide man possesses. Jocasta's recommendation of thoughtlessness is not really an option. Even omens and prophesies must be interpreted, and a plan of action must be formulated. In that task, there is only reason to rely on. Omens are just more appearances in the world, requiring the application of man's reason. Oedipus proves this by solving the riddle of the Sphinx. But just because one riddle can be solved hardly means that all the riddles of existence can be solved. Oedipus has done all that he can to avoid the terrible deeds that are his fate. The fault may be his but not because he is blamewor-thy. That is precisely the point: it is fault without blame.

Oedipus does those things that are most horrifying to man, family, and city. He destroys the very conditions of order of each. Human values rest on a necessary order—the divine conditions of all that exists. There is not some city in which it is permissible to kill one's father or marry one's mother.[16] These relationships are the foundation of a human world. Outside these basic norms, we are not living in a human world at all. Oedipus breaks apart the ordered universe of man. He is cast off into the wilds of nature, the space between organized human communities. He is literally no longer of this world. Whether that makes him sacred or savage is an open question.[17]

That the wisest of men, the best of political rulers, and the most loving of fathers can rend the universe in two suggests the failure of human knowledge. The true order of the world moves to a system of causes that is beyond our grasp. Plato may have thought that being and the good are one and the same, but Sophocles did not. Why do the gods so hate Oedipus? We cannot answer that question without

---

[16] Thus the early anthropological interest in incest, in the pursuit of a kind of human science of myth. See, e.g., J. Frazer, *Totemism and Exogamy* (1910); S. Freud, *Totem and Taboo* (1918); C. Levi-Strauss, *Elementary Structures of Kinship* 24 (J. Bell, trans. 1969).

[17] See Sophocles, *Oedipus at Colonus*. For a modern investigation of the double character of the excluded figure, see G. Agamben, *Homo Sacer: Sovereign Power and Bare Life* (D. Heller-Roazen, trans. 1998).

literally entering a Sophoclean world in which our ordinary understandings of the order of reality are profoundly disturbed. We cannot
know if Oedipus is the victim of earlier actions by the House of Laius,
as if the gods keep their own tally of action and revenge. Oedipus asks,
"Was I not born evil?" and "What have you designed, O Zeus, to do
with me?"[18] Alternatively we might think that Oedipus's fate is the
response of the gods to Oedipus's own hubris in thinking he could
outsmart them. When time loses its order, as it does with the immortal
gods, we can no longer distinguish cause from effect; an effect can
constitute its own cause. But if Oedipus's predicted fate is a consequence of choices not yet made and character not yet formed, he can
do no more about it than if he were suffering for the deeds of his
ancestors. Or perhaps there is no reason at all for Oedipus's suffering.
We moralize endlessly about our lives, but perhaps the gods do not
really care. Oedipus's fate may be only ill luck without any explanation at all. All these possibilities terrorize.

The issue raised by these competing interpretations of the reasons
for Oedipus's fate is the question of the dimensions of human blindness. All converge on the idea that man's knowledge is not adequate
to the field upon which he acts. That field is one that is constituted by
the gods, and about this man can know nothing. Outside the theater,
we cannot see as the gods see, so we might as well not see at all:
Oedipus puts out his eyes. Reason marks the point of man's hubris:
his belief that there is a symmetry between what he can know and
what he can do. Man's reason, however, is nothing more than cleverness, and cleverness runs out. Whether we have eyes or not, blindness
is the human condition. In the end, riddles define the scope of human
action because of the incapacities of human knowledge.

The terror of the play, then, lies in the dimension of the sacred. Man
may be a plaything of the gods; he may be the object of the gods'
antagonism. In neither case is he a subject who can control his actions
through reason. The human order that we create in good faith through
politics and family may, at any moment, be shown to rest on a founda-

---

[18] Sophocles, *Oedipus* 822, 738. The translator's use of the word "evil" for the Greek
κακος should not be confused with the Judeo-Christian conception of evil. Its meaning is
closer to bad or ignoble.

tion as terrifying as that of Thebes. We cannot know, because the ultimate reality against which our actions are measured is impenetrable
to reason. "What man, what man on earth wins more / of happiness
than a seeming / and after that turning away?"[19] No man can be proclaimed happy until he is dead, for all that he thought to constitute
his happiness may be shown to be nothing but disaster. In an inversion
of the Platonic claim that the best life, philosophy, is a practice of
dying, the Chorus proclaims that those who live are "equal with those
who live not at all!"[20] This is not a reassurance but a statement of
terror in a world in which the gods may not be benevolent forces.

We can, of course, read the play as not really about divine causation.
Prophesy can be seen as just another form of knowledge, not as a form
of divine intervention.[21] In that case, Oedipus brings his own fate upon
himself, and the gods merely see into the future. While today we might
be attracted to a reading that strips the play of its sacred dimension,
such a reading is hardly adequate. There is no moral puzzle to solve
in Oedipus's behavior, as if the lesson is to take a bit more care before
one acts. To make it that is to turn it into comedy: mistaken identity
is the very stuff of comedy.

There is, however, a closely related reading that is more compelling.
This reading aligns the play with Plato's inquiry into political psychology in the *Republic*. The narrative line of the play begins with the
prophesy to Laius, the ruler of Thebes and Oedipus's father. He is
warned of the future behavior of his son. He tries to prevent this behavior, but he fails. He cannot prevent the appearance of a son who
will slay him, claim political authority, and take possession of his family. That such a son will arise is not a product of chance—secular or
sacred—but a necessary consequence of the structural conditions of
power in the city. The possibility of parricide haunts every royal family. It is unavoidable as long as authority exists in city and family. Now,
the play is not about Oedipus but about the structural conditions of
politics, and how the structure of political authority shapes the psy-

---

[19] *Id.* 1190–92.

[20] *Id.* 1188–89.

[21] For another dramatic representation of this problem, consider Macbeth's response to
the prophesy that he will be king. Shakespeare, however, poses the issue in terms of a psychological drama—exactly the terms that Oedipus lacks.

chology of those who are ruled.[22] Oedipus as a unique person, characterized by his disfavor with the gods, disappears from view in the political-psychological account. The subject of this account is not the failure of reason but the workings of intergenerational ambition and jealousy: the son will assert himself in order to seize authority.

By murdering his father, Oedipus claims a power equal to, if not greater than, the source of his own being. By marrying his mother, he claims a kind of agelessness. He spans generations, confusing the chain of orderly succession. This is the ultimate rebellion of the powerless— to attempt to control time itself in the ages of man.[23] The child has become father to the man. In an age of science fiction, he would be represented as literally father to himself.[24] He comes as close to being the uncaused agent—the first cause—of his own existence as is possible in Greek representation. The violation of the order of the universe is the violation of the fundamental order of life and death. Oedipus claims the power of the gods themselves.

Yet Oedipus cannot claim this power without suffering horror at his own actions, for fundamentally he believes in the norms that he has violated. He would be the good son, the good ruler, and the good father. His character is to be hero, not antihero. The horror Oedipus feels is the affirmation of the city's order in the face of rebellion. Thus the play begins with Oedipus, as King, announcing the penalty for the unknown murderer of Laius:

> Upon the murderer I invoke this curse—
> whether he is one man and all unknown,
> or one of many—may he wear out his life
> in misery to miserable doom![25]

If we read the play as an assertion of Oedipal power rather than as a meditation on the failure of reason, then we see that power to be insubstantial. Lacking divine foundations, this new power cannot sur-

---

[22] This is the common reading of Antigone after Hegel. See G. W. F. Hegel, *Phenomenology of Spirit* 221 (A. V. Miller, trans. 1975).

[23] Oedipus's intergenerational character should be considered in relation to his insight into the riddle of the Sphinx.

[24] Consider the movie *Terminator* (1984), or Orson Scott Card's *Children of the Mind* (1997).

[25] Sophocles, *Oedipus* 246–49.

vive in any dimension: the city expels him, his mother/wife kills herself, and Oedipus physically blinds himself. In this condition of affirming the city's order through his own suffering, he becomes a point of manifestation of the sacred.[26] Through him, traditional order has overthrown rebellion and thus shown its own foundational power. In Freud's account, this reassertion of civilization against the rebellious child occurs through the vehicle of guilt, which serves as the foundation of law.[27] For him, the play gives outward expression to the internal suffering of a soul that wills its own existence by denying every limit on its own power.[28]

Freud and Sophocles agree that Oedipus violates the conditions of political/familial order. Freud would locate the principles of order and disorder in man himself. He internalizes Nietzsche's account of the moral history of the Christian West as a battle between the powerful and the powerless. For Freud, the outcome depends on the feeling of guilt by which the superego controls the id. Civilization is only as powerful as the resources of guilt. Evil, accordingly, is that force within the self that would destroy the conditions of the subject's own repression. Knowing this about ourselves, we know that we have the capacity for evil. Psychologically we are already guilty by virtue of that very knowledge. Part of the subject wants to be Oedipus, while another part is terrified by the possibility. The triumph of civilization is the self-binding of the id, such that the subject affirms the orderly life of family and polity.

If we read the play in this Freudian way, we do turn Oedipus into an evil character. His suffering is now the appropriate response to his moral failing, and that failure is located in the will to be the source of his own being. This is a will that would make of the universe an image of the self, such that one never sees anything other than a reflected image of one's own power. To accomplish that end, one must murder and violate ordinary moral norms. The suppression of this evil is, for Freud, the source of civilization. He, too, believes that the normative order is a tenuous affair, built on a kind of self-induced blindness.

---

[26] See Sophocles, *Oedipus at Colonnus*, which portrays a contest between Thebes and Athens for possession of the body of Oedipus after his death.

[27] See Freud, *Civilization and Its Discontents* 79–80.

[28] Again, a comparison to *Macbeth* is appropriate.

For Freud, man cannot bear too much knowledge of himself.[29] For Sophocles, he cannot take too much knowledge of the world.

That the play is accessible to such a reading may explain something of its enduring quality. Nevertheless, it is wrong to project this reading back into the classical context, for at the center of this reading is an assertion of the will in the face of death. This is indeed the problem of evil in our world, but to get here from the classical era our analysis must take up the myth of Adam and Eve.

For Sophocles, Oedipus's conflict is not located in the soul. It is, rather, a battle between man and the divine but not the divine within man himself; this man is not created in the image of God. For Sophocles, the divine still inhabits the world. Oedipus lives in a sacred world that is not of his own creation. Oedipus is not striving for autochthony—killing his father and claiming his mother. He is striving to lead a virtuous life within the ordinary intergenerational cycles of politics and family. He has not been found out; he has been turned out. Oedipus is not responsible for this inversion of power. If anyone is responsible, it is the gods. In fact, every effort to assign responsibility is left indeterminate in the play, for evil is not at issue.

What is so terrifying here is the showing forth of a divine order that sets aside as mere empty appearance the objects of human understanding. The horror of Oedipus is mixed with the sacred from the very beginning. Prophesies and omens are needed to clarify exactly who Oedipus is. Oedipus shares that double quality of the divine as simultaneously sacred and polluted. In the presence of the polluted, we are very close—perhaps too close—to the sacred. For this reason, Oedipus's broken, blind body becomes the object of a battle for possession between Athens and Thebes in *Oedipus at Colonus*. What is truly terrifying is the manifestation of the divine as a principle of sacred destruction. Indeed, this is too much to see; the terror is too great. Oedipus blinds himself and takes himself away from the sight of the human community. We can take just so much exposure to the sacred. Whether the divine shows itself as ordered creation or endless horror is beyond our control. To the human actor, it is one and the same

---

[29] Nietzsche would take hold of this knowledge in the pursuit of a transformation of values. See F. Nietzsche, *Genealogy of Morals* (W. Kaufman, trans. 1989) [1887].

world. It is only the difference between looking at life and at death. Both are equal parts of our world.

This showing forth is the point of the *mysterium tremendum*.[30] Oedipus truly is touched by the gods. That makes him simultaneously sacred and terrifying. Man's duty is to maintain the order of the world by expelling the polluted. It is to repair the rent in the universe by which the sacred shows itself in its full and terrifying force. But there is no rational theory by which to understand how the universe comes to be torn, just as there is no theory by which we can understand how mind becomes embodied or why life ends in death. Because the world is torn, the world is terrifying. That it is so is simply a fact that we experience. This fact is denied by the philosophers.

The rent in the universe is a measure of the gap between man's knowledge and the order of existence. Ultimately, we are all as blind as Oedipus. Ritual must replace reason; prophesy, deliberation. If the ritual fails—as it always will—all that is left is the horror. The truth Oedipus learns, and the truth that he represents, is the truth that he becomes: man is blind. We know no more about life than about death. About death, it is always as if we are blind. We cannot see beyond life to death; we cannot make sense of the presence of death. The stories we tell about life turn out to be no more substantial than the stories we tell about death. Oedipus thinks he is father, king, husband. These are only words in an impenetrable universe.

Man experiences pollution as terrifying, but it makes no sense to describe the polluted as evil. It is not up to Oedipus to avoid the deeds he committed; it is not up to him to overcome them. His problems are metaphysical, not psychological and not moral. He does not prescribe a course of treatment for himself. He takes on a ritual of banishment, not a therapeutic intervention that will allow him to return to the norm.[31] His behavior is the source of the disturbance, but we cannot say that he is evil.

Oedipus would move from a polluted figure to an evil actor were he to take up what he has done as his own actions, were he to assert

---

[30] See R. Otto, *The Idea of the Holy: An Inquiry into the Non-Rational Factor in the Idea of the Divine and Its Relation to the Rational* 12–18 (J. Harvey, trans. 1958).

[31] For a general theory of the scapegoat, see R. Girard, *Violence and the Sacred* (P. Gregory, trans. 1990).

a power to overcome death, were he to assert that he is the cause of his own existence and deny the principles of order within which he finds himself. In short, were Oedipus to affirm the person that he is, we would confront evil.[32] To make any of these affirmations, however, Oedipus would have to understand himself as fundamentally free. He would have to understand his identity as the product of his own free will. He would have to define himself through his relationship to his will rather than to the gods. That person he would become is at the heart of the Judeo-Christian tradition. Indeed, we are that person.

TERROR AND THE INVENTION OF EVIL

Sophocles leaves us no dream of a perfect world, a world in which the problem of Oedipus is solved. Pollution is a fact about the world, not a problem of human agency to be solved through knowledge or cleverness. Oedipus is doomed to wander from place to place, always reminding men of the terrifying truth of their own condition before the gods. The Oedipus myth has a shape much like that of Cain. We cannot know why Cain is disfavored or why Abel is favored. Like Cain, Oedipus is marked by his pollution, which arises from killing a family member. Each wanders the earth. For both, the divine sanction also has a sacred power: the power to found and protect a city. Oedipus and Cain always draw the attention of the gods—for good and bad.

This structural homology of Oedipus and Cain suggests that evil steps into the category of the polluted. Just as the polluted is simultaneously terrifying and sanctifying, so is evil. There is a danger of getting too close but also a danger of losing contact entirely. The double character of Oedipus—polluted and sacred—is replaced by a new double in the Judeo-Christian word—evil and love.

Something new appears in the idea of a covenantal religion. There could not be a concept of evil until there was a concept of the will. This is exactly what the classical Greeks lacked, which is why the Oedipus story is not about evil but about the confrontation of reason

---

[32] Compare Edmund in *King Lear*, particularly the opening of act 1, scene 2, where Edmund literally affirms his bastardy and directs the gods to "stand up for bastards!"

and revelation, of order and pollution.[33] In the Judeo-Christian tradition, a metaphysics of the will displaces a metaphysics of the hiero-
phantic. The sacred no longer shows itself in the things of this world—
for example, omens and rituals—unmediated by the human will.[34] The
very concept of pollution is rendered difficult, for the world is the
creation of God's will and that which He creates is good. Nor is the
sacred a matter of knowledge, as if we can reason ourselves to God—
although a classical tradition of reason survives even within the
Church. The relationship to the sacred is now founded on faith, and
faith is a matter of the will.[35]

Faith is beyond reason, but, like reason, it opens us to a world of
meaning outside ourselves. The opposition of faith to reason appears
with clarity in the story of the sacrifice of Isaac: Abraham must have
faith in the unreasonable promise that he will found a nation even as
he sacrifices his only legitimate son. Other immediate examples of this
opposition include that most concrete expression of Christian faith,
the catechism, which proclaims belief in a proposition that defies reason: the "consubstantial Trinity."[36] Or in the even simpler incantation,
in the mass for the dead, of Jesus's statement, "He who believes in me
shall never die."[37] If faith in God is a product of the will, then failure
of faith is no longer a matter of "weakness of the will"—what the
Greeks termed *akrasia*. Rather, the failure of faith is sin made possible
by a free will.

Sin is the failure to place the self in a world of sacred meaning. It is
not the violation of a norm but the turning away from God. Of course,

[33] On the lack of a conception of the will in classical thought, see H. Arendt, *The Life of
the Mind* Vol. 2, *Willing* 18 (1978); P. Kahn, *Putting Liberalism in Its Place* 147 (2005);
M. Forster, "The Christian Doctrine of Creation and the Rise of Modern Natural Science,"
43 *Mind* 446 (1934).

[34] Of course, not completely. There remains, for example, the tradition of sacred relics,
and the sacraments remain central to Catholicism. Pollution, too, remains a part of the
Jewish tradition. Generally Christianity is competing with—and absorbing—elements of an
earlier occultism in much of Europe right up to the early 1700s. See J. Butler, *Awash in a
Sea of Faith: Christianizing the American People* 7–30 (1990).

[35] A classic expression of the subordination of understanding to faith is Saint Anselm's:
"I do not seek to understand that I may believe, but I believe in order to understand."

[36] "The mystery of the Most Holy Trinity is the central mystery of the Christian faith and
of Christian life. God alone can make it known to us by revealing himself as Father, Son
and Holy Spirit." *Catechism of the Catholic Church*, 2d ed., 261 (2000).

[37] John 11:25–26.

one form of that "turning" can be violation, but there is a fear that even those who follow the law may still be in a state of sin. Sin is not the outward act but the inner failure of faith, that is, the inner turning of the will.[38] That failure can result from the pride of reason as easily as from the desires of the body. In both cases there is effectively a turning in upon the self, a claim that the goal of the will is to express individual subjectivity; whether that subjectivity is thought of as the consequence of deliberation or of interest is not as important as the initial turning.

This idea of sin as a product of the subject's will makes no appearance in the Oedipus drama. Pride is a virtue in a classical world. It could, of course, lead to a hubristic overreaching, but hubris is not sin. Pride suggests autonomy, independence, and self-reliance. Sophocles' Oedipus begins the play full of pride for his accomplishments. That pride comes to appear as hubris, because he has a misplaced belief in his own reason: he has lived in a world of false appearances. In its place, Oedipus takes up an attitude of horror toward himself. Yet he does not overcome himself; there is no impulse toward self-transcendence. He does not move from a position lacking faith to one of faith; his problem is with the gods, not with his will. We can use neither the language of faith nor that of will to describe his condition.

Oedipus shows us one set of classical antinomies: sacred and polluted; Plato another: mind and body. Philosophy was seen as an attack upon the gods at least in part because it would substitute the latter antimony for the former. Philosophy would pursue contemplation in order to free the soul of particularity, whether that of the desiring body or that of the sacred. Neither of the dualisms of antiquity—mind and body, sacred and polluted—is adequate to a world in which the soul is experienced through a faculty of will. If the quality of the subject—his or her moral character—is a product of a free will, then the battle is not between body and mind but between the divisions of the soul itself. In this very sense, man has become a deeper problem to himself.

---

[38] Immanuel Kant secularizes this idea when he insists that the measure of moral worth is not the outward act, which may be in accordance with law (civil and moral), but in the quality of the maxim the subject gives himself—for example, "maxims which neglect the incentives springing from the moral law." I. Kant, *Religion with the Limits of Reason Alone* 25 (T. Greene & H. Hudsen, trans. 1960) [1793].

It is no longer enough to control the body's intemperate desires. Nor is it enough to educate reason alone. A free will is subordinated only by its own free act.

Knowledge and evil, we know all too well, are no less compatible than desire and evil. In *Genesis*, knowledge follows the willful act. Indeed, knowledge of good and evil is the product of the violation. If so, knowledge cannot be the answer to the problem of will. Man gains knowledge but loses the presence of the sacred. Knowledge no longer leads to the universal, to transcendence of the body. Just the opposite: knowledge now appears as bound to the body and to individual subjectivity. Oedipus had reason but was defeated by an unreasonable universe; in the Judeo-Christian tradition, man has reason but is defeated by his own free will.[39]

In place of the classical dualism of the sacred and the polluted, we confront a new dualism of love and evil. Neither love nor evil can be understood apart from the relationship of the subject's will to his own death—not the fact of his death but the subject's awareness of his own finitude. Thus the knowledge that Adam and Eve gain and that defines their fallen condition is the knowledge that they will die. Evil arises out of the flight from death, whereas love expresses a faith in the possibility of the transcendence of death. Both express a metaphysics entirely different from that derived from conceptions of the sacred or of reason available to the Greeks.

All this is already present in the biblical myth of creation. God creates a universe that is good. It is perfect in that it is complete in itself; it needs nothing else. God creates Adam and Eve just as he creates the other beasts, in pairs.[40] These original pairs are not unique subjects but rather contain the entire life of the species. This is the creation of Forms in the Aristotelian sense.[41] All that the horse is or will be is

---

[39] See *Romans* 7, 15.

[40] In this discussion, I run together two different accounts of creation in the text. Distinguishing between these two accounts is important to the argument I develop in later chapters. At this point, however, I want to emphasize only certain elements present in the general account of creation.

[41] Modern fundamentalists who insist that all species were fully present at creation are closer to Aristotle than they realize. On the importance of Aristotle's metaphysics in understanding the nature of Christ and the Eucharist in medieval thought, see D. MacCulloch, *The Reformation: A History* 24–25 (2003).

present in the original creation. That particular horses appear in the order of time is irrelevant to what it is to be a horse. The garden is a world of essences, of paradigms, only instances of which could be repeated through all future time. In the absence of free will, nothing new is to happen. Indeed, nothing could happen, for there is no ground or source of the new. Accordingly, naming the individual originals of creation is naming all instances of the species for all time. Adam does not assign the beasts proper names.

Like the other species, Adam and Eve can themselves be thought of as plural beings. In them, all men and all women are already present. But unlike the other beings, their state of perfection requires an exercise of the will; that is, they must will their own perfection. In mythical terms, they must exercise will to remain in the presence of the sacred. They fail, as does all mankind that follows them.[42]

Death is not present before the Fall, because death has no meaning for the species. Death is not yet an event; neither is birth. An event has a before and after, but at creation all time is present. Time itself would be only iteration, not change. Of perfect iteration, however, there is no measure. We literally could not tell one moment from another. Sin breaks the temporal character of creation. Human time—a measure of past, present, and future—begins with the Fall. This conception of time as moving from present to future is implicit in the dual meanings of labor, which is the source of the sequence of generations and of the world of production. Before the Fall, Adam's present is like the immortality of medieval European kings: deathless in its form but sustained through successive iterations. That a species can die, let alone that a new species can appear, is knowledge that must await nineteenth-century science. The knowledge that man can be the agent of such species disappearances, as well as of new appearances, creates one of the great moral burdens of the twentieth century.

In the beginning, Adam has one great discursive task: the naming of species. Even after Eve's creation, there is nothing further to talk

---

[42] Augustine insists on the "corporate" character of Adam, from which follows his doctrine of original sin. In Adam's sin, we all sinned because the Adam who sinned contained the entire human race. See E. Pagels, *Adam, Eve, and the Serpent* 108–9 (discussing Augustine's *City of God*).

about. If nothing happens, what is there to say? There is no history to record and no future to plan. Life in the Garden is life without male or female labor. From our perspective, there is a sense in which Adam and Eve lack seriousness. For this reason, they are associated with the innocence of childhood. What they say in the Garden—apart from the naming and before the temptation—is not worth recording. It is ephemeral; it is of no consequence. Their talk to each other could not advance beyond idle chatter. The only object of their talk that could be serious would be the praise of God. But here words fail. There is nothing to reason about, no counterpoint against which to judge creation, no need to pray for anything further. Prayer could be nothing other than a naming of God. All that could be said is already said in the name itself.[43]

Discourse begins with temptation.[44] Only now does something happen. The serpent appears. This serpent is not the species' representative: snake.[45] (The serpent is singular—an individual—in a garden of plural beings) He does not appear in order to be named. Rather, when he appears, he speaks. As an individual, the serpent has speech. That speech is hardly idle chatter. The serpent is the symbol of man's will, for its appearance marks the possibility of action. With its appearance, creation breaks apart into individual subjects, each of whom has a unique place in the sequence of time. There is no will in the abstract, no moment of pure will that corresponds to that denial of the individual self which reason seeks through unity with the abstract universal. Will has already individuated in the myth, because will is always the possession of a subject. With the appearance of the serpent, we move immediately from a world in which speech is naming to one in which speech is narrative. The possibility of the willed act marks a before

---

[43] Something of this remains in the Jewish service. While it does present the fundamental narrative of divine intervention in favor of the Jews, at its center is an act of naming the unnamable, of speaking what cannot be said. There is an asymptotic approach to this mysterious center—the more Orthodox the congregation, the more the central act of naming recedes into "what cannot be said." In the Garden we imagine the constraint lifted, which means that all speech would converge on the single name of God.

[44] See M. Luther, "Lectures on Genesis" in *Eve and Adam* 273–74 (K. Kram, L. Schearing & V. Ziegler, eds. 1999) (imagining Adam and Eve's conversation after the Fall).

[45] Interestingly, he becomes that only after the original sin. This is his punishment.

and an after, and that is the domain of narrative. Thus the origin of the subject brings together discourse, will, action, and time.[46]

The serpent's speech is neither that of reason nor that of the desiring body. It is the speech of action. There is not yet knowledge by which to judge the serpent's speech. There is only authority, on the one hand, and temptation, on the other. These are the boundaries of the will. The serpent, accordingly, deploys the vice of the will: jealousy. Jealousy is temptation's response to authority. It is a kind of self-construction that simultaneously involves recognition and denial of the authority of an other. Eve would be like God in the knowledge of good and evil. To be such, she must deny God's authority.

The result of this dialogue of temptation is an act: something new happens in the Garden. Its newness is symbolized in God's failure to know of it. Here, the suggestion is that not even God can foresee a free act. His omniscience does not include the product of a subject's free will.[47] His knowledge corresponds to the perfect and timeless state of creation before the act. Thus God learns of the act only after he sees the evidence of its occurrence. He finds Adam and Eve hiding in the Garden and ashamed of their nakedness.

Tempting Eve, the serpent speaks to her. We cannot separate the temptation from the speech. Entering into a dialogue, she is constituted as an individual. She becomes an individual when speech opens a range of choices. Confronting possibility, she thinks of herself as a subject who can exercise her will. This is the sense in which dialogue creates the subject.[48] If we spoke only the language of mathematics— that is, the language of abstract deduction—speech would not be linked to action. We would, in that case, be in the classical world of pure reason. In *Genesis*, speech, action, and subjectivity are all created at once. This speech that is not naming shows forth a world of possibility: Eve has a choice whether to eat of the apple.

[46] We could push the exegesis back further, noting that even before the serpent's appearance God commands Adam and Eve not to eat of the trees. The command assumes the possibility of the willful act; it, too, is speech linked to action but in the authoritative-prohibitive mode. The possibility of the act is realized with the appearance of the serpent.

[47] This is a highly contested reading, resolving the "paradox of omniscience" against God. Augustine argued that divine omniscience included knowledge of the free act, as did those Protestant sects that took a strong view of predestination. See Augustine, *On Free Choice of the Will* 92 (A. Benjamin & L. Hackstaff, trans. 1964).

[48] See, e.g., C. Taylor, *The Ethics of Authenticity* 33 (1992).

Just as this speech is a necessary condition of subjectivity, action is a necessary condition of dialogue. Speech directed at reason, rather than action, tends toward the null point of dialogue. Beyond a certain point, dialogue gets in the way of truth, which is the goal of reason. Truth makes a claim to settle speech; it closes down discourse.[49] After a successful mathematical proof, there is nothing more to be said. Similarly, claims to truth tend to undermine political communities, which are built on free speech. A world of action, however, is a world of speech.[50] Action has, for this reason, traditionally been associated with rhetoric, which is the art of persuasion. The Serpent's speech, we might say, is the first rhetorical performance. God's speech was creative, not rhetorical; Adam and Eve's speech prior to the Fall was naming, prayer, or chatter. The Serpent shows us speech as action, which is the domain of rhetoric.

Because we are called upon to act, we are called upon to speak and to listen. Every act has its source in a subject. Every subject has his or her reasons. We try to persuade others to exercise choice one way or another by appealing to those reasons. What appears internally as choice appears outwardly as the object of persuasion. Both Adam and Eve succumb to persuasion. We need to refer to that speech—we listen to the narrative—to understand their actions. Action and speech, accordingly, are reciprocal phenomena. They are the constitutive elements of a subject whose defining feature is the will. Because action requires speech, an individual who understands that the source of the self lies in the will necessarily understands himself as a part of a community, for there is no speech apart from a community of speakers.[51] The serpent, we might also say, is the original founder; politics begins in an act of the will.

Adam and Eve speak because they face a choice. If they can choose, they are subjects. The Oedipus story, too, begins with speech, but that speech is prophesy. That divine prophesy stands in sharp contrast to the *Genesis* account in which God lacks knowledge of Adam and

---

[49] See Plato, *Republic*, VI 506d–e (truth itself is beyond the capacity of language).

[50] On action and speech, as mutually constructive of the political realm, see H. Arendt, *The Human Condition* 197–98 (1958).

[51] See P. Flathman, *Willful Liberalism: Voluntarism and Individuality in Political Theory and Practice*, chap. 3 (1992).

Eve's sin until after the fact. Prophesy does not open up a moral domain of action; it undermines the very idea of action. Oedipus is not commanded to do—or not to do—anything. Just the opposite. A prophesy is made that opens up the paradox of free choice in a deterministic world. Oedipus's vice, if he has one, is not of the will; he does not disobey.

Oedipus and Adam provide us with two very different mythical representations of man's place in the world. Oedipus's story always points outward toward the divine conditions within which reason and action go forward: speech becomes riddles, choices accomplish their opposite. The problem for Oedipus is his inability to know what is real and what is not. The play poses the question: "What can we know?" The biblical story instead turns inward. It forces us to ask: "What is the source of disobedience?" The answer to that question is found not in a failure of reason but of will. Both stories tell us that we live in a disordered, unsettled world. Both are stories of failure: one of reason, the other of will. One denies us knowledge, warning that reality may be only a seeming. The other recognizes knowledge—we have eaten of the tree—but at the cost of a disobedient will. One is a story of necessity, the other of freedom. One puts us at the mercy of forces outside ourselves, over which we have no control; the other puts us at the mercy of our own will over which we fail to exercise control.[52] We seem to have to choose between the failure of reason and the failure of will. Modern science may well have solved the riddles of knowledge that were impenetrable to Oedipus, but it has not taken us one step closer to solving the problems of the will. Natural horrors may have receded in a disenchanted universe, but the terrors of evil have only grown in the modern period.

In the Judeo-Christian tradition, every action, even the mythical first act, is the act of a subject, because every action is the product of a choice between possibilities. Only with the introduction of a free subject can we speak of "what might have been."[53] Of course, we speak loosely in this way when we ask, for example: "What would the world

---

[52] Interestingly, for Augustine the consequence of the original failure of the will is a loss of control of the body, particularly in its sexual function.

[53] A traditional problem of theology comes from anthropomorphizing God at this point: Could God have created a different world?

have been like had it not collided with the meteorite that wiped out the dinosaurs?" But this is only a confusion of categories made possible by imagining ourselves as observers of—and thus free agents with respect to—the event in question. The category of "what might have been" is a human category that shapes the narrative of history, not the evolution of prehistory. But it is precisely this category that the prophesy of Oedipus denies.

The category of "what might be" has no existence apart from its imaginative construction in discourse. Without this category, however, we cannot speak of choice. Action, in other words, requires the possible. To understand an event as an act, we have to understand it in relation to possibilities that were not, in fact, realized. That which has been chosen is always seen in the light of that which has not been chosen. Both are equally real from the perspective of the subject. Discourse refers both to what is and what might have been. It refers equally easily to both, because each is necessary to the other. Thus the subjunctive is as necessary a condition for language as the present tense. Contemporary theoreticians make the point that there are no internal marks by which we can distinguish history from fiction: both are narratives.[54] Precisely because the account of human action—history—must refer to what might have been, there is a necessary element of fiction in every narrative.[55]

In the narrative we construct of our own lives, we experience an endless longing for what might have been. This does not mean that we regret the choices we have made. Still, no one fails to feel the enduring pull of at least some of the possibilities those choices excluded, for example, a choice to have no more children or to have none at all. We experience metaphysical, if not psychological, regret. This "might have been" exists in quite a different way from the "might have been" of another ice age,[56] for these unrealized possibilities are as important

---

[54] See, e.g., L. Mink, "History and Fiction as Modes of Comprehension," 1 *New Literacy History* 556–69 (1969); H. White, "The Value of Narrativity in the Representation of Reality," in *On Narrative* 1–23 (W. Mitchell, ed. 1981).

[55] See C. Geertz, *The Interpretation of Culture* 15 (1977) (anthropological writings are "fictions"); M. Foucault, *Power/Knowledge: Selected Interviews and Other Writings, 1972–1977* at 193 (C. Gordon, ed. 1980) ("I have never written anything but fictions").

[56] Games of chance pair these two categories by making the consequence of choice—for example, a bet—dependent on an event rather than an act.

to who I am as are the actual choices made. They are inseparable, because every choice gains its meaning in substantial part from that which has not been chosen.

Having acted, Adam and Eve feel shame toward each other. Shame necessarily accompanies action, because every action exposes the limited character of the subject to him- or herself. We not only choose, but we judge the choices we make. We take ourselves as subjects of an internal discourse. Indeed, we do so endlessly. We invest the limited resource that is the self one way rather than another, and we hold ourselves accountable. We make judgments about our judgment. We know that every choice is partial, and thus we know ourselves as vulnerable—as failing to be complete—at the very moment that we know ourselves as subjects of a particular character. Every choice for something is a choice against other possibilities. Because we must be less than we would be, we are ashamed. This is not a matter of violating a moral rule. We feel shame even when we have done nothing wrong.

At creation Adam and Eve do not know shame, because, without discourse or choice, they are not yet individual subjects. Shame is a reaction to the realized judgment, but there is not yet anyone or anything to judge. Shame first arises when the subject imagines himself to be observed, for in the thought of observation is that of judgment. We think of ourselves as "exposed." An internalized sense of shame requires that the subject imagine himself standing in the place of another who is observing him. To feel shame, accordingly, is to feel simultaneously bound to and estranged from the self. I cannot take that position in the imagination until I have engaged an other in discourse. But we cannot enter into dialogue without being judged and without judging the other.[57] Speaking and being spoken to, we are ashamed. As subjects engaged in the narration of our own lives as the product of free choice, we feel shame.

We cannot experience choice as something that matters without experiencing the subject as a finite, limited asset. Choosing x means giv-

---

[57] Contemporary proponents of discursive communities, for this reason, find themselves interested in "shaming" theories of punishment. See, e.g., J. Braithwaite, "Reintegrative Shaming, Republicanism, and Policy," in *Crime and Public Policy: Putting Theory to Work* 191 (H. Barlow, ed. 1995); D. Kahan, "What Do Alternative Sanctions Mean?" 63 U. Chi. L. Rev. 591 (1996); D. Kahan, "Social Influence, Social Meaning, and Deterrence," 83 Va. L. Rev. 349 (1997).

ing up y forever. To speak of what might have been is to speak of the limited conditions of a human life; it is to invoke death. When we do not think choice matters, our decisions fail to register as elements constitutive of our own subjectivity. They do not enter into our own narrative. Indeed, we rapidly forget the content of such decisions; we do not long for them at all. Nor are we ashamed for having made them. We make countless decisions throughout the day: moving one way rather than another, eating one thing rather than another, flipping through the channels or scanning the newspaper. None of this is remembered; it all could have been otherwise. None of it matters, because nothing is at stake. It is not really chosen, although it may be preferred. Tomorrow we could behave differently; the decisions of today do not preclude their opposite tomorrow. But not everything is like this.

The subject emerges only when the understanding arises that choices matter because they do not come again. Possibility may be infinite, but choice is not. Action differs from behavior in just this element of choice. Of course, there is no defined domain of choice, as if some options are in and of themselves appropriate for choice and others only for behavioral preference. The diversity of human subjects allows for anything at all to become a matter of choice constitutive of the subject. Things or acts become valuable when they become constitutive of a subject who, in the very act of choosing them, must sacrifice other possibilities. We are "invested" in these choices. This investment cannot be measured in economic terms, for it rests on a distinction between value and preference.

The consequence of choice, then, is the knowledge of what might have been and therefore of the reality of death. More precisely, knowing of our own death, we confront choice. Choice matters, because we die. The objects of our choice are valuable, because they make us something rather than nothing. We know that nothing as death. One way to flee from the knowledge of death is to flee from choice.[58] If we lived forever like the Greek gods, we might have personal decisions to make, but they would not matter. That we might be playthings in their

[58] The ethos of entertainment and the pathology of depression are both forms of the flight from choice and recognition.

deathless world is, in part, the horror of Oedipus. It is death that makes us serious. The human subject, as well as the human world, is constituted by choice in the face of the knowledge of a personal death.

In the biblical account, death is the consequence of choice. That representation projects the necessary conditions of human action into a mythical narrative in which conceptual conditions are reified. Death becomes the punishment for choice. That is more or less how we experience our own subjectivity: constituting ourselves as unique by virtue of our freedom to choose, we always appear to ourselves as having failed in that choice. We must fail, because every choice is equally a negation. For this failure, we believe we suffer the burden of death. We are always already fallen. Our sin appears to be original. We are ashamed.

Choice means that we have some control over our will: a capacity to evaluate our plans and to decide what the principle of our action should be. Looking forward, our actions always seem to us to be the product of our plans, that is, we think about what we will do and thus "plan ahead." Accordingly, our actions always appear to us to be the result of choices already made. Kant correctly insisted that free choice represents a break in the chain of physical causality, because there is no scientific or empirical explanation of an action based on a principle. To account for it, we must provide a narrative of the subject, an account of the deliberative process by which the subject chose and thus of the values and principles which he affirmed in that process.

That events in the world can have their source in principle is a complete mystery from the perspective of knowledge. Yet, to the acting subject, it is no mystery at all. It is just the necessary condition of the moral task he finds himself confronting at every wakeful moment. More than that, because he experiences his action as the product of his plans, the world of practice appears as one already imbued with principles. To have beliefs about what we should do is, at least implicitly, to have principles that are separate from the acts themselves. Those principles are available not only to inform our future choices but to evaluate the choices we have already made. We understand ourselves always already to have acted—or failed to act—on principles. We question whether these were the "right" principles and whether they have been applied correctly. Because man is a problem to himself, inevitably he perceives errors. The principles as well as their applications are contested by the subject himself.[59] Again, death makes us see that every life is bought at the cost of what might have been.

We cannot experience choice without experiencing the dread of choosing—or, indeed, of having chosen—wrongly. Again, with choice comes shame. To choose wrongly is to be the wrong person; it is to miss the one chance of being that which we "know" we should be. There are any number of ways this thought is expressed in the Western tradition: the Romantic idea of realizing a true inner self, the Jewish idea of a self constituted by following the law, the Christian idea of being born again, the existentialist idea of taking responsibility for the self. Having the capacity to choose, and caring about choice, we reflect upon the principles that should guide choice. But we have no uncontested source by which to measure the correctness of our choice. The only measure of that choice is the life we lead. By the same token, the measure of the life we lead remains the life that might have been. We can no more escape the one than the other.[60]

Possession of a capacity for choice does not, in the abstract, tell us why we should care about the choices we make or fail to make. We care because we appear as a project to ourselves, and we appear as such a project because of the knowledge of our own finitude. Each of us, as the saying goes, "has just one life to lead." We care about choice, because we care about the constitution of the self as a unique subject.[61] Knowledge of death is the condition of our awareness of ourselves as unique subjects. Only a subject aware of his own death has a moral

[59] The paradigmatic example of this self-contest is Christ's experience of doubt. For a classical version of radical self-doubt, see Plato's *Phaedo*, 60e–61b, where Plato describes Socrates composing songs just before his death. When asked why, Socrates responds that it is just possible that his philosophical mission in life had been based on a misunderstanding of an oracle that told him to "make music."

[60] This is the message of the final myth presented in Plato's *Republic*, the Myth of Er.

[61] See the discussion of "self-love" in H. Frankfurt, *The Reasons of Love* 97 (2004) ("[Self-love] is a condition in which we willingly accept and endorse our own volitional identity. We are content with the final goals and with the loving by which our will is most penetratingly defined")

responsibility for creating his life. We would eat of the tree of knowledge, but we cannot do so without taking up the burden of death. Had Adam and Eve chosen instead to eat of the tree of life, there would be nothing to say. Nothing would have changed. There would be only the timeless replication of the species.

After the Fall, sin is constitutive of what it means to be a subject. This is Adam's real sin: he becomes a person. Before that, he was man, not a man. The subject experiences himself as already fallen because he always experiences himself as a project that is only partially accomplished and that has already partially failed. One never finds the self in a state of perfection to be maintained but always in a state of yearning, a state of dissatisfaction with the present. This is the existential condition of shame. The absence of such a yearning appears to the moral agent not as a state of beatitude or peace but as a kind of moral stupor. It is a forgetting of the urgency of life in the face of death.

If Adam's sin is that he becomes a person, then there is an infinite longing for a return to that state in which there was no subjectivity, no differentiation of the subject. One traditional expression of that longing is to imagine the self beyond death. The Platonic myth dissolved the individual subject into a pure knowledge of Ideas. In the Judeo-Christian world, in which the subject is the product of the will, that answer is not possible. The will requires an affirmation of the subject at the same moment that there is a transcendence of finitude. The longing of the subject must be responsive to the sense of self as fallen, which means an understanding of self as an individual facing the reality of his own death.

Self-transcendence—at least in the West—is not the dissolution of the finite in the infinite but the affirmation of both, that is, of the infinite in and through the finite. For this reason, no explanation of heaven has, or could, overcome the problem of the one and the many: Would we be one or many in eternity? We must be both. That collapse of the one and the many is at the center of Christianity: God is one and three. The Son is both apart from and the same as the Father; he both dies and lives. The sacraments replicate this ambiguity of the one and the many in the daily life of the members of the Church. To participate in the sacraments is—until the next moment of action—to be without sin. To be without sin is to be without subjectivity; one exists not as a subject but as a part of the body of Christ, which is the Church.[62] To be without sin is to approach the point at which the will disappears. This, however, is not the human condition. So the mystery of the sacrament can never be anything but episodic. We are thrown back into our individual lives, facing the limits of our own choices and the knowledge of our own death. This longing of the finite self for the infinite opens a space for good and evil. We know the "good" form of this self-transcendence as love; its pathological partner is evil.

The metaphysics of will is impenetrable to the Enlightenment mind and to the whole movement of modern rationalism. Enlightenment means to take responsibility through the exercise of choice under the guidance of reason's identification of right principles.[63] If we believe that a domain of action can be perfectly ordered by reason, not only evil but love, too, slips from view. There is neither love nor evil in the conceptual world of the laboratory or the market. If we believe that politics could be perfectly ordered by reason, then politics, too, could be a domain without love and evil. Liberals often entertain this dream, banishing that which resists reason to the domain of the private. What remains would be a politics of administrative rationality, on the one hand, and judicial reasonableness, on the other.[64] Reason may dream of such a perfected politics, but reason has always been a weak force in the face of the will—exactly the point of the myth of the Fall. Liberals are always shocked by the resistance of politics to reason. We forget at our peril that politics remains a domain of love and evil.[65] Reason alone will not take the self from deliberation to action.

The world imagined from the perspective of the will does not end with an account of reasonable deliberation and its failure, or of rationally justifiable principles and enlightened institutional design—or their failure. Rather, the world of the will includes ideas of the macro-

---

[62] The miraculous powers of the saint are related to this magical quality of a "subjectless" soul. The saint becomes an intermediary between the praying subject and God.

[63] See I. Kant, "An Answer to the Question 'What Is Enlightenment,'" reprinted in *Kant: Political Writings* 54 (H. Nisbet, trans., H. Reiss, ed. 1971).

[64] This emphasis on the marketplace and the courtroom is just what Larry Siedentop finds emerging in the European Union. See L. Siedentop, *Democracy in Europe* (2001).

[65] See Kahn, *Putting Liberalism in Its Place*.

cosm in the microcosm, of self-transcendence, of temporal simultaneity, of mystery and magic. If we imagine self-transcendence not as unification with the other through love but as the destruction of the other, then we approach the domain of evil.

CONCLUSION: LOVE AND EVIL

The inquiry into evil begins from an awareness of the experience of sin as the condition of a finite being with an awareness of the infinite. In this chapter I have begun the elaboration of the elements of a theory of evil. These include the self-creation of the subject in the face of a knowledge of death, the place of the will in the constitution of that subject, and the endless need to transcend the conditions of subjectivity. Evil is never far from death: not biological death but the existential condition of knowing of our own death. Nor, however, is it far from love. The metaphysics of our normative order—the structure the world must have to support the values we find there—seems always to leave open two possibilities: love and evil. Both show us the continuing presence of forms of experience that are not accountable to reason. The outbreaks of evil in the last century remind us that reason had not penetrated deeply into the sources of meaning that actually motivate political orders and individuals.

Man is, by nature, an incomplete being within which the whole of existence—what is and what might be—shows itself. He always combines the finite and the infinite. Knowing that we will die, our condition is beyond the possibility of repair by reason. In the Judeo-Christian tradition, man experiences the human condition as a metaphysical scandal. He is, we might say, metaphysically jealous of God. This scandal continues in a secularized form today. That a being who contemplates the whole of creation from the Big Bang to the Cosmic Crunch is limited to the merely material conditions of his experience is no less shocking than Adam's fall. Adam's condition after the Fall is a mythical representation of this shocking antinomy for he has eaten of the tree of knowledge—and is thus like God—but he is condemned to the conditions of his own singularity in time and space. In short, he combines knowledge and death.

Man would encompass the whole of the universe, but he is always thrown back upon the very real limitations of his own subjectivity, his own choices, and his own time. From the perspective of reason, there is no way out of this antinomy, except by denying one side or the other. One either affirms the whole and thereby denies the conditions of subjectivity, or one affirms the limits on the subject and denies the possibility of the infinite. This is a familiar antinomy in the West, one that appears in various domains and guises: epistemic (transcendent vs. empirical accounts), ethical (deontological vs. utilitarian accounts), and ontological (idealist vs. realist accounts).

No particular choice we make can overcome the burden of our own death and the awareness of finitude as an experience of shame. To overcome this state of fallenness, we seek a state of being beyond choice. Evil is the effort at self-help by the fallen will. It is an effort to overcome the conditions of finitude and thus of death itself. It is, however, a strategy of denial, of projecting shame and death on to the other. Evil claims for the self the power of life and death. The motion of evil is the flight from death through murder. The motion of love is self-transcendence through sacrifice for the beloved. Love invokes a power over death by turning death into sacrifice. Sacrifice and murder, love and evil, mark the basic antinomy of the will in the Judeo-Christian tradition. The sides of this antinomy, I argue, are perilously close to each other. A politics of sacrifice is also one of murder.[66]

The particular, finite being we know ourselves to be has an unlimited capacity for love or for evil. This intimate connection of love and evil is the reason that all our cultural creations are suspect. With only the slightest change of perspective, our highest accomplishments can be revealed as structures of evil. Thus Walter Benjamin famously proclaimed, "There is no document of civilization which is not at the same time a document of barbarism."[67] Whatever we do, we are "ashamed." This double sense is carried forward in postmodern theory in the ambiguous quality of the central concept of power. Is power good or evil? Is it the source of cultural productivity or the source of

---

[66] This is the central claim of chapter 5 below.

[67] W. Benjamin, "Theses on the Philosophy of History" in *Illuminations* 253, 256 (H. Arendt & H. Zohn, trans. 1969).

individual constraint? Is some power good, and some evil, or is it always a question of where one stands in relationship to the assertion of power?[68] The entire world can, in a moment, appear as a structure of evil.

Evil is not simply a condition to be eliminated. It is the point of the "all too human." Man cannot conceive of his death without conceiving of a self that can overcome death. This is what it means to experience the self as fallen. We exist in that ambiguous moral state that is the intersection of the human and the divine, the profane and the sacred. This is the point at which the possibility of evil emerges simultaneously with the possibility of love. A study of evil, then, is a study of the human condition from beneath. It is a study of love gone wrong.

---

[68] I explore this double-character of power in Kahn, *Law and Love*.

CHAPTER TWO

■   ■   ■   ■

EVIL AND THE IMAGE
OF THE SACRED

Liberalism fails to understand evil for just the same reason that it fails
to understand love. Its horizon of explanation is framed by reason, on
the one hand, and personal well-being, on the other. Between reason
and interest, it can find no third term. It has no conception of the will
that is not absorbed either by the universalism of reason or by the
particularism of interest.[1] These always appear to be in a state of actual or threatened tension: reason must rein in interest, which will
always seek more than reason allows. This tension remains as long as
individuals find themselves living under conditions of moderate scarcity, because even under the best of arrangements they cannot have all
that they want.[2] Evil, accordingly, can appear to liberalism only as a
failure of reason or as unconstrained desire—two perspectives on the
same phenomenon.

Liberalism can see pathologies to be cured, but not evil beyond repair. Its effort to explain evil focuses on the social or psychological
conditions that lead to the failure of the ordinary constraints of reasonableness. The acts that result are addressed as pathologies subject
to the criminal law, on the one hand, or to therapeutic intervention,
on the other. When evil appears as a political rather than a personal
phenomenon, liberalism's response remains the same: enforcement of
law may now require an army; therapeutic intervention may require
foreign assistance and institutional reorganization. In each instance,
evil is understood as the collapse of the mechanisms of reasonable
restraint, resulting in or caused by the outbreak of irrational desires.

---

[1] See P. Kahn, *Putting Liberalism in Its Place* 15–16 (2005).

[2] See B. Ackerman, *Social Justice in the Liberal State* 31–33 (1980); J. Rawls, *A Theory
of Justice* 127 (1971) (on moderate scarcity).

To many, the great surprise of the twentieth century was the simultaneous extension of the empire of reason and the reach of evil. To the liberal sensibilities of the nineteenth-century Victorian, the political disasters of the next hundred years were beyond imagining.[3] Having discovered the principles of political rationality, the next hundred years should have been a period of moderation and reform as reason spread throughout the world. Even colonialism was understood as an aspect of this process of bringing civilization—that is, reason—to its full practical extension. Nevertheless, the science of politics did not save Europe from a self-destructive frenzy of violence, and the spread of civilization proved quite compatible with evil both before and after the process of decolonization.

When the political failure came, liberal thought was not prepared for it. Predictably its explanations tended to move in two directions. In part, it saw a problem in the identification of the principles of reason. The problem with fascism or communism was that they were false sciences of the political. A false science could not do the work of reason to restrain interest. Political disputes were thereby assimilated to other forms of scientific disagreement. But scientific disagreements do not ordinarily lead to violence and slaughter. Why would the United States and the Soviet Union threaten to destroy each other— and incidentally the rest of the world—over the question of who should own the means of production in a technologically advanced society? Such destruction surely would not be in the interest of either, just as the earlier great wars of the century could not be explained in terms of the advancement of the state's ordinary interest in citizen well-being. If the false-science explanation was not adequate, then the problem had to be located in particular individuals who abused their positions of power because of their own psychological pathologies. Now the problem was not wrong reason but too little reason. The problem, on this view, was not Germany but Hitler; not the U.S.S.R. but Stalin. These were unreasonable men driven by personal pathologies, even when they were responding to real political circumstances.

---

[3] See I. Berlin, "The Bent Twig: On the Rise of Nationalism," in *The Crooked Timber of Humanity: Chapters in the History of Ideas* 247–48 (1990) (on failure to foresee twentieth-century nationalism).

Their appeal to political ideology was only a rhetorical form; real explanation could be found only in an analysis of individual psychology.[4] Under some circumstances, political situations arise that empower leaders who themselves lack the internal mechanisms of reasonable restraint. A policy designed to prevent evil should therefore be one that intervenes to prevent these situations from arising in the first place or, if such leaders nevertheless arise, devises institutional mechanisms for their removal. This gave us the postwar, double agenda of development aid, on the one hand, and international criminal law, on the other: the Marshall Plan and the Nuremberg trials.

Of course, both these sorts of claims might be true, even if they do not provide an adequate account of evil. There can be false sciences of the political. Fascism and communism, from the perspective of the twenty-first century, certainly do look like false sciences. So, however, does laissez-fair capitalism, as well as the varieties of social Darwinism that accompanied our own liberal politics one hundred years ago. Belief in eugenics was widespread at the start of the twentieth century, but it did not lead to genocide everywhere. We have little reason to think that a science of politics explains much in the operation of actual polities. The gulf between science and practice, between theory and action, remains too large; the relationship of each to the other is, at best, reciprocal, with practice affecting theory as much as the reverse. Consider, for example, the contemporary transformation of Chinese communism into a form of capitalism.

Similarly, a political leadership can no doubt demonstrate psychological pathologies. Yet that is hardly an explanation of national political action. All the questions remain as to why and how such individuals are seen as heroic rather than sick, as leaders rather than criminals. After the fact, we might treat such political leaders as criminals. We often do so in order to separate their moral responsibility from that of the larger political community.[5]

Whether it is effective or not as a transitional strategy for overcoming the burden of political evil, criminal accountability reflects the con-

---

[4] A closely related view projected the pathology of interest not on a particular individual but on an entire class, for example, European aristocrats, capitalists, or the working class.

[5] See, e.g., J. Malamud, *Game without End: State Terror and the Politics of Justice* (1996); J. Sklar, *Legalism* 155–56 (1964) (on Nuremberg).

ceptual resources available to liberal thought. Liberalism can understand individual criminality; it resists a discourse that speaks of the body politic as an evil actor. It will assimilate such groups to criminal conspiracies.[6] It is committed to an individualism that is both metaphysical and moral. It will always be inclined to reduce the political to the psychological, to view evil as a problem of criminality, and criminality as a problem of the failure of reason to restrain interest. Liberalism will pursue the calculus of punishment—a just measure of retribution and an effective amount of deterrence. Outside this calculus, liberalism fears that the dignity of the individual—even that of the wrongdoer—will be lost.

In the liberal world, evil slips from view. Instead, we see mistake and crime, or false science and psychological deviance. None of these is adequate to account for the presence of evil in the world. For this reason, liberalism is always surprised by the failure of reason. In the public order, liberals will continue to pass laws and establish tribunals; in the private, they will support more education and more therapeutic interventions. But they never seem to be able to get ahead of the problem of evil. There is always the hope for one more institutional reform—a constitutional court, an international criminal court, universal jurisdiction, open markets, or increased foreign aid—or one more form of therapy—psychological, sociological, pedagogical, or pharmacological—that will finally usher in a well-ordered world in which the individual can exercise his or her own reason in the establishment of a moderate life plan that each perceives to be good. It never seems to work. Our actual world is one in which nuclear-equipped armies stand facing each other, in which genocide and torture regularly appear, in which ethnic nationalism leads to civil war, and in which individuals regularly abuse others.

A contemporary approach to evil, accordingly, must also be a critique of liberalism—not a critique of liberal political policies, as if the correct alternatives were conservative policies, but a critique of the

---

[6] Accordingly, at Nuremburg, group criminality was conceived under the model of a criminal conspiracy. See, generally, G. Fletcher, *Romantics at War: Glory and Guilt in the Age of Terrorism* (2002); A. Danner & J. Martinez, "Guilty Associations: Joint Criminal Enterprise, Command Responsibility, and the Development of International Criminal Law," 93 Cal. L. Rev. 75 (2005).

philosophical approach upon which those policies rest. The policy disputes between political liberals and conservatives are little more than disputes over the best application of broadly liberal principles. The pattern of liberal thought on evil was already established in the philosophical framework offered by Immanuel Kant. His fundamental insight was to turn away from the metaphysical task of trying to understand the possibility of moral freedom in a world governed by universal causality: How can we be free in a law-governed universe? Rejecting metaphysics, he asked what we can know about our world and what we must believe about our own actions. We are not in a position to say anything at all about an ultimate reality. We do not have God's view of creation; we have only the structure of our own experience, which spans facts and values, causal accounts and free choice. His turn away from metaphysics, however, was not a turn to particular, individual experience. It was, instead, a turn to the universal capacity for reason. Kant argued that we experience both science and morality as deployments of reason. Both appeal to law: the laws of nature, on the one hand, and the moral law we give to ourselves as free agents, on the other. Both kinds of law rest on reason. Liberalism, too, is committed both to individual responsibility under a moral rule of reason and to scientific, causal explanation. Thus the practical and the natural sciences have existed side by side for two hundred years.

This double schema applies at the macro level of politics as well as the micro level of our own behavior. When we address the issue of future behavior, we cannot help but appeal to our deliberative resources organized under principles of moral reasoning. We ask what it is we should do. We have to convince ourselves and others that our answer to that question is the correct answer. So we deploy arguments that appeal to common ground of reason. We find ourselves making arguments about what all rational beings would agree to, whether the maximization of utility or adherence to a set of common rules. All such debates assume that in and through the deployment of reason, the question for free action—What should I do?—can be answered. The same is true when the task of free action is political. Here, too, the modern, liberal approach is first to write a constitution, which means to deploy reason to specify a set of institutions, rights, and obligations. We enter into these debates believing that, in our common appeal to reason, we will reach agreement on a political order.[7]

When we look back on this same behavior, however, we organize it under causal patterns of explanation. We theorize about the influences on individuals or even about the relationship of brain chemistry to behavior. On the macrolevel of the political, we speak of economic, geographic, sociological, biological, or countless other causes. Looking back, we are never satisfied with an explanation that simply says it was a free choice; looking forward, we are never satisfied with causal predictions. These two perspectives are always set in tension with each other.

In offering his solution, Kant himself falls victim to an earlier metaphysical puzzle: Is it possible to theorize evil without making it simply the appearance of an absence? As long as being and the good are one and the same, a failure of the good must appear as a failure of being. While Kant has nothing to say about being or nonbeing apart from human experience, he nevertheless takes up a modern version of this position when he identifies moral failure with the absence of reason. If action is not the product of reason's self-direction, then it must be the causal product of desire. In this claim, Kant replicates the classical opposition of soul and body. Body without reason is, for Kant, not really the subject at all, for the subject only shows itself—only exists— to the degree that he or she gives the self a principle of action. This produces a kind of baseline principle of modernity: the truth of the Kantian subject resides in his or her universality, not individuality. My character as a particular subject is a product of the body—its desires, pleasures, and pains—which may be part of the world but fails to represent the truth of the subject. Kant's transcendental idealism is not all that far from the metaphysics of the Fall.

For Kant, in the absence of the principled choice of reason, we are thrown back into a causal world, and thus to explanations of behavior that point to laws of nature rather than moral laws. We speak, accordingly, of "influences," not choices. Only when reason controls action does the subject realize freedom. Without freedom, the subject is not really present at all. What appear to be actions are to be explained as

---

[7] For a paradigmatic theoretical expression of this approach, see Rawls, *A Theory of Justice*.

merely phenomena in the world. Because action is always possible, for Kant the failure of the subject to appear is not an excuse: one could always have acted. Nevertheless, we approach moral failure as if it were a negation or an absence of the subject.[8]

Even Kant understands that this explanation is not adequate to the appearance of evil, which most certainly does appear as action by a subject.[9] But neither Kant nor his liberal successors have a conceptual apparatus adequate to the problem of evil. Freedom, the subject, and reason all coincide: if a subject is present, it must be because she is giving herself a rule of action. To understand evil, Kant falls back on the only alternative left to him: it must be action based on a wrong maxim. He cannot easily explain, however, how mistakes or irrationality can ground a free act. It is, he says, "inscrutable."[10] Is not the application of a wrong principle an empty set? It can determine nothing. A mistake in mathematics, for example, is a mere nullity. Is it not the same with moral law? There seems to be no space left for the free act that is constitutive of an evil subject. If so, the appropriate response is again therapeutic, which means to replace nothing with something.

Kant understands the Enlightenment as the moment of recovery of man's wholeness. The subject is now to give to himself the principle of his own being: reason. Man becomes a project to himself. He is to act as reason demands in all his relationships. This is the principle incorporated in the categorical imperative: "act only according to that maxim by which you can at the same time will that it should become a universal law."[11] Indeed, after the Enlightenment, anything of practical importance becomes a project for reform based on reason: self-construction, on the one hand, and political, economic, or social construction, on the other. All our practices, habits, and traditions should be subject to the test of reason. Politics, no less than individual action,

[8] On Kant's problem of reconciling his conception of evil with his understanding of the conditions of freedom, see generally R. Bernstein, "Radical Evil: Kant at War with Himself," in *Rethinking Evil: Contemporary Perspectives* 55–85 (M. Lara, ed. 2001). Bernstein quotes John Silber precisely on the point "[Kant's] evil is expressed in abandoning the conditions of free personal fulfillment in favor of fulfillment as a creature of natural desire." *Id.* at 80.

[9] See I. Kant, *Religion within the Limits of Reason Alone* 25 (T. Greene & H. Hudson, trans. 1960) [1772] ("The wickedness or . . . the corruption of the human heart is the propensity of the will . . . to [reverse] the ethical order [or priority] among the incentives of a free will").

[10] *Id.* at 17.

[11] I. Kant, *Foundations of the Metaphysics of Morals* 39 (L. Beck, trans. 1959) [1785].

should be a product of deliberation and choice under the guidance of reason. Kant can dream of "perpetual peace" in such a world.

Not only does God have little to say in this world, man is constitutionally incapable of hearing him—unless he speaks the language of reason. There are no more miracles. If that is all God has to say, however, man no longer has need of him in order to discern what must be done. Man already has all the reason he needs both to understand the world and to shape his own free actions in that world. Modern liberals still dream of this world, but this was not the world the Enlightenment produced.

Before the First World War a powerful imaginative effort was needed to overcome the liberal confidence that evil was only a failure of reason and that the West was moving in the direction of a common culture of science, the rule of law, and administrative rationality in place of an earlier history of political conflict, authoritarian rule, and religious prejudice. After the war, evil haunted the ordinary imagination as well as the actual political landscape.[12] Today, however, as the great wars recede from memory, we hear again from the same sort of apostles of Enlightenment who wholly failed to foresee the latent potential for evil that erupted in the twentieth century. Not surprisingly, Kant's theory of perpetual peace among reasonable, well-ordered states is again invoked.[13] Today the shock of terror is the equivalent of the shock of the outbreak of war in 1914. This time, however, we have no excuse for failing to explore the nature and source of evil.

CONTEMPLATION AND LABOR BEFORE THE FALL

From what point does the explanation of evil begin? It begins not with the Fall but with creation. We cannot understand the Fall without understanding what it is from which man fell, for in the identification

---

[12] See, e.g., E. Remarque, *All Quiet on the Western Front* (A. Wheen, trans. 1996) [1929]; W. Owen, "Dulce et Decorum Est," in *The Complete Poems and Fragments*, vol. 1 (J. Stallworthy, ed. 1983).

[13] See M. Doyle, "Kant, Liberal Legacies, and Foreign Affairs," 12 Phil. & Pub. Affairs 203–34, 323–53 (1983); A. Slaughter, "International Law in a World of Liberal States," 6 Eur. J. Int'l. L. 503, 504 (1995).

of sin, there is always an aspiration for recovery.[14] In the *Genesis* account, however, it is as if there were such uncertainty about the truth of man's nature that the myth of origins had to be written twice.

On the first account, God, man, and nature stand in a continuous relationship with one another. God first creates the natural world and then creates man "in our own image, after our likeness." This man who is the image of God is created male and female. Neither in the relationship to God nor in the relationship to the things of the earth is there a distinction between man and woman. Man who is the image of God has "dominion over . . . all the earth, and over every creeping thing that creeps upon the earth."[15] Man is not just an image of God as a sculpture might be an image of someone. It is not a question of appearance but of power, that is, of "dominion." To all the rest of creation, man represents God's power on earth. Man is the point at which the authority of the creator shows itself within the created world. Man's rule, moreover, speaks directly to the goodness of God: "God saw everything that he had made, and behold, it was very good." Prelapsarian man and woman live within a world perfectly suited for them: "And God said, 'Behold, I have given you every plant . . . and every tree.' " Accordingly, they need only be themselves to realize the principle of meaning in the world: it is all an expression of God's goodness. This man, who is an image of God, is content with his own divine origins, for he lacks nothing. He may have dominion, but he has no needs that require labor. What remains for him is what remains for God after creation is complete: to contemplate the goodness of creation. Paradise, we might say, is the indefinite continuation of the seventh day, the day of rest and contemplation.

Yes, but not quite, for a second account follows rapidly on the first.[16] In this account, God most emphatically does not give man "every

[14] See G. Anderson, *The Genesis of Perfection: Adam and Eve in Jewish and Christian Imagination* 8 (2001) ("*Genesis* is not only about the origins of sin; it is also about the foundations of human perfection").

[15] Luther expresses this idea as follows: "Here the rule is assigned to the most beautiful creature, who knows God and is the image of God, in whom the similitude of the divine nature shines forth through his enlightened reason, through his justice and wisdom." Lectures on Genesis, in *Eve and Adam: Jewish, Christian, and Muslim Readings on Genesis and Gender* 267 (K. Kvam, L. Schearing & V. Ziegler, eds. 1999).

[16] On the subsequent history of the two accounts, see E. Pagels, *Adam, Eve, and the Serpent* (1989).

tree." In this account, God's creative act does not end with man, who then mediates between creation and divinity by virtue of being an image of God. Instead, God's creation of life begins with man. Man's end is no longer to reflect upon the goodness of creation. Instead, from the beginning, man must work. Labor defines man's existence even before the Fall: "The Lord God took the man and put him in the garden of Eden to till it and keep it." Man does not look out over all creation but over only a limited domain within which he has a particular task. That domain is circumscribed from without—Eden is a geographically defined location, set among four rivers—but also circumscribed from within—man may not eat of the tree of good and evil. Nor does God look upon his creation as complete and good from the start; rather, creation appears as a project to be perfected as the need arises. In this second account, both man and God are seen from the perspective of action, not contemplation. Thus God reflects, "It is not good that man should be alone; I will make him a helper fit for him." Even this task of finding man a helper is presented as a project subject to a process of trial and error. God first creates animals in the search for man's helper but is unsuccessful. This causes him to adopt a new strategy in the creation of woman from a part of man. Man as actor stands in constant need of divine assistance. The presence of this divine succor—not the absence of labor—marks this as paradise. Tending creation is a joint project of man and God. It must be, as long as man himself does not know good and evil.

We find in these two myths the elements of a fundamental ambiguity that has haunted the Western mind for millennia. In the first ("Genesis one") there is a "natural" correspondence between subjects and their world. A world made for man and woman is fundamentally a knowable world. Man is not a stranger in this world. Knowing this world, he knows it as good, just as God judged it to be good: being and goodness are inseparable. This is already built into the ideas that the world is a product of divine creation and that man is at one with the creator. To create is to act with regard to a final cause. For God, the final cause of creation can only be goodness itself. Since it is creation *ex nihilo*, there is no impediment or resistance to the realization of the good in the material cause of creation; there is no separate material cause. Thus it is neither accident nor skill that leads God to conclude that his creation is good. In Genesis one, the goodness of God's act is also its goodness for man. To be an image of God is to share in the divine purposes. We find here a series of fundamental equivalencies: knowledge, creation, and goodness. Fully to know is simultaneously to realize the truth of the subject's own existence which is the goodness of creation. On this view, man's Fall results in the breaking apart of these equivalences. His recovery would be to regain this knowledge. This line of thought reaches its ultimate fruition in Hegel. If we knew what God knows, we would again overcome the distance between the creator and the created. We would again be an image of God.

In the second myth ("Genesis two"), we find a set of reflections on man who always experiences himself as out of place in the order of nature. Even the things made for him must be subdued by him. He must labor in the garden from the first; there is not yet a helper "fit for him." This man experiences himself as always threatened by need. Similarly, he must name the creatures of the earth. Naming is another way of appropriating and subordinating to his own will; it is a form of labor, a kind of taxonomic task. Everything about Genesis two points to the future as anticipated need; labor, not contemplation, defines man's character. Being and goodness never coincide once creation includes the self-consciousness of a needful being. From the perspective of Genesis two, the Fall is not a failure in the dimension of knowledge but in that of action. God is no longer there to help man with this endless task. Man is on his own, and this is truly terrifying.

In Genesis one, man sees the present as complete and thus good. There is no need for labor or speech; man does not see his own death. Instead of death, he sees continuity—"be fruitful and multiply"—and endless dominion. Man has no need beyond that of realizing the principle of his own being, which is to be the image of God. He is that simply by being the point at which creation gains awareness of itself. Being, reason, and the good all intersect in the mind of man, which at this moment of contemplation approaches the mind of God. This has remained the aspiration of much of our philosophical and religious tradition: to know that which God knows. Man is the finite creature in which the infinite shows itself. One strand of this aspiration is expressed in the various mystical traditions within Judeo-Christian thought; another strand is expressed in the turn to "natural philosophy"—which develops into modern science—with its idea that the world itself expresses the mind of God.[17] There is always something divine about knowledge.

It would make little sense to say of this man that he could not eat of the tree of knowledge of good and evil. For God possesses knowledge and power. Man certainly does not possess the latter. If men and women are an image of God, it must be because of their capacity for knowledge. As the myth says, this man is given the fruit of "every tree." Satisfying as this image of completeness may be from the perspective of contemplation, it fails to account for man's experience of himself as subject to an indeterminate future, as somehow radically incomplete, that is, as in need of a helper. In Genesis two, even before the Fall, man appears to himself as suffering need. Man of the second myth is neither a natural philosopher nor a mystic; he is a laborer. One does not experience need as universal but as most intensely personal.

Each myth provides a theological/metaphysical account of a familiar experience: the awe that man stands in before his own consciousness of creation and the unease he experiences before the endless task of labor. This double perspective within the creation accounts of *Genesis* is reflected in traditional approaches to evil. In the first myth, man is complete simply in and through his consciousness of being. If the object of contemplation is creation itself, and creation is the product of a divine act that is good, then there is simply no room for evil. This follows from God's pronouncement of the goodness of creation—not good in part but fully and completely. The Fall signifies a failure of comprehension, a substitution of appearance for reality. Such a failure of apprehension is a failure of man to be fully that which he is essentially—an image of God. There is a long history of this form of theodicy in the West. If all creation is good, then the appearance of the bad—misfortune, natural disaster, and even evil behavior—must be a false appearance. Evil is a problem in the knower, not in the object of

---

[17] On the connection of these two strands in the early modern period, see D. MacCulloch, *The Reformation* 658–62 (2003); C. Webster, *From Paracelsus to Newton: Magic and the Making of Modern Science* (1982).

knowledge. The created world is, and must be, the best of all possible worlds. As Pope famously said, "Whatever is, is right."[18] That we fail to see this is a consequence of our character, not a fault in the world.

For man as actor, the world appears quite differently. He moves not toward withdrawal from, but rather investment in, the world. He does not see the wholeness of the good at once but experiences an endless demand placed upon him from without and an endless need arising from within. Looking forward, not backward, he sees a constant threat of failure. He sees a need that ultimately he cannot meet in the threat of his own death. He appears to himself as a wasting asset, pregnant with nonbeing.[19] He cannot secure a world without need or pain even for those he loves. On his own, the best he can do is to improve conditions "for the time being." He can reform but not cure the disorder of the world. From the perspective of need, the apologetic character of the first view approaches moral irresponsibility and metaphysical nonsense. It is an appropriate subject of ridicule as in Voltaire's *Candide* and Hume's *Dialogue*. Laboring man stands in need of that which he had before the Fall: divine assistance.

From the perspective of labor, knowledge appears inadequate to the task of meeting need. Indeed, it is knowledge that delineates need. Knowledge of good and evil gives man the charge, the direction, in which he must move, but it does not give him the resources fully to meet that need. After all, God links knowledge to death, telling Adam that, if he eats of that tree, "you shall die." At best, man can produce more—more of the fruits of the ground and more of the fruits of sexual union—but neither form of production is able to meet the endless need that the future presents. Looking inward, man finds a kind of empti-

---

[18] See A. Pope, "Essay on Man" in *Selected Poetry and Prose* (W. Wimsatt, ed. 1951). See generally S. Neiman, *Evil in Modern Thought: An Alternative History of Philosophy* 18–36 (2002).

[19] Kant's "Speculative Beginning of Human History," which is his "fanciful" reading of *Genesis* 2–6, emphasizes this line of interpretation. He sees the first human couple discovering an awareness of freedom through the deployment of reason. This leads quickly, however, to "anxiety and unease" in the face of the "infinitude" of choices that reason reveals and then to a vision of endless need leading inevitably to death. Man finds himself "[thrown] into the world, where he was awaited by so many crises, burdens, and unknown evils." Man's hope is for a paradise in which "he could dream or trifle away his existence in peaceful inactivity and permanent peace." See I. Kant, *Perpetual Peace and Other Essays* 49, 51–53 (T. Humphrey, trans. 1983) [1786].

ness: he sees finitude—death—not the infinite. Not surprisingly the symbol of this failure, which arises with the knowledge of good and evil, is the awareness of man's sexual nature. For even more than economic labor, sex is the sign of man's endless longing in the face of his own death.[20] Accordingly, the serpent becomes a sign of sexual threat and danger. The serpent is the false promise of divine assistance, but man needs the real thing.

On the first account, then, evil is a mere appearance to be explained by a failure of knowledge. If we knew what God knows, then we would not see evil. God's knowledge, exercised at creation, is easily reconfigured as the objectivity of a scientific account. For this reason, there was a direct move from the eighteenth-century deist, who believed that God's creation was limited to the original act of getting the universe going, to the twentieth-century scientist, who believed that if that were so, then there is no reason to refer to God at all. If God is done with us, then we can be done with him. There is no need to think about the author as long as we have the text. The monk contemplating the unity of being and the good is the premodern form of the physicist contemplating a unified field theory.

If the world works according to scientific laws—if all that happens can be accounted for by causes that are independent of moral judgment—then there is no room left for evil. From the perspective of evil, there is not a large difference between saying that this is the best of all possible worlds because it was created by God and saying that it is the only possible world because it is causally determined under universal laws. True, one account emphasizes final causes; the other, efficient causes. But the final causes are God's: to man's knowledge they add nothing beyond the abstract character of the good; that is, no particular good is at stake. Tracing back in time the course of efficient causes will take us just as rapidly to the uncaused origin of the whole: creation ex nihilo or the big bang. Either way, the universe seems indifferent to any moral valuation of man's labor. Whether we speak of divine providence or scientific laws of causation, evil disappears from sight because human freedom disappears.

---

[20] Diotima's speech in Plato's *Symposium* (201d–207a4) provides a classical expression of this view.

The scientific/contemplative account, however, is no more complete in modernity than it was when offered in Genesis one. As Kant saw, it misses the equally fundamental experience of man as actor.[21] We have no particular reason to begin the account of ourselves from the experience of contemplation rather than from that of labor and need. We can no more deny the experience of ourselves as free actors, who must labor to produce the good, than deny that the universe is fundamentally accessible to reason and reason's laws. From the latter perspective, we must deny the possibility of miracles; that is, everything that happens is explainable within the terms of a scientific inquiry, even if we are not yet fully capable of giving the explanation. But then free action itself and the moral demand with which we experience the possibility of freedom looks like a regular recourse to miraculous intervention. Nevertheless, this is a miracle in which we are constitutionally required to believe: we cannot help but believe that we can and must labor to produce the good. This double character of our necessary beliefs was not the discovery of Kant in the eighteenth century. It was already present in the double character of the myths of creation in *Genesis*.

It is often said that evil is a failure to recognize the common humanity in the other. Nazis, for example, failed to see Jews as human; American racists fail to see African Americans as human. But this just pushes the inquiry back to what it means to be human. Doing so, it avoids the hardest part of the inquiry into evil, for there is not just one way to be human. The Genesis account of creation already suggests two ways: thinking and acting. To the subject as actor, thinking is never enough, for the aspiration for the infinite presses upon him as a fear of his own death. To be assured that he already possesses the infinite is not reassuring at all. To the contemplative subject, on the other hand, labor is never enough, for in that direction there can be no completeness.

This tension of the infinite in the finite often appears in the Western tradition as the tension of soul and body: the immortal soul and the

---

[21] Kant begins the conclusion of the *Second Critique* with a reflection on the inescapable connection of thought and action: "Two things fill the mind with ever new and increasing admiration and awe . . . the starry heavens above me and the moral law within me." I. Kant *Critique of Practical Reason* 166 (L. Beck, trans. 1956) [1788].

mortal body. Kant's theory of heteronomy and, more generally, liberalism's understanding of the irrational character of interests represent modern versions of the myth of the Fall as the subjugation of the soul to the dying body. The double creation myths of *Genesis*, however, suggests that the focus on the body is misplaced. That focus substitutes a classical idea of the opposition of soul and body for the biblical idea of an existential tension in the subject, who appears to himself as the infinite within the finite. This tension does not arise with the Fall but is already represented in creation itself. Man has both an immediate relationship and a mediated relationship to the infinite. He possesses the whole as resource, origin, and goal. Yet he labors to achieve its realization, knowing that nothing he can do is adequate to the ultimate meaning he intuits. No life ever realizes its full potential; no state policies or actions are a full realization of a state's sovereignty; no work of art is adequate to the artist's full aesthetic vision; and no narrative is adequate to the fullness of experience. In every direction, man knows himself to be more than he can realize. If we begin with this tension, the problem of evil has less to do with the body's uncontrolled desires than with the problem of a finite will that seeks to realize an infinite meaning. Evil is not the pathology of the body but of the sacred.

Man has a metaphysical aspiration to make the finite self an image of the infinite. This image of the sacred inspires fallen man, who can suppress neither the knowledge of his own death nor the knowledge that he is linked to the infinite. It is this image of the sacred that powers faith in Christ and in the mystery of love. This image of the sacred is also at the heart of evil.

If the aspiration for the infinite lies behind both love and evil, then, we can learn a great deal about both by examining the forms of the sacred. The sacred always shows itself as the infinite in the finite. Corresponding to the changing conceptions of the sacred in the West have been changing conceptions of evil. Evil for the Jews is different from evil for early Christians; both are different from that of the Protestants. In each instance, the positive conception of man's relationship to the sacred is reflected in the conception of evil. Because the myth of Adam and Eve serves as a constant resource for Western reflections on evil, tracing the shifting readings of that myth provides a point of comparison of the different conceptions of evil. This is not merely an exercise in theological history, as if one form dies and is replaced by another. Remnants of each conception continue today even as we have secularized good and evil. Thus genealogical inquiry is a path to understanding ourselves.

A RELIGIOUS GENEALOGY OF EVIL

The Old Testament God of the Jews is separated from man by an unbridgeable gap. Man may have been made in the image of God, but the created can never be equal to the creator. A made object can never overcome the gap between maker and made.[22] Making is specifically not reproduction: a child grows into a man; a made object only deteriorates after the moment of its production. This sense of separation of God and man is reflected in the myth of an original proximity lost. In the Garden, Adam was able to speak directly to God. That very proximity, however, was too close. Brought near to God, man wanted to be like God. For that, he is banished. The gap that was always there is now given temporal and geographical—as well as moral— representation. Excluded from the Garden, man is now of the earth from which he came and to which he will return. In classical terms, matter, not form, defines the conditions of his relationship to the sacred. Man may have walked with God in the Garden, but now man confronts God as completely distant from, and other than, himself.

The gap between creator and created is nevertheless crossed by transmissions in both directions: through the authority of God, on the one hand, and the obedience of man, on the other. God does not fully withdraw behind the gap. Rather, God appears to man in the form of the authoritative declaration of law, that is, he commands. The creator God leaves a constant mark of his own presence in the command, "thou shalt not . . ." God as lawgiver appears first in the words, "And the Lord God commanded the man, saying, 'You may freely eat of every tree of the garden; but of the tree of knowledge of good and evil you shall not eat.' "[23] Conversely, man reaches across the gap by

[22] Locke will derive ownership from the act of making. See J. Locke, *Second Treatise of Government* 111–12 (I. Shapiro, ed. 2003) [1690]. The same impulse is there in Old Testament faith: man is God's possession, never the other way around.

[23] Indeed, Jewish law retains a focus on eating.

obeying those commands. By complying with the divine command, he shows himself to be again an image of the divine: he is that which God would make of him. Conversely, to fail to obey is to entrench the gap, just as a failure of God to command would entrench the gap. To comply with law is to maintain the divine order of creation, without which man has no more meaning than the earth of which he is made. That which was required of him in Eden is still required: to obey the divine command. A failure to follow law replicates Adam's fall. Man cannot give himself his own end; he cannot recover Eden on his own. His end is always death. Thus he should seek to follow God's law even in his fallen state. That is not just the best he can do; it is all he can do. Nothing else has any value.

Jewish history is the fate of a people who have been banished from their home because of their violation of God's command. There can be no other explanation of suffering in a world in which facts follow law, and a world that is the product of God's act of making is exactly one in which "is" follows "ought." Suffering must therefore be a consequence of disobedience. Conversely, what unites Jews of the diaspora is that all live under the same law, regardless of where they might be.[24] To follow the law is to reach across the gap, which is represented geographically and temporally in the diaspora. Man cannot himself close the gap, but he can show himself morally ready for the reciprocal, divine reaching across the gap.

Not surprisingly, Jewish readings of Adam and Eve emphasized the perspective of divine law: How is it that God has ordered men and women to live? If Adam and Eve were not yet fallen, then they must have been living in perfect compliance with law. We can therefore read that law out of their behavior. "For centuries Jewish teachers built from the passage [*Genesis* 2:23–24] the basic laws of moral behavior. Certain rabbis actually formed these lines into a code of sexual conduct."[25] Jewish thought turned to the myth to understand the laws of marriage and procreation, the appropriate relationships within the family, and, more generally the relationship between the sexes. The

---

[24] The thought of obedience to law is, inevitably, linked to a territorial idea of return: "next year in Jerusalem."

[25] Pagels, *Adam, Eve, and the Serpent* 13.

centrality of the obligation to procreate, for example, comes directly from the text of *Genesis*. The text figured dramatically in the construction of rules regulating not just marriage and divorce but homosexuality, adultery, public displays of nakedness, childbirth rituals, and gender hierarchy.[26]

The point is not merely heuristic; it is deeper than using the myth, as we might appeal to diverse sources, to develop the content of law. There is a single form of understanding that connects man and law. Both law and man are created images of God; both have their sole source of meaning in their character as created. God spoke both into being; both always point toward their creator. Thus each derives its meaning from the same source outside itself. If we ask what is the ground of the authority of law—what we would call the source of its "legitimacy"—the answer is that it is God's command. If we ask what is it that gives ultimate meaning to a life lived with labor, suffering, and pain, the answer is God's care. Thus the Jews are "chosen." Because God cares, he commands the law. To follow the law is to live as an image of God, for it is to make of oneself an objectification of God's will.[27]

For the Old Testament Jews, living in the law is the symbol of reciprocal action across the gap: man reaches toward God, who has given the law. Man lives under the threat of destruction from without and from within. His world can fall apart either because God withdraws—that is, he abandons the Jews—or because man fails to place himself in the proper relationship to the divine. The latter failure, the myth tells us, is the violation of law. Law establishes an economy of the sacred—a point of exchange between the infinite and the finite.

The diaspora is the point at which there is a shift in Jewish practice from ritual sacrifice in the Temple to law among decentralized congre-

---

[26] See *id.* 12–13 (citing rabbinic tradition, and *Mishna Gittin* 9, 10); *The Book of Jubilees* 3, 8–31.

[27] This idea is hardly anachronistic. There remains an intimate relationship between sovereignty and law: the legitimacy of law, on this view, flows from the will of the sovereign. This is particularly true of a constitutional democracy that is committed to the idea that the popular sovereign—the people—wills the constitution into being. They are the source of its legitimacy. For the individual citizen, to follow the law is to give expression to popular sovereignty; it is to make oneself an "image" of the popular sovereign. See P. Kahn, *The Reign of Law: Marbury v. Madison and the Construction of America* 234–35 (1997).

gations. But a religion of law and one of sacrifice are deeply intertwined, and not just because the ritual of sacrifice is a law-governed
activity that must be done exactly right if it is to propitiate God.[28] The
connection runs deeper. Sacrifice is not simply a gift. The ritual of
sacrifice is the paradigmatic act of crossing the gap in both directions.
To sacrifice is to make sacred by making an object a point of revelation
of the divine. The sacrificed object is a divine image not as a reflection
but as a presence: it literally brings God's presence into the community. The sacrificed object suspends the gap, drawing man to God and
God to man. For this reason, the sanctified object is often consumed
by the faithful. Unless the offering makes present the divine, it has not
yet worked in the domain of the sacred. But this showing forth of the
sacred is not within the power of man alone.

We can still see something of the relationship of law to sacrifice in
the modern property regime. Property is misunderstood if seen only
as an object or discrete area in the world. Rather, for an object to
become property requires that one see through it to an entire domain
of law and legal regulation, including contemporary rituals, for example, registration, good-faith purchase, and title. Knowledge of all these
background conditions may not be explicit—one sees the property as
an object—but it can be made explicit. It is maintained in the "social
imaginary," and it will be called forth when and if a problem arises.[29]
Property presents, in a reified form, not just the legal order as a system
of rules but also an image of the sovereign authority to make law, for
the sovereign is the source and guarantor of that law. For this very
reason, early modern political theory locates the function of the sovereign in the establishment of a property regime.[30] Property differs from
possession just in this relationship to the sovereign. Property carries
the "warrant" of the sovereign; it does so by being created and conveyed according to law. The sovereign not only creates the possibility
of property but has an underlying claim on all property, which can

---

[28] See H. Hubert & M. Mauss, *Sacrifice: Its Nature and Functions* 28 (W. Halls, trans.
1964) [1898]; M. Eliade, *The Myth of Eternal Return* 34–37 (R. Trask, trans. 2005).

[29] On the concept of the social imaginary, see C. Taylor, *Modern Social Imaginaries* 23–
30 (2004).

[30] See, e.g., J. Locke, *Second Treatise* 101 ("Political power, then, I take to be a right of
making laws with penalties of death, and consequently all less penalties for the regulation
and preserving of property").

always be exercised to save the nation. The value of property is present both in its maintenance and its destruction.[31] The sovereign can only partially bind itself to act according to law in its seizure of property—a "just compensation clause."[32] In times of emergency—the Schmittian exception—property just is the expression of the power of the sovereign. The sovereign shows itself by its demand for sacrifice of property; it creates an exception to the ordinary law. This is why property only appears from within the legal order of the state. To the outsider—particularly the enemy—what appears as real property from within, appears only as the state's territory. From this perspective, the geographical extension of the state is identified with the political sovereignty of the state.[33] Similarly, for a religion of sacrifice, God constitutes the value of and has a claim upon every finite object and place.

Obedience to a law understood as divine command always has the potential of appearing as a form of sacrifice, for it is both a means of propitiating God and of making the divine present. It is reordering the world as an image of the divine. Thus the sacrifice of Isaac allows fallen man a hint of the return to, or at least the possibility of a full recovery of, that life that is an image of God. The only authority for the act of sacrifice is the divine command, but that is the only authority there ever is in the world of image, law, and sacrifice. This is a world in which the only subject is God. All else gets its meaning by virtue of its relationship to God's will. This is what it means to be "chosen."

---

[31] L. Strahilevitz, "The Right to Destroy," 114 Yale L.J. 781 (2005).

[32] See, e.g., *United States v. Caltex (Philippines)*, 344 U.S. 149 (1952) (destruction of private property to prevent it from falling to the enemy does not constitute a compensable taking); *United States v. Pacific R.R.*, 120 U.S. 227, 238 (1887) (quoting veto message of the president: " 'It is a general principle of both international and municipal law that all property is held subject, not only to be taken by the government for public uses, in which case, under the constitution of the United States, the owner is entitled to just compensation, but also subject to be temporarily occupied, or even actually destroyed, in times of great public danger and when the public safety demands it; and in this latter case governments do not admit a legal obligation . . . to compensate the owner. The temporary occupation of, or injury to, and destruction of property, caused by actual and necessary military operations, is generally considered to fall within the last-mentioned principle.' Cong. Globe, Forty-second Cong. (2d Sess.) pt. 5, p. 4155.")

[33] When property is owned by a foreign national, conflicts inevitably arise when the sovereign exercises this residual claim to all property within its jurisdiction. International law has long struggled with conflicting views over the appropriate regulation of foreign expropriation. See R. Dolzer, "New Foundations of the Law of Expropriation of Alien Property," 75 Am J. Int'l L. 553, 557–72 (1981).

This is also a world that is squarely within the myth of Genesis two, that is, a world in which man's relationship to the sacred is mediated through the paradigm of labor. Man's truest labor always appears to be sacrifice: sacrifice for loved ones, for community, and for God. Law, accordingly, represents the promise of the divine assistance that was lost with the Fall.[34]

A world of sacrifice is equally a world in which the miraculous is routine. God actively shows himself in the world. Coordination between action and its consequences remains a subject for the Creator's will. Obedience to law brings man security, if not happiness, only because God wills that consequence. There is no explanation for God's commands, only the threat of destruction for failure to comply and the hope for his beneficence with compliance. Paradigmatically, this is the story of Abraham and Isaac. God appears to man in the form of command; the act of obedience is sacrifice. Obedience fueled by faith leads to the miraculous reordering of nature itself.

Old Testament faith is characterized by this gap between man and God. Every bridging of that gap is miraculous. Thus law is miraculous, in just the same way that sacrifice is. They are the same exchange between man and God; the finite becomes an image of the infinite. Accordingly, the narrative of the Old Testament is, on the one hand, an account of the miracles that have linked the Jews to God, and, on the other, a narrative of a people's effort to comply with law. Because fulfillment of law is never more than partial, the miracle, which is always the appearance of the divine within the ordinary conditions of space and time, is both threat and promise: we cannot know in advance whether the God that appears will be vengeful or protective. God may save Isaac, but he destroys Sodom; he saves Noah and his family but destroys everyone else. Indeed, the biblical history of mankind is overwhelmingly a history of punishment. There is not an alternative metaphysics that explains suffering evil. There is only disobedience followed by the vengeance of a just God. Suffering must be deserved; it is the consequence of disobedience. The suffering of the Jews, right up through the Holocaust, is frequently read in just

---

[34] Judaism is sufficiently diverse also to include traditions squarely located within the framework of Genesis one. There is, for example, a long tradition of Jewish mysticism.

this way. It is not the evil done by others to the community but rather an affirmation of community identity by virtue of God's special concern for the Jews. That concern is special even when God acts in the form of punishment. If we suffer, we must ourselves be the source of that suffering.

In such a world, moral failure appears as disobedience: the failure to obey God's commandments. The narrative of the Jews is a history of a failure to follow law—at least, this is the repeated lesson of the prophets. But evil has a still more palpable face in Old Testament faith: idolatry, or the worship of false gods. Disobedience to law—an ordinary failing—becomes evil when it is grounded in idolatry. Thus the First Commandment has a normative priority. Indeed, that priority is represented temporarily as well, since idolatry and divine law-giving appear simultaneously. While Moses ascends to obtain the law, the community, left on its own, turns to idolatry. Law will be the vehicle of mediation between fallen man and God.

In a world enthralled to the divine, the failure to worship one god always rests on a decision to worship another. The belief that other gods have the power to coerce and reward is the necessary foundation of disobedience in a world watched over by the divine. Evil, accordingly, is belief in the wrong god. Man's suffering is not evil, for suffering may be justified punishment or it may be merely natural. To believe that some other god has the power to alleviate that suffering, however, is evil. To turn for succor from Jehovah to Baal—or any other god— is to locate the truth of one's self outside God's will. It is to make of the self an image of some other god, to become a citizen of some other sacred space. To believe in other laws and other rituals of sacrifice is to place into competition a set of ultimate beliefs that determine the life and death of the individual, as well as the community. "In general the war against idolatry in the Bible is a war against forms of ritual worship imported from foreign nations."[35] A religion of law and sacrifice can always be challenged by an alternative conception of the object of sacrifice and the requirements of divine law. Today we often describe sovereignty as the authority to make laws for a particular

[35] M. Halbertal & A. Margalit, *Idolatry* 108 (1992).

jurisdiction. Sovereignty always appears to itself as exclusive.[36] When conflicting claims of sovereignty are set forth, war is often the result; when a citizen changes sovereign allegiance, it can appear as the secular evil of treason. Idolatry is the religious form of treason, just as treason continues to carry the religious aura of idolatry.

The Jews of the Old Testament must maintain the distinction between the moral failure of disobedience to law and the evil of idolatry. Violation of the law can be mundane, an ordinary failure characteristic of all members of the community. Idolatry, on the other hand, threatens to redefine the sacred character of the community and the self. Not all crime is treason, although there is always a kind of pressure to move in this direction, since all illegality disregards the sovereign command.[37] The categories are necessarily confused: all crime is a betrayal of an obligation of loyalty to the sovereign. Idolatry, like treason, is prohibited as a matter of law, but idolatry is always more than a particular crime. The turning away from law is a turning away from God and thus a turning toward another god.

More broadly, what positive meaning can we give to worship of another god in the face of the claim that there is only one God? Worship of other gods must be worship of nothing at all, not a competition among alternative sources of the sacred but really just a negation of the source of all meaning. Thus the Jews must deny the very existence of that which they fear most.[38] The charge of idolatry simultaneously suggests the power of other gods and undermines any such claim by asserting that they are not gods at all.[39] A golden calf has no power to construct or to destroy, no power to bridge the gap between the finite and the infinite. The meaning of worship of the false god is reduced to a violation of the true law of the one God. The calf is an empty

[36] This is why the American constitutional idea of federalism, in which the states were to retain some aspects of sovereignty, appeared so conceptually difficult. See F. MacDonald, *Novus Ordo Seclorum: The Intellectual Origins of the Constitution* 277–78 (1989) (on the problem of *imperium in imperio*).

[37] Traditionally crime was a breach of the king's peace. See M. Arnold, "Accident, Mistake, and the Rules of Liability in the Fourteenth Century Law of Torts," 128 U. Pa. L. Rev. 361, 370–72 (1979).

[38] Halbertal and Margalit find the earliest biblical meaning of idolatry in the metaphor of the sin of adultery. This is to locate the wrong in the turning away of the believer rather than in the object toward which he turns. See Halbertal & Margalit, *Idolatry* 11–14.

[39] See *Jeremiah* 2:11.

image, and its very emptiness becomes the ground for divine retribution. This is an important characteristic of our perception of evil. Evil is a reaching toward the divine, but at the same time it is a negation. It is both there and not there—the action of negation or a false transcendence. Evil is an image of the divine, but it is also nothing at all.

The evil of idolatry is, accordingly, twofold. First, it is a violation of God's law set out for members of the Jewish community. Paganism is not idolatry, for pagans are not bound by that law. The analogy to treason is again exact: it is not treasonous for the noncitizen to support a state opposed to my own. Second, idolatry differs from other violations of the law because of its assertion of a divine power in place of God. That which we recognize as evil has this double character of violation and power. To identify evil as idolatry is more than a descriptive act; it is already the assertion of a strategy of repression and denial. If the idol is not really a god, then it is only the creation of man. The idol has no power at all. The evil of idolatry, accordingly, includes the idea of man attempting to make his own gods, that is, he would himself be the source of the sacred. This, not merely the violation of law, is what makes idolatry evil.

Idolatry is the face of evil in a world in which polytheism is still imaginable. To label a practice idolatrous is to defend one set of beliefs about the sacred by condemning another. What we might call the "dialectic of idolatry," however, extends more broadly. That dialectic has the following character: first, the appearance of a new source of ultimate meaning; second, the violation of the community's existing norms for the sake of that new source; and, third, the community's negation of the positive claim, leaving only the wrongful conduct. Evil is recognized but then is reduced to mere sin. This dialect of idolatry is seen today in the political evil of treason: first, a claim is made for a new source of political meaning; second, the community's law is violated; and, third, that claim is negated, leaving only the illegal act. The failed revolutionary becomes the common criminal; his execution is simultaneously a recognition and a suppression of the alternative claim to power. Treason is recognized to be not just another illegal act, even as it is forcefully assimilated to crime.[40]

---

[40] See G. Fletcher, *Loyalty: An Essay on the Morality of Relationships* (1992).

The proliferation of conflicting claims about the sacred is not just a problem of lingering polytheism. A community based on the interpretation of a sacred text always threatens to fragment into diverse communities of interpretation. The text itself—the point of entry of the sacred—has no capacity to stop this proliferation of interpretations. Authority works against interpretive diversity, but it has no more claim on the text than any of the interpretations it denies. No interpretation can itself ground an authoritative claim to the truth of the text.[41] It is always possible for a prophet in the wilderness to arise and claim that the community labors under a misinterpretation of its own sacred text. How and when such interpretive disagreement will arise, and whether a new interpretation will attract its own community of faith, remain mysteries. We cannot say whether any particular crisis—assuming there is a relationship between the turn to faith and crisis—will lead to an affirmation of traditional beliefs or spawn a new interpretation. It depends not just on the felt force of the new interpretation but on the real force—coercive, punitive power—of the existing authorities. Truth is as much a function of power as power is of truth. Sometimes the revolutionaries win; sometimes they are hanged as traitors.

Judaism spawned just such a diversity of interpretations and interpretive communities.[42] Yet the birth of Christianity is not just the appearance of another interpretation of a common, sacred text. Christianity claimed to offer something more than another interpretation. Christ's relationship to the sacred text is not interpretive at all. His relationship to that text is as the superceding truth that the text prophesizes. For the new community of faith, Christ is the miraculous appearance of the Word within creation. He is described as himself a text, the *logos*—not like the law, a lingering marker of God's presence, but the thing itself; not a made image of God, the product of a creator, but the divine Son. To the traditional community of the Jews, who did not accept Jesus as the Messiah, such a claim could not help but appear

---

[41] See S. Fish, *Is There a Text in This Class? Interpretive Communities and the Sources of Authority* (1982); R. Cover, "The Supreme Court, 1982 Term—Foreword: Nomos and Narrative," 97 Harv. L. Rev. 4, 16 (1983).

[42] See, e.g., E. Pagels, *The Gnostic Gospels* (1979); see also *Second Corinthians* 11, 4–5 (Paul warns of those who preach "another Jesus").

blasphemous, for it denied the fundamental gap between man and God. That gap had been mediated by law. Now Christians proclaimed the end of law.[43] Those who affirmed belief in this new God appeared to the traditionalists as idolaters: worshiping nothing at all, they violated the sacred law. The dialectic of idolatry would have Christ executed as a common criminal.

New Testament faith radically reconceptualizes the relationship between creator and created, the infinite and the finite. The Old Testament concept of that relationship as one of a made image to its maker is replaced by an image of the Son and the Father. The gap has been overcome in the person of Christ, who is both man and God. Thus the Nicene Creed specifically declares that Christ is "begotten, not made." Whereas a made object can never be the same as, and is always subordinate to, its maker, an organic relationship is one of identity across difference. Father and Son are of the same form, substance, or essence: "God from God, Light from Light, true God from true God."[44]

The model of craft or making is not only the earliest model of order—order exists because it was established by an intelligent act of making—it is also the most pervasive and easily accessible. It is at the root of all anthropomorphic conceptions of the sacred. This model of making continues, for example, in the powerful intuition behind the argument from design: the finely articulated order of such things as the hand or the eye "shows" us that there must have been an intelligent act of creation. We cannot easily imagine an intelligent act apart from an anthropomorphized intelligence. This was and continues to be the argument—and image—that Darwin and all his successors have had to defeat. Darwin did so by linking reproduction to change.[45] Until that point, reproduction had been conceived as the mechanism for maintaining identity through difference.

Mythically, Christ's displacement of Adam is the displacement of a made image by a begotten son. God as father displaces God as maker.

[43] *Romans* 10, 4.

[44] Nicene Creed. One sees here the attraction of the later theological turn to Aristotle's understanding of form or substance.

[45] This revolutionary thought is conveyed in the very title of Darwin's work: *Origin of Species*.

Both are anthropomorphic images: man is by nature both a maker and a begetter.[46] Neither has priority over the other; neither can do away with the other. Despite their common basis in ordinary experience, each invokes a different conceptual frame: a model of making versus a model of organic unity. The appearance of the idea of Christ marks a movement from the former to the latter in imagining the relation of man to God.

Prior to Darwin, the organic was a model of the relationship of the part to the whole. Each part gains its meaning only from the relationship to the whole, and the whole is nothing apart from its elements. Organic models work both synchronically and diachronically. Synchronically, the hand is only a hand by virtue of its being a part of the entire body. Detached it is only the "remains" of a hand.[47] Parent and child are constituent parts of the organic unity of the family; citizens are constituent parts of an organic nation. The principle of the whole is more than, but not separate from, the constituent parts. An artisan may have a blueprint or an abstract idea of the whole before he begins his work, but there is no idea of the horse or of the family prior to the existence of particular horses or families.[48] Diachronically, the child succeeds to the parent, carrying forward the same unmediated principle or form. Nations, as well as other corporate bodies—for example, churches, ethnicities, and institutions—also reproduce themselves across generations. Reproduction appears as the temporal maintenance of the continuity of complex form. The relationship is not causal but synecdochic. At each instance, the whole is present in the particular. Thus an organic entity maintains sameness in difference across both space and time.

---

[46] Arendt's ordered typology of human behavior would have making—"work"—succeed begetting—"the labor of the body." H. Arendt, *The Human Condition* 79–93 (1958). The genealogical order of Western religion suggests that she gets the order wrong. That genealogy is repeated endlessly in Western institutional self-understandings, including American constitutionalism. Institutions begin with a moment of the sovereign act of law making; they maintain themselves as organic—that is, corporate—entities. See P. Kahn, *Legitimacy and History* 5–7 (1992).

[47] See Aristotle, *Parts of Animals* 1.1640b34–641a10.

[48] With biotechnology, the line separating the organic from the made is shifting, but this was always a blurred line with respect to social formations: a constitution is both a made object and an organic whole. The framework of understanding we use depends upon context.

A craft understands the form of its product as something separable from the material in which it is executed. The Old Testament God first had the idea of man before he made him: He made him in the image of Himself. The elements of the organic are not similarly "put together" according to a plan. We misconstrue this organizational form—that is, its principle of intelligibility—if we continue to offer efficient causes to explain its temporal sequence and spatial organization. To understand the organic, we have to explain not how it came to be but what its nature is. There is no understanding the "how" of Christ, only the "what" of the Church, which is his body. Of course, theologians will continue to speculate about the how, producing two thousand years of doctrinal controversy, which is all that can be expected when one asks the wrong question. Christ is outside all temporal sequence and geographic division: he fills all time and space. His particular appearance is simply a mystery, for chronological sequence is itself the temporal form of making, and Christ is not made.

The religion of the New Testament begins with the disappearance of the gap that informs the Old Testament ideas of image, law, and sacrifice. After Christ, man no longer relates to the sacred as to a maker/creator God.[49] Christ announces the end of law; he takes on to himself the entire demand for sacrifice under which the Jews had labored. Just as he is the Word, he is the sacrificial offering. This is literally the end of time, because the sacred is present not as a ritual object but as man himself. The presence of the divine among men marks the end of man as a made image of God. That man dies and is born again as something entirely new. This new man reconceives himself as a participant in the body of Christ. He is a part of a sacred whole, the unity of which is not an aggregation of divisible parts but completely organic. The end of time, accordingly, is the end of man's conception of himself as a laborer in need of law, on the one hand, and of sacrifice, on the other. With that, there is a new focus on Genesis one, in place of Genesis two. For Christ is the new Adam through whom individuals now achieve that perfect realization of the infinite in the finite—the unity of being, knowledge, and the good—which was Adam's in the first myth of creation.

[49] See *Romans* 8, 1–8.

The Church is the body of Christ in precisely the sense of an organic community. The Church is not made; there is no blueprint, no plan, no model against which it is measured. Participation is unmediated by a craftsman, even by the divine creator who had always to mediate between command (law) and consequence for the Jews.[50] Thus the Church is not a historical phenomenon in the same way that the narrative of the Old Testament records the history of miraculous interventions for the sake of the Jewish community. Rather, the Church exists at once everywhere and in all time. One must be born again into the Church, which means to be born again as a part of the body of Christ. Man is no longer a finite body—an image separated from the divine, living in a fallen world of geographical space and temporal succession. In Christ, man is no longer of this world.

To be of the body of Christ is to experience personal salvation not as a promise for the future but now as an eternal present. It is to escape history in a way unavailable to Old Testament faith. This is spoken of as the "end of time," but the eschatological impulse can confuse a phenomenology of religious experience with a metaphor. The relationship to the sacred has already changed; the time of fallen man is already over. A religion of law waits for the end of time as a historical event that corresponds to the giving of new law. New Testament faith abandons linear history for the immediate presence of the sacred in and through the body of the Church itself. This is the movement from a religion of sacrifice to one of self-sacrifice. To be a part of the body of Christ is to have suffered the crucifixion and resurrection. It is already to have sacrificed that self which was the finite body: "We know that our old self was crucified with him so that the sinful body might be destroyed, and we might no longer be enslaved to sin."[51]

Evil in the Old Testament, I argued earlier, appears in the form of idolatry, which is best understood as a conflict between claims of sovereign allegiance: whose law does one obey? What is evil after the

---

[50] Historically and institutionally, of course, claims for mediation do arise and a priestly class develops, which is, in turn, rejected in the Reformation. The Church, as a temporal institution, has a political life—internally and externally—as a competitor for power. See, e.g., G. Wills, *Why I Am a Catholic* (2002). My discussion is not a social or political history of the Church but a genealogy of conceptual models.

[51] *Romans* 6,6.

appearance of Christ? It is the failure to take up the offer of Christ to be born again as a part of the organic unity of the sacred. It is to remain within the Old Testament conception of the gap; it is to continue to labor under the law. This is the evil of the Jews, who reject the divinity of Christ as if his worship were only another form of idolatry. The killing of Christ, of which the Jews are long accused, is symbolic of treating Christ as another false idol, that is, treating him as nothing at all.

If Christ is no more than a false appearance of the sacred, then man himself remains bound to death. That is an intolerable thought and the implicit threat that motivates the millennia of anti-Semitism. Just as the Jews saw the idolater as a combination of power and nothingness, so does the Jew—the paradigmatic nonbeliever—appear as that same combination to the Christian. By denying Christ, the Jew proclaims the continuing power of death over life; he stands, therefore, within the emptiness of an unredeemed life. He can follow law, but to what end when life brings only death? Luther writes "When the Law stands alone without the Gospel and the knowledge of grace, it leads to despair and ultimate impenitence."[52] Man can mark himself with the sign of the Covenant, but he remains separated by an unbridgeable gap from the divine being.[53] We see in this opposition between Christian and Jew a basic structure of evil—not simply relativism but a conflict over the source of meaning adequate to overcome death itself. Each side claims for itself all the meaning that there is; each sees the other as pursuing death in place of life.

Man longs not just to be good—to follow the law—but to be a part of the sacred. He wants not just to sacrifice according to divine law but to be the object of sacrifice himself. Only then can he become the point of transparency to, and participation in, the sacred. Thus Christ is exactly what Isaac is not: Christ is sacrificed; Isaac is saved for the law. But in the economy of religious belief, Isaac is denied what Christ achieves: Isaac is not saved but dies. To the Christian, everyone has a choice whether to follow Isaac on the path of law or to be a part of

---

[52] Luther, *Lectures on Genesis* 272.

[53] The failure of law to provide meaning appears in the familiar opposition of law and love, a timeless theme of Western literature. See P. Kahn, *Law and Love: The Trials of King Lear* (2000).

the sacrifice of Christ. Death has literally changed places. Paul writes, "All of us who have been baptized into Christ Jesus were baptized into his death. Therefore, we have been buried with him by baptism into death."[54] The turn to Christianity is, accordingly, marked by the move from sacrifice to self-sacrifice. Christ says, "He who wishes to follow me, let him deny himself and take up his cross." Only a religion founded on an organic conception of unity can support a practice of self-sacrifice: it is that form of self-destruction which is rebirth. Again, Paul writes, "I have been crucified with Christ; it is no longer I who live, but Christ who lives in me."[55]

This is not a conflict over the intensity of religious belief. Both Christian and Jew can be fully enthralled by the sacred; both claim to locate an ultimate meaning in the realization of the sacred in and through their own lives. It is rather a question of the forms of religious belief: Do we experience the sacred as a transcendent power miraculously showing itself across the gap or as immanent and participatory? Is the sacred found in law or in self-sacrifice? This same form of conflict intrudes on the West in the confrontation with Islam. Like Judaism, Islam is a religion of law: the Sharia marks the miraculous appearance of the divine within the finite conditions of life. Mohammed is a prophet, not a god. Islam and Judaism, for this reason, have far more in common than Christianity and Islam.[56] This has been reflected in the history of conflict.[57] For much of European history, the face of evil—when it was not the Jew—has been the Muslim. Not surprisingly, as anti-Semitism is suppressed, it is replaced by an anti-Islamic sentiment. This remains a conflict between a covenantal community and an organic community, a community of law and a community of the Eucharist. There is no common ground in such conflicts: where

---

[54] *Romans* 6, 3–4.

[55] *Galatians* 2, 20.

[56] This close relationship of Islam to Judaism is symbolically represented in their mutual appeal to the story of Abraham's sacrifice of his son. Jews believe that son to be Isaac; Muslims believe him to be Ishmael.

[57] The recent appearance of the suicide bomber as a tactical weapon used by certain Islamic groups should not be read to suggest that self-sacrifice is central to Islam. The suicide bomber appears first as a tactic within a nationalist struggle of the Palestinians. Some of the bombers, for example, are Christian Palestinians. Moreover, one would have to know about the expectations of the bomber: Does he expect a future reward, and of what sort?

one sees ultimate meanings, the other sees only negation; where one sees God's presence, the other sees only the obstinate refusal of belief; where one sees the sacred, the other sees idolatry; where one sees life, the other sees death.

To the Christian, to remain bound to law is to choose evil; it is to choose to remain fallen in the face of the presence of divine salvation. The Christian sees here a kind of repetition or recurrence of the original sin of turning away from God. From this perspective, the problem is not disobedience to law but rather the idea of law itself. Law suggests an enduring gap between God and man.[58] Law provides order in the place of the chaos of mere change; it provides meaning where otherwise there would be nothing at all. Law is the measure of meaning—and therefore of action—in a world still pregnant with death. This is a world that is bound to history: to realize meaning within history is to live in accordance with the divine law. The lesson of Isaac's sacrifice was that compliance with divine command is the foundation of the nation of Israel. That nation is suspended between the divine foundation and the not-yet of the divine return. Law is the structure of order in this intermediate time and space. With Christ, however, God is now present in the world. The gap expressed by law has itself dissolved through the final and complete miracle of Christ's appearance. This is the fundamental belief of Christianity. To live as if the world continues as before is the fundamental evil. It literally kills the soul. Like idolatry, it seeks power in what is only negation.

An entirely new calculus of good and bad is required in this transformed world. This is the lesson of the early Christian martyrs, who invert the moral valence of pleasure and pain, of life and death. Even the phenomenon of torture is transformed. Living already as a part of the body of Christ, they are no longer of this world. Their bodies have already exhausted themselves on the cross of Calvary, for they are His body. Their actual torture is nothing more than a replay, in finite time, of a death already suffered. The transcendent self-sacrifice that spans all time and includes all others is Christ's suffering on the

---

[58] This gap remains even when we think of law as the expression of the popular sovereign. Law is never the actual presence of the sovereign but only a kind of marker that the sovereign had been present. Law always marks the absence of the sovereign, even as it claims to be the product of the sovereign act. See Kahn, *Reign of Law* 69–74.

cross. Thus the Christian martyrs have no concern for life itself, no concern for the painful deaths they are forced to suffer. Or, not exactly no concern; rather, suffering is martyrdom and is thus the celebration of the soul over the body, of redemption over fall, of rebirth in the body of Christ.[59]

Suffering is no longer a sign of God's displeasure, His response to a failure to comply with law. Suffering is now testimony to transcendence: through suffering one testifies to the reality of Christ's presence. Thus sacrifice moves from an external object given up to God to the body itself. Sacrifice is no longer an act under law designed to bridge the gap. Rather, self-sacrifice is the presence of the divine and thus the disappearance of the gap. Abraham could not literally sacrifice Isaac, his only legitimate son, and still found a great nation. There must be a miraculous substitute. With Christ's appearance, there is no longer any distance between sacrifice and suffering; there is no substitute. The very meaning of the nation of Israel has come to an end, for history itself has come to an end.

Earlier I argued that we see remnants of the Old Testament idea of sovereignty in our understanding of the popular sovereign as the source of law, in property as the reification of a legal order, and in treason as the paradigmatic political evil. We find a parallel remnant of the New Testament idea of the Church as the body of Christ in the idea of the popular sovereign as a transtemporal, organic whole—that is, a unified subject composed of all citizens at all times and in all places. Participation in the popular sovereign is simultaneously an act of self-sacrifice and the realization of the ultimate truth of the self. Citizens are exhorted to be "selfless"—that is, wholly public regarding—in their relationship to the state. They are asked literally to make the "ultimate sacrifice," when the nation needs them.

No words thrill the modern citizen more than "We the people," which is always a single subject, never a mere aggregate. The European sovereign traditionally was the mystical corpus of the state; the popular sovereign retains this mystery of a transtemporal, single, collective subject. Evil now appears as that which would deny the reality, or

---

[59] See P. Brown, *The Body and Society* 72–76 (1988); Pagels, *Adam, Eve, and the Serpent* 55.

threaten the life, of this organic whole. Archetypically, evil is seen in the regime of law that preceded the emergence of the popular sovereign. In postcolonial states, including the United States, the prior regime was the order of law that bridged the gap between sovereign and colony.[60] In the European ancien régime, that same gap was present in the relationship of sovereign to subject. In the contemporary experience of the nation-state, evil is located in the enemy who, by threatening the existence of the sovereign, calls up a demand for self-sacrifice on the part of the citizen. In this imaginative construction lies the reason why so much of the modern experience of the nation-state has not been that of a peaceful, well-ordered legal regime but rather one of self-sacrifice in war.

Once life and death changed places, the moral foundation of the prohibition on murder is no longer secure. Christ may have preached peace and a universal love, but we know the organic community as a potentially dangerous and destructive form of belief in ultimate meanings. The deepest source of that danger is its own belief in self-sacrifice. Killing those outside the body politic does not appear as murder at all, for it occurs within a context in which members show their own willingness to die. War appears as a competition in self-sacrifice rather than a murderous impulse directed at the nonbeliever. In a community of self-sacrifice, death expresses the character of the sacred.

The popular sovereign has a literal claim on the body of every citizen. It has the power to conscript. This is true regardless of whether any particular state currently has a law in place granting the government this power. Such a law could be passed. Thinking of conscription as a legal power fails fully to capture the place of self-sacrifice in the citizens conception of the ultimate character of political meaning in the modern nation-state. Conscription is not just an allocation of legal authority; it is the power of life and death.[61] The modern nation-state actively cultivated an ethic of self-sacrifice; countless citizens realized a kind of self-transcendence on the battlefield.[62] Under conditions of

[60] Consider how much of the American Revolution was driven by reaction to British laws, e.g., the Townshend Acts, The Quartering Act, the Stamp Act, and the Intolerable Acts.

[61] On self-sacrifice and sovereignty, see Kahn, *Putting Liberalism in Its Place* 91–92.

[62] See J. Glenn Gray, *The Warriors: Reflections on Men in Battle* (1970); C. Hedges, *War Is a Force That Gives Us Meaning* (2002).

modern warfare, the battlefield expanded to the entire state. Despite the efforts of international humanitarian law, modern warfare eroded the distinction between soldier and citizen. This was true of both the great wars of the twentieth century but also of the wars of decolonization and the Cold War, with its policy of Mutual Assured Destruction, which occupied the second half of the century. All citizens in every part of the state were at risk; all could be called upon to sacrifice themselves for the state.

This changed set of ultimate beliefs represented by the appearance of Christ is reflected in the new meaning drawn from the story of Adam and Eve. In place of the Jewish readings that found in the story the moral law for the family dedicated to procreation, early Christian readings, beginning with Paul, tend to understand the story as an account of sin that must be overcome. They read the story from the perspective of the Fall rather than from that of creation. Adam and Eve can have nothing to teach us about how to live in a world informed by the presence of Christ, the new Adam. In Augustine's view, they can have nothing to teach us for we are not even similarly situated with respect to freedom of the will, that is, in our capacity to obey law. Through their sin we have all been condemned, and law cannot redeem us.[63] Living as Adam and Eve did, following the law that informed their actions before sin, is not a possibility for men. Moreover, to attempt to do so would be to ignore the presence of the new Christ. For Augustine, the authority of the Church now stands in place of the authority of the Genesis myth as a source of law.

Rather than replicating the sin of Adam and Eve through sexual union, Paul—following Christ himself—preaches the normative priority of celibacy.[64] In place of the reproductive family, Christians speak of marriage to the Church and of becoming one flesh in the body of Christ. The sexual family of Genesis—"man and woman become one flesh"—is to be overcome through the family of Christ. Christ is the bridegroom and the Church his bride.[65] This new family rests on a

---

[63] Augustine, *City of God* 13, 3. Augustine is continuing Paul's claim that "no human being will be justified in his sight by works of law, since through the law comes knowledge of sin." *Romans* 3, 20.

[64] *First Corinthians* 7.

[65] See *Ephesians* 5, 29–32 ("We are members of his body").

denial of the flesh rather than a lawful ordering of desire: "I appeal to you . . . to present your bodies as a living sacrifice, holy and acceptable to God."[66] To follow Christ is to act in the awareness that the Kingdom of God is at hand, which means that the body is viewed through its negation in the act of self-sacrifice. The injunction to be fruitful and multiply no longer applies in a world where the meaning of the body is now found in its sacrifice.

Paul's vision of the immediacy of the end of time does not come to pass. The Church necessarily becomes a historical institution concerned as much with maintaining its own authority as saving souls. Not everyone can give up family for Christ—at least not for long, if history is to continue. The austerity of Paul's vision and the self-sacrifice of the martyrs must be moderated by the recovery of the value of family as the source of reproduction and maintenance of the culture—including the culture of Christianity. The asceticism of Jerome is necessarily challenged by the moderation of Jovinian.[67] Nevertheless, the understanding of the body as the medium for self-sacrifice and for participation in Christ remains a powerful theme of Christian belief. Augustine puts the corruption of the flesh at the very center of his theology, which becomes central to the doctrine of the Church, with its continued insistence on clerical celibacy. The appropriate attitude toward the body, which carries the taint of sin, is that of self-sacrifice. The West remains deeply attracted to this idea, as well as to the idea of the moral virtue of suffering. True life remains not of this world.

The mark of an organic understanding of the sacred, I have argued, is the shift in the character of sacrifice from an object offered across the gap to self-sacrifice as the displacement of the finite body by the presence of the infinite. The subject no longer makes an offering to an angry God but becomes literally a part of the godhood. Organic communities—including the Church—are often characterized by violence directed both within and without.[68] The enemy that threatens the life of this community will be called evil. But precisely because the community finds itself in the act of self-sacrifice, there is a certain

[66] *Romans* 12, 1.
[67] See Pagels, *Adam, Eve, and the Serpent* 90–96.
[68] See chapter 5 below.

ambiguity in regard to an enemy that calls forth the sacred. The enemy at war is never quite so evil as that which denies the very foundation of the sacred character of the community. For the early Christian community, the Jewish Pharisees represented the paradigmatic evil of insisting on law as the only measure of the sacred.

We cannot rank the forms of evil as if there is a better and a worse. The critical point is that every form of belief in the sacred sees evil as the negation of itself—as a false infinite. Jewish faith will see Christianity as just another, and more vicious form, of idolatry. To worship Christ, in place of the law of Moses, is to believe in false gods or mere idols—all the more so to the degree that Christianity includes worship of relics and the rituals of the sacrament. Christians can return the favor, accusing the Jews not just of a failure to recognize Christ but of following their own sacrificial rites, for example, drinking the blood of Christian children.[69] Christian accusations of Jewish idolatry are complemented by accusations of Pharisaism. The dynamic of evil remains the same: to turn away from sacred truth and put in its place a false claim of the divine.

We cannot get beyond our own beliefs in order to identify an "objective" form of evil. For religions of law and sacrifice, evil is recognizing a new source of sovereign command. For religions of sacrificial participation, evil is insisting that life can have meaning outside the organic body of the Church. Wars are fought over the power of idols or the meaning of the Eucharist. These are not "small things," for at stake is the ultimate meaning of man. Evil always moves from the normative to the ontological; it begins with a perception of violation but proceeds to a controversy about the nature of being—of life and death—itself. We may have lost much of our religious sensibilities, but our political conceptions bear remnants of their genealogy. Our world remains very much one in which we trade charges of idolatry and engage in our own attacks upon Pharisaism.

It is no harder to believe that man is the product of a divine act of creation than to believe that the subject is born again as a part of the body of Christ. Elements of both sets of belief—the models of making

---

[69] This is generally referred to as the "blood libel" myth and dates back to 1144 in England. See *The Blood Libel Legend* (A. Dundes, ed. 1994).

and of the organic—are present from the beginning of Judeo-Christian thought. Each is a subtheme to the other as they trade places as the dominant form of explanation of man's relationship to the sacred. Arguably, both are needed to comprehend the experience of the sacred. The infinite is separated from the finite self as maker is to made, and yet it is so close that the subject appears to himself as an aspect of the infinite. Religious doctrine is an effort to give conceptual form to the experience of the sacred as that of the "infinite in the finite." It cannot do other than use the conceptual tools at hand. These tools always include the models of made order and of organic order, for these are the double meanings of labor already set forth in *Genesis*. They are, of course, fundamental to all human experience.

To modern, multicultural sensibilities, we cannot be sure if the evil is located in the other—the idolater or the Pharisee—or in the negative reaction to the competing claim to the sacred. We cannot be sure, because both sides of this antithesis invoke conceptions of the infinite of which we are skeptical. The miracle of divine intervention presented in the narrative of the Jews is not the same as the presence of the Holy Ghost, but both beliefs require a leap of faith. If God saves Isaac, surely He will follow that act with a set of commandments—laws—setting forth how the nation that derives from Isaac is to conduct itself. If we can believe that God created Adam, then it is no harder to believe that Christ is the Second Adam come to redeem man from the sin of the first. Both forms of belief are equally hard to maintain once the confidence in the possibility of the miraculous disappears. That disappearance is the phenomenon of the Enlightenment, which is both a product of and then an influence on the developing culture of Protestantism—the third moment in the Western genealogy of the sacred.

The Enlightenment has multiple strands, but its most important characteristic is a turn toward critical self-reflection.[70] Man finds himself with certain beliefs, that is, representations of himself and of a world outside himself. But what exactly is the relationship between representation and represented? What is it that man can know? Are his representations to be trusted? This is the point of origin of

---

[70] See I. Kant, "What Is Enlightenment?" in *Kant's Political Writings* (H. Reiss ed., H. Nisbet, trans. 1971) [1784].

Cartesian doubt: Can we find a firm foundation for true belief? The Enlightenment deepens as the critical instrument of doubt is applied ever more widely until no belief whatsoever—scientific, political, moral, or religious—is secure from the application of the corrosive force of doubt. One direction of doubt is empirical; the other is conceptual. The former leads to an effort to return to unmediated experience, that is, to the phenomena themselves. On this view, what we can know about the world is only secured through the immediacy of direct experience. The latter leads to the various forms of idealism. What we can know, on this view, is only that which we can grasp through reason itself. Logic, not sensation, is the only secure ground of knowledge. Thus the philosophy of the Enlightenment is characterized by an antithesis between the empiricists and the idealists.[71] We cannot say whether Hume or Hegel is more representative of Enlightenment thought. We can say, however, that both are responding to the Cartesian challenge: What can we know beyond doubt?

Protestantism began with an effort to apply the lessons of a recovered classical humanism to the content of inherited religious belief. Later, that recovery will lead to a more general Enlightenment skepticism toward unsupported claims of knowledge and authority. Before that, however, it powered the effort of the Reformation to purge Christian faith of false representations. Symbolically, this is evident in the attack on pictorial images of the divine, which is characteristic of Reformed Protestant sects. More important, we find the fundamentalist impulse to return directly to the biblical text itself. Religious belief is to be grounded in that text which carries still the aura of the miraculous. To add to that text—for example, with the history of Church teachings—is to replace a direct manifestation of the divine with man's interpretive acts, which can always be in error. To move beyond doubt, we have to separate the sacred text from all other claims of religious authority. That text is the only warrant for authority; all other claims to authority fail to survive this process of doubt and critique.

In this sense, Luther shows the way toward an empiricism of faith. He seeks to get to the phenomenon of faith itself, stripping away the layers of interpretation added by the Church over the centuries. Lu-

[71] Of course, there are positions in-between, the most important Kant's.

ther, who remains committed to infant baptism and to some artistic representations, goes only so far on this path.[72] Nevertheless, he sets a direction quickly pursued by Zwingli, Calvin, and other Protestant reformers who would strip away all beliefs that lack biblical warrant. There is no logical explanation of why the text, but not, for example, the sacraments, is seen as the base point of miraculous revelation. And, of course, a majority of the Christian community remains enthralled to the Church as the body of Christ, as well as to Church doctrine. There is nothing about religious experience in itself that points to a text over any other possible point of miraculous appearance, wherever and whenever it might have occurred; that is, there is no explaining from within the hermeneutics of faith. There are ample explanations from within the historical sociology of the Church: for example, the presence of political corruption and the abuse of religious authority for the ends of personal power. Luther did not set out to found a new faith but to reform an existing one.

The scalpel of Enlightenment self-criticism cannot, however, be contained within the parameters of traditional faith. Once belief becomes the subject of doubt, there is an unbounded character to the question, "What can we know?" The answer that we can know only that which God has directly revealed is necessarily an unstable answer, dependent on a faith that remains outside the engine of Enlightenment criticism. Hume, for example, directly applies the corrosive character of doubt to the reports of the experience of the miraculous upon which religion had traditionally been based.[73] Both Old and New Testament faiths were rooted in the experience of the presence of the divine: one in the form of law, the other in the form of the mystical corpus. But Hume shows that neither reports of the miraculous nor even the experience itself can authoritatively support the religious claims. Were we today to experience the miraculous, we would register it as merely the "yet to be explained."[74] The tools of explanation we would bring to the

---

[72] See MacCulloch, *The Reformation* 138–39.

[73] D. Hume, *An Enquiry concerning Human Understanding* 175–86 (T. Beauchamp, ed. 1999).

[74] See *id.* at 184 (imagining a uniform report of an eight-day darkening of the earth, Hume writes that "our present philosophers . . . ought to search for the causes whence it might be derived"); see also R. Fogelin, *A Defense of Hume on Miracles* 25–28 (2003).

phenomenon would be those of modern science. That we do not understand a phenomenon is hardly proof of the existence of God but only of an unsolved problem for further scientific inquiry. If we can no longer read our own experiences as proof of the existence of God, then the content of our religious belief, if it is to be secure or warranted belief, must be generated by the deployment of reason itself. This is not Hume's position—he is a thorough agnostic—but it is Kant's response. He announces this Enlightenment ambition in the title of a critical work, *Religion within the Limits of Reason Alone.*

For Kant and many others, the God of Protestant faith must be a God of reason. The authoritative quality of the moral law comes not from its miraculous source in the sacred word but rather from its quality as a norm that expresses the nature of reason itself. Reason is objective and universal. Accordingly, the moral law is the content generated by the form of reason alone. This is summarized in the categorical imperative: "Act only according to that maxim by which you can at the same time will that it should become a universal law."[75] On this formula, moral belief becomes self-warranting: reason must believe in the truth of its own command. Man's capacity to give a law to himself, to determine the maxim of his own action by reference to reason, is the practical reflection of the divine within finite existence. An irrational god is unimaginable at a time when the reason of the world is being revealed by science and when reason is working a revolution in reordering the productions of social life. If reason links man to the divine, then it is exactly as a rational agent that man is an image of God.

Kant argued that we can know nothing about the existence or nature of God in and of itself, since we can only know that which we experience in space and time—so far Hume was right. Nevertheless, we put ourselves in the position of the divine legislator when we determine our intentions by reason alone. Here Hume was wrong, for he failed to see that reason can be an active force and thus a source of our own freedom.[76] God is not distracted by interests or desires, and

---

[75] See above at note 11.

[76] The practical side of this dispute between Hume and Kant is foundational for the modern period. Hume founds the belief in negative freedom, under which the task of reason is to strip away false idols, whether internal or external. Kant founds the belief in positive freedom, under which the task of reason is to ground an authentic intention stripped of the influence of heteronomous forces whether from within or without the body.

neither should we be. However, where God's reason would order creation, our own reason can order nothing beyond our own individual wills—not even the small world within which the self acts. The hope that a well-ordered will can be successful in action remains a matter of religious faith—a necessary faith for man.

Thus the larger Enlightenment project for religion must be to locate the grounds of faith in the conditions of true belief. In this domain, the goal of Cartesian doubt is the reconstruction of a sure faith. Christian belief is to reemerge from a rigorous examination of man's own capacity for reason and representation. Religion will no longer be based on faith in authority but on propositions whose truth cannot be denied. Such was the hope of the Enlightenment faithful. After all, if God made man in his image, critical self-reflection should lead man back to God even more surely than relying on the inherited traditions of the community. An enlightened, mature man must have an enlightened faith.

Enlightenment man is thus an inquirer into the nature and scope of justified religious belief. Religion must be put on the same foundation as other beliefs, which means that religion and science must have a common root in man's reasoning and representational capacities. Thus the founders of modern science—for example, Descartes, Newton, and Leibniz—do not see any break between their scientific and their religious inquiries.[77] There is just one world, which they are exploring by examining the truth conditions of man's representations of that world. They had every reason to believe that the end of that inquiry would reveal the divine truth. As long as they believed in creation, they could not imagine any other result.

Through the early nineteenth century this project was more or less successful. Philosophy had not separated from theology, on the one hand, or from natural science, on the other. Metaphysics remained the "queen of the sciences."[78] What we call science was pursued as "natural philosophy." To understand the world was to understand God's creation. Institutionally we see that many of the great modern universities have their origins as religious seminaries. Sociologically we see not just the unity of philosophy, theology, and science but,

---

[77] See Webster, *From Paracelsus to Newton.*
[78] The expression is taken from the opening page of Kant's *Critique of Pure Reason.*

more generally, that the most learned man in a community was usually the minister whose education likely spanned the entire reach of philosophy.[79]

Protestant thought is caught between reason and experience. On the one hand, there is the desire to put religion on the same ground of rationality as all other justified belief. One form of this quest is Kant's moral law; another is Newton's effort to understand the miraculous through scientific inquiry. Contemporary versions of the latter range from creationism to the archaeological search for Noah's ark. On the other hand, there is the effort to return to the biblical text itself, which is to be approached without interpretation, that is, without the intervention of the doubtful capacities of human explanation. Fundamentalism is never far from scientism in Protestantism. This is nothing more than the theological version of the tension in modern thought between the impulse to seek a foundation for belief in the immediacy of experience and the contrary impulse to seek it in the systematic quality of reason. When we turn to experience, we find religion as easily as we find desire; the "oceanic feeling"—a sense of transcendent unity—is as elementary as pleasure and pain.[80] When we turn to reason, we might find systematic theology or critical social theory. The forms of inquiry do not themselves account for the content of the phenomena to be explained.

The fundamentalist strain of Protestant thought reads the myth of Adam and Eve not as a source for law nor as a kind of negative counter to the institutional community that is Christ's body but as a literal account of our current situation. The text is not only fundamental to an understanding of our condition, it is the only source of understanding: "The Fall took place at the beginning of human history, and all

[79] The convergence of learning, faith, and public service is seen, for example, in that provision of the 1780 Constitution of the Commonwealth of Massachusetts regarding Harvard College, referring to graduates who were "initiated into those arts and sciences which qualified them for public employments, both in church and state; and whereas the encouragement of arts and sciences, and all good literature, tends to the honor of God, the advantage of the Christian religion, and the great benefit of this, and the other United States of America." Part II, Chap. V, sec. I.

[80] See, e.g., R. Otto, *The Idea of the Holy: An Inquiry into the Non-rational Factor in the Idea of the Divine and Its Relation to the Rational* (J. Harvey, trans. 1925); C. Taylor, *Varieties of Religion Today: William James Revisited* (2002).

individuals born since then suffer these same consequences, are fallen, sinful and lost and are in need of the saving grace of God."[81] There is a recognition of the religious idea of the gap between the finite and the infinite but a rejection of the institutional forms—law and the Church—of overcoming the gap. Instead, what is required is a personal avowal of faith in Jesus and, correspondingly, a direct response from Christ: "There is no salvation apart from personal faith in Jesus Christ as Lord."[82] In place of institutions, we have a religion of immediacy: Christ either appears to the believer or he does not. The relationship to Christ is personal and self-validating. Christ is the believer's "personal savior." This is Protestantism as a phenomenology of religious experience. The fundamentalism of the text is paralleled by a fundamentalism of experience: both exist only as unmediated, miraculous appearances of the divine.[83] Belief is not mediated through the report of old miracles or through the authoritative traditions of the Church. Rather, the miraculous is located within the individual believer. Each person must be seized by the Holy Spirit; each must be personally born again. Thus a religion that takes a text as fundamental can curiously appear to be without language—the personal experience of being saved can take the form of "speaking in tongues." Every deification of a text—every fundamentalism—puts at risk language as an expression of dialogic form and intersubjective engagement. It must do so precisely because of the skepticism it directs toward interpretation.

The rationalist strain of Protestant faith, on the other hand, reads Adam and Eve as a myth urging self-reliance and the deployment of reason. Adam and Eve may be on their own, but they are in possession of knowledge of good and evil. The task of man is to apply reason within the domain of his own experience. For Kant, that domain begins with the lawful ordering of the individual will. For his followers

---

[81] Grace Evangelical School of Theology: Detailed Statement of Belief; see also Southern Baptists Convention, 2000 Baptist Faith and Message (Adam "fell from his original innocence whereby his posterity inherits a nature and an environment inclined toward sin. Therefore, as soon as they are capable of moral action, they become transgressors"). These themes are already present in Augustine, but he remains committed to the authority of the Church as a response to the Fall.

[82] Grace Evangelical School of Theology: Detailed Statement of Belief.

[83] On the fundamentalism of the text, see "The Chicago Statement on Biblical Inerrancy."

along the path of positive freedom, that domain expands to include the entire sociopolitical order. Recovery is no longer waiting on divine intervention. The post-lapsarian utopia will be the kingdom of reason, which will arrive as soon as man puts it into place.[84] A God that demands that we act under the guidance of reason is asking no more than that we subject our practical selves to the same critique of reason that we apply to every other form of belief. The fundamental meaning of the myth now shifts to a message of equality: each person is equally an image of God, because every individual possesses reason. The new Protestant rationalist is paradigmatically Jefferson, whose most famous statement is that "all men are created equal." Jefferson is followed by all those who claim a Christian foundation for the modern idea of individual dignity. This is the sense in which modernity itself is a deeply Protestant project. This is true not just of modern forms of economic organization but also of the commitment to democratic government under the rule of law.[85] The autonomous, rational agent is the ideal upon which this conception of the citizen depends.

The end of this line of development is the morality of liberalism, for liberalism is the commitment to ordering practical affairs through the direction of reason. Only when we understand the religious genealogy of the reason-governed will can we make sense of "liberal passion," that is, the fervor with which these beliefs are held and the proselytizing character of their adherents. Liberalism, like every other version of Judeo-Christian belief, is a fighting faith. At stake is not merely a prudential reasonableness, but the realization of that unity of the finite and the infinite for which fallen men strive. No doubt part of the intuitive attraction of Rawls's idea of reaching a knowledge of justice behind the veil of ignorance is the symbolism of leaving this fallen world of particular concerns and returning to a purer space of undifferentiated, equal individuals. Rawls's argument is a modern myth of overcoming the Fall by returning to that moment just prior to expulsion in order to determine the conditions that should govern the labor upon

---

[84] Modern social contract theory is just the latest version of this appeal to reason. See Kahn, *Putting Liberalism in Its Place*.

[85] See M. Weber, *The Protestant Ethic and the Spirit of Capitalism* (T. Parsons, trans. 1958).

which man is about to engage.[86] In the end, Rawls appears as a New England Congregationalist replicating the covenantal communities of his Puritan forbearers.

What do these new forms of religious experience suggest about evil? For each, evil arises out of the failure to apply the Enlightenment demand for doubt to the content of religious belief. Again, at stake is a false faith—a mistaking of nothing at all for the infinite. Of course, each finds its self-evident foundation—its point beyond doubt—in opposite ways. Thus the Protestant rationalist sees evil in the failure of the fundamentalist to entertain any doubt of his or her claim of Christ's presence in text and experience. The fundamentalist, on the other hand, sees evil in the failure of the Protestant rationalist to doubt the capacity of reason itself.

Evil is refracted through these two conceptions of Enlightenment faith: experience and reason. Each now takes the other as the primary object of fear and the threat of evil. For the fundamentalist, contemporary evil is likely to take the form of "secular humanism." This is understood as the claim that reason can inform a moral practice quite independently of religious belief. The fundamentalist understands this claim as the modern form of Adam's effort to be the source of his own ultimate meaning. Luther already identified the source of sin in man's desire to be wise: "That is what the devil wants to bring about in all his temptations, that the farther man draws away from the Word, the more learned and the wiser he appears to himself."[87] Faith in reason stands in contrast to faith in the Word. Secular humanism appears as the end point of this development.

Religious belief for the secular humanist is reduced to private faith, and private faith is seen as essentially irrational, a matter of taste. The secular humanist does not need to deny the phenomenon of religious experience but only to declare it irrelevant to the projects of creating a public order or of articulating norms of justice, equality, and liberty. This denial of a public space to religious faith is intolerable to the

---

[86] Rawls does his best to disavow such a "metaphysical" reading of his work. See J. Rawls, "Justice as Fairness: Political Not Metaphysical," 14 Phil. & Pub. Aff. 223 (1985). My point, however, is not about Rawls's own views but about why those views seem so compatible with the fundamental beliefs of many.

[87] Luther, *Lectures on Genesis* 271.

fundamentalist who finds Christ's presence to be not a matter of personal feelings but a new foundation of the world. The fundamentalist sees the same threat to the transformative character of faith from the privatization of religion in liberal democracies as from the suppression of religion in the old communist states. The contemporary Eastern European experience suggests that faith can thrive in adversity, yet wither with tolerance. Contemporary fundamentalists do not want to be "tolerated"; they want to construct a public order infused with the sacred.

Accordingly, the fundamentalist finds himself locked in a battle with those who would construct a public order based on the same kind of critical thought that characterizes science. In contemporary America, the secular humanist is identified with a broadly liberal political and social culture. But that is not the source of the fundamentalist's complaint. He would have the same complaint against other secular, political ideologies, whether socialism or libertarianism. The arguments between them are family disputes over the shape of a politics founded on reason. None is open to the fundamentalist's claim for the primacy of the experience of the Word.

Conversely, the Protestant rationalist sees the source of evil in the claim to a personal experience of God's grace, that is, the claim that some individuals are saved and others lost. A *personal* savior is an affront to the universalism of reason, which finds its contemporary moral and political expression in liberalism. Claims of religious privilege always appear as a ground of distinction for favoring some over others. This distinction between the saved and everyone else becomes a ground for injury, abuse, and hatred. Because this religious claim is inaccessible to reason, it appears as an irrational prejudice incompatible with the public norm of justice. Accordingly, the particularism of religious faith must be expelled from our public life. Moreover, the state must be ready to intervene even in private life where fundamentalist faith violates norms of autonomy and equality.

Both sides in this conflict have much history to draw upon. They are continuing the old battle of Genesis one and two. The fundamentalist seeks that unity of being and the good that had been Adam's; the Protestant rationalist takes up the task of ordering the world through labor.[88] Nor does recent history allow us easily to choose between them. We know that efforts to remake society on the basis of science have produced some of the worst evils of the last century. Liberalism is not the only science of the political that has characterized modernity. Its competitors included those varieties of totalitarianism that produced the paradigmatic instances of modern political evil. Claims for reason may have their origin in the faith of the Enlightenment that man can be released from the irrational bonds of tradition and the customary practices of power. But, for most people, the result has hardly been a new age of personal freedom. We also know, however, that those who hold themselves to be privileged in their relationship to God are capable of terrible acts against those with whom they disagree.

CONCLUSION

Religious faith is always one thing and not another. Too often we think of faith as primarily a matter of tradition, as if there is a single narrative of a community of faith that anchors it to the past. But, like any other conceptual formation, the structure of a group's faith emerges in response to the circumstances of belief within which it finds itself. Religious forms, no less than political formations, have a history of belief, crisis, and recovery. I have argued in this chapter that Western belief moves from a conceptual model of making to a model of the organic to one of self-reflection. This dialectical shape characterizes the search for order across many fields of experience. We start by thinking that the order we find is the product of an intentional act of making. We move beyond that when we realize that we are not just observers of the whole that we seek to explain but rather are a part of it; we stand within, not outside, the whole. The principle of intelligibility does not come from without but sustains the whole from within. Finally, we turn our capacity for critique upon the structure of our

---

[88] Of course, neither side to this dispute will leave uncontested the alternative reading of *Genesis*. Above I argued that the rationalist side of Protestantism claims the "image of God" for its vision of rational equality; surely the fundamentalists want to take up the burden of labor in order to refound the world.

thought itself. We create some distance between faith and reflection, and take responsibility for our commitments.

No religious conception ever gives way entirely to its successor. Earlier forms of belief continue right alongside those forms that develop in reaction and opposition. Jews do not disappear with the appearance of a new form of religious belief in and through Christ; Protestants do not defeat their predecessors in New Testament faith. Rarely, however, do these diverse forms of belief view each other from the perspectives of benign indifference, of multicultural celebration, or even of modus vivendi accommodation. They see in each other threats to the foundation of their own beliefs; they see each other as evil. Because each stands as a challenge to the other's beliefs about the meaning of life itself, each grounds a distinctive conception of evil. In each instance we see that evil is not the failure to meet the internal norms of a system of belief. Rather, it is the external assault on the claim to have located the point of the sacred in a fallen world.

These three moments in the history of Western monotheism, accordingly, provide the groundwork for our understanding of evil. Experience of the sacred can take the form of following the law, participation in the mystical corpus of Christ, personal salvation, or the pursuit of what used to be called "natural philosophy." Each form generates a double perception of evil—synchronic and diachronic. The synchronic supports what Freud called the "narcissism of minor differences."[89] Those with whom we share a worldview can become our deepest enemies and the incarnation of evil. This is the history of civil wars and religious factionalism but also the personal history of intra-familial dispute. These disagreements offer familiar patterns of the perception of good and evil, but not every difference is minor. Entire worldviews shift. The diachronic clash of worldviews, of entire patterns of understanding the ultimate meaning of experience, can be the locus of good and evil. The alien other can be no less evil than my alienated brother.

We can name the synchronous model of evil after its first appearance: the charge of idolatry in a polytheistic world. Idolatry is that form of evil that appears within a single conceptual model or category

---

[89] S. Freud, *Civilization and Its Discontents* 61 (J. Strachey, trans. 1961); see also M. Ignatieff, *The Warrior's Honor: Ethnic War and the Modern Conscience* 34–71 (1997).

of belief. As interpretive communities splinter, they inevitably charge each other with false belief, with substituting a false god for the truth, an empty idol for the sacred presence. Analogously, we can label the diachronic form of evil after its first appearance: the Christian attack on Pharisaism, that is, the condemnation of the Jewish failure to recognize the new Adam in place of law and ritual. It is that form of evil that appears across forms of belief. So used, idolatry and Pharisaism are categories, not particular practices. Thus the charge of Pharisaism can take the form of antipapism for Reformation Protestants, and charges of idolatry can occur across the schism between the Catholic Church and the Eastern Orthodox.

Used most expansively, these terms can describe the deepest conflict of the contemporary period. Idolatry expands to include the very core of the religious experience: faith in the manifestation of the sacred. Once every claim to the sacred is rejected, an appearance of the divine has no more power than a golden calf. The history of religious experience is described as a history of "illusion." Not the wrong god, but all gods lead to behavior that disrespects and ultimately destroys the only true source of value there is. That value is the application of reason to the well-being of the subject—every subject. The history of evil, on this view, is not just parallel to the history of religion; they are one and the same. Evil threatens to reappear whenever and wherever people give up the practice of a secular reason aimed directly at well-being and, instead, place a religious-like faith in a leader, a group, or an institution.

Just as charges of idolatry expand to cover every manifestation of the divine, charges of Pharisaism expand to cover all who would rely on law in place of an organic, participatory faith. The characteristic of the Jew that anchored Pharisaism was his insistence that man was separated from God by a gap that could only be partially bridged by law. This meant that history could never be more than labor. Laboring man still has to wait for the appearance of a savior. If history is only the domain of labor, then we remain doomed to death. The Jew, then, is easily assimilated to all who reject the claim that man has been offered the opportunity to be reborn free of the finite conditions that characterize the Fall. The Jew becomes the symbol of the pathologies of modernity—whether economic, epistemic, political, or cultural.

This is, for example, already the role of the Jew in the *Merchant of Venice*. The deepest dispute of the contemporary period remains that between the biopolitics of reason and the biopolitics that is the body of Christ. What else should we expect for Western man who must struggle to locate a transcendent meaning within a finite body.

What unites all these forms of evil is their proximity to a set of ultimate beliefs. "Ultimate" refers to matters of life and death—Adam's sin brought death to the world—as well as to matters of infinite value. Every idea of evil in the religious tradition arises at the point of intersection of these two senses of the ultimate: Is there a meaning that can save us from a life of labor leading only to death? Evil is not measured by disregard for the life or the well-being of others. Such disregard may be criminal; it is certainly immoral. We enter the domain of evil when such disregard is the product of a contest between beliefs about ultimate values. These are the beliefs by which we respond to the awareness of our own finitude by asserting a faith in the sacred. If we are without any faith at all, we will not see evil but only criminality and pathology. We will be where this chapter began: with liberalism's incapacity to understand evil.

Evil arises at the intersection of death and faith. So, of course, does love. The myth of Adam and Eve locates all four—death and faith, love and evil—at the point where man realizes he is condemned to finitude. We are an infinite consciousness caught in a finite body. Today many would contest the idea that the forms of evil can be read directly out of religious belief. That belief has become both too various and, after Darwin, too tenuous. Darwin teaches the nineteenth century that order can emerge from disorder without the intervention of Providence. Accordingly, we do not need final causes to explain our own origins. Chance operating within a world of finite resources is a more powerful source of explanation than any appeal to divine plans. If we no longer need God to explain our origins, perhaps we do not need God to explain our fate. It may very well be that we have no fate at all. We may be alone in a universe driven by chance. There may be nothing at all on the other side of the gap. Religion is to be explained now not by God's revelation across the gap but by man's very human activity of projecting an image of God across the gap.

The end of this line of thought is found in Nietzsche and Freud—a disenchanted world.

Yet the religious genealogy of evil offers fundamental insights that remain relevant in our more secular age, for this genealogy points to two fundamental ideas: first, evil arises in the flight from a meaningless death; it is finitude we cannot bear. Second, we find evil in close proximity to love. These are the claims I pursue in the following chapters, which trace the continuing presence of evil in our secular world.

To understand contemporary evil we must understand the contemporary forms of our own beliefs about ultimate meanings. If we would use the language of Enlightenment to say that man's maturity is marked by his capacity to accept his own death, we can say that the source of evil is the continuing presence of man's immaturity. This immaturity, however, like original sin, may be a condition beyond our capacity to outgrow.

CHAPTER THREE

■　■　■　■

LOVE AND EVIL

The second Adam and Eve myth of Genesis ("Genesis two") is usually read as a story of disobedience and punishment. The magnitude of the disobedience is heightened by the authority of the source of the rule. We can also read the myth, however, as a story of love. Read as a tale of punishment, it offers a one-dimensional account of man: he is to be measured only in his relationship to God's command. As a tale of love, however, the myth broadens, rather than narrows, our understanding of ourselves, for it asks us to reflect on the tension between authority and love, or justice and meaning.

THE TWO-BECOME-ONE OF LOVE

In the first Genesis myth ("Genesis one"), woman is created simultaneously with man. Both are created as images of God. Their joint creation is a necessary condition of God's procreative ambition: "be fruitful and multiply." Genesis two approaches Eve from a completely different perspective. The story of Eve's creation now begins with God's observation that "It is not good that the man should be alone; I will make him a helper fit for him." What is the deficiency for which the man needs a helper? It is not the need to labor; labor is not yet a burden.[1] Nor is it the task of naming; naming does not require dialogue. It is not even the necessities of procreation. The injunction to procreate figures in the first Genesis story of man's creation, not in the second. A procreative god does not overlook the female of the species.

The source of need in the second story is not procreation but loneliness: man "leaves his father and his mother and cleaves to his wife,

---

[1] Of labor in the Garden, Luther remarks that God gave man this task "that he might not be idle." M. Luther, "The Freedom of a Christian," in *Selections from His Writings* 9 (J. Dillenberger, ed. 1962).

and they become one flesh." Eve's creation is a story of separation of a part of the self—the metaphorical rib—and recovery—becoming one flesh. This is much the same story as the myth of the circle-men told by Aristophanes in Plato's *Symposium*. Aristophanes explains that once we were whole, but we have been split apart. As we are metaphysically constituted, we are lonely. It is as if we have lost a part of ourselves. Happiness depends upon recovery of our other half. When we find that other half, we will cleave to it and become "one flesh." Thus our loneliness arises from the limits of the body itself. We experience the body as a source of isolation, of separation from the world. In Aristophanes' myth, man experiences the body as literally a wound. We can only overcome the injury of loneliness through love, which is the recovery of our other half.

The account offered in a myth must resonate at two levels. First, it has to have its roots in the range of ordinary experience. These are stories of passion, anger, conflict, and revenge. Aristophanes' myth, for example, is so attractive because we know exactly what he means in referring to the circle-man's search for his other half; the same is true of the Genesis idea of becoming "one flesh." Second, the object of the myth is to provide a narrative—an account of reciprocal demands and actions—to explain the subject's experience of the self in the world. The story tells us "how" we got to where we are. The explanation of our current sense of ourselves as guilty, for example, must be found in an earlier violation. Similarly, if we are looking for love, we must have lost an earlier love. Thus man finds himself always already to have eaten of the tree—he knows good and evil—and already longing for his other half—he needs the completeness of love. He finds himself always and already at the end of the mythical narration. The point of the myth is not simply to offer an explanation of our condition but to dispose the listener to take up a certain attitude toward his or her present situation. The account is not neutral. It offers meanings, not facts.

In both the biblical and the Platonic stories, the completeness of love is experienced as both promise and threat. Both myths suggest that love is not just the goal we seek but also the origin or foundation of our present world. Man longs for that completion through union, which he feels as the recovery of the truth of the self. Nevertheless, to believe in the achievement of that union is dangerously hubristic. For Aristophanes, the prelapsarian love of the other leads to a direct challenge to the gods; in *Genesis*, it leads to disobedience to God's command. The point is the same: a fully accomplished love is complete in itself; it has no need of the gods. In both myths, a divine sanction follows. The wholeness is lost; individuals are separated, doomed to an endless longing for their lost, other half. We can never fully recapture that complete love. Put more directly, love is never complete; there is always some remainder of the self beyond or outside love.

The image of becoming "one flesh" symbolizes a life in which need no longer figures. Not because we are sated but because we are complete. Thus Aristophanes appeals to the image of a circle, complete in itself. Lovers know exactly who they are. They do not wonder if there is more to life or if they are being true to themselves. For them, love is experienced as the point at which being and meaning are one and the same. What I am is exactly what I ought to be, for it is as that subject that I both love and am loved. Such a convergence of the "is" and the "ought" ordinarily appears as an attribute of the sacred; about love there is always something sacred.

Both myths suggest that love provides the plot for the narrative of our lives. Since we cannot search for what we do not know—or at least know of—love has somehow preceded us. If sin is original, then so, too, is love. We are thrown into our world as a consequence of love. For Western man, love, like sin, is a necessary condition of the life within which we find ourselves.[2] Without speaking of love, we cannot explain who we are; neither can we explain our relationship to each other or to the world. We cannot speak of love, however, without speaking of guilt, sin, and fall. Love appears as the truth of the self, but it is a truth we never quite realize. We cannot fully shake the sense of guilt; we cleave to the other, but we cannot quite become "one flesh." Love is the aspiration to overcome the loneliness of the finite self. Through the beloved, love remakes our relationship to the world. Yet somehow we are not quite adequate to love.

[2] In the Kantian sense, love is a "transcendental condition" of our experience of ourselves.

Man has need of a "helper." Without that, even in the presence of God, man is lonely. This creates one of the great paradoxes of the Judeo-Christian tradition. God creates a being that alone is not perfect and that cannot find its perfection in the single relationship to God. Perfection of man requires the creation of the beloved. But with love, man no longer needs God.[3] Hegel's myth of the master who has control of the slave but can never obtain from such a subordinated creature the recognition he wants has its archaic origins in the biblical creation myth. God faces the same choice as the master: He can have a less than perfect man who worships only Him or He can have a perfect man who no longer needs Him. In much of the Judeo-Christian tradition, God is to be the object of man's love. Jews speak of the relationship of the nation of Israel to God as one of marriage; Christians speak of Christ as the bridegroom to the Church. But this is just the state of prelapsarian man: the state in which God saw that man needed a helper. Love is so powerful that once it appears we can read man as hubristic—he no longer needs God—or we can read God as jealous—He would take up the position of the beloved. This is a paradox not just for God but for man as well. How can man have the completeness of love without offending the authority of God?

The lovers lack of need for divine assistance is symbolized by their transgression: they would be like God in eating of the tree of knowledge. The serpent promises Eve that "when you eat of it your eyes will be opened, and you will be like God, knowing good and evil." They do indeed learn good and evil, but they do not become like God. After the Fall, lovers no longer fully realize that escape from loneliness, which Adam found in Eve. Their world is now one of labor, not in place of, but despite, their love. Knowing good and evil—possessing moral knowledge—is a problem for love.

Aristophanes claimed that love has a daimonic power to make us whole. In *Genesis*, the ambition for wholeness remains love's aspira-

---

[3] This paradox generates two thousand years of theological dispute over the place of celibacy in the relationship of man to God. Is not the celibate—whether monk, saint, or priest—at best in the same relationship to God as was Adam? Did Adam not need a helper? The three stages of Western monotheism resolve this puzzle in different but always unstable ways. See G. Anderson, *The Genesis of Perfection* 43–62 (2001).

tion, but now our loneliness is beyond love's capacity to repair. For love itself is implicated in the sin. Loving Eve, Adam cannot abandon her once she has eaten of the apple.[4] Adam knew a life without Eve: it was one of irredeemable loneliness. No relationship to an asymmetrical authority, even that between God and man, can be complete. Completion requires the two-in-one of love. Thus, for the sake of love, man will do anything; he will even disobey God.[5] For this they are expelled from the Garden. Piercing the narrative form of the myth, we can say that through love we learn of good and evil; we learn that our actions have not met the standard of justice.

This conflict between love and authority—even divine authority— is deep and true.[6] It appears even when we believe that the demands of authority are entirely just. For the sake of love, we place ourselves against the demands of justice. We privilege our own children over the just demands of equally deserving children; we protect our own families at a cost to others, even when there is no just reason to make others bear that cost. For love of nation, we protect our own community while we ignore the equally just demands—indeed, even more just demands—of outsiders. We will, if necessary, injure innocent others for the sake of protecting those we love. Every loving relationship privileges the beloved in a way that is incompatible with the obligations of justice.[7] Morality always makes a claim to speak in the universal language of reason, but love is never reasonable.[8] Sometimes we speak of a love of all mankind. That can mean putting justice ahead of love of anyone in particular; it can also mean acting toward a particular individual for no reason other than his or her humanity. A selfless love might be universal, but it would not speak to the longing for

---

[4] To put love at the center of Adam's choice is to follow Augustine's reading: "the man could not bear to be severed from his only companion, even though this involved a partnership in sin." *City of God* 14.11 (M. Dods, trans. 1950). This reading was, in turn, at the heart of Milton's *Paradise Lost*, 9:955–59. See generally Anderson, *The Genesis of Perfection* 105–11.

[5] The theme of betrayal of a sovereign authority for the sake of love is a constant of Western literature. But the moral quality of the act is open. It can be represented as an affirmation of love or as treason against the state. See *Anthony and Cleopatra*.

[6] See P. Kahn, *Law and Love: The Trials of King Lear* (2000).

[7] See *id*. 169–70.

[8] On the tradition of associating justice with Satan and mercy (love) with God, see Anderson, *The Genesis of Perfection* 167–68.

completeness experienced by the subject acutely aware of his or her own limits. Such a love might be Christlike, but it is beyond us. As long as there is a particular content to oneself, love must be bound to particular others.

We do not ask of love that it meet a measure of justice either internally or externally. Rather, love operates under the standard of care.[9] Internally, the demands lovers make upon each other are not just; the demand for care is never a just burden. It is not just that my parents, my spouse, or my children have extraordinary needs. It is not just that some lovers are happy and others are in pain. We do not demand compensation for the burdens of love—although, when love ends, we look to justice for a standard for the distribution of assets. Externally, too, the reciprocal care that lovers bestow upon each other looks like an unjust allocation of resources. No doubt more good could be done by a more equitable distribution. Nevertheless, every utopian scheme that has tried to substitute justice for love—from Plato to Mao—has failed. This is true not only of familial love. Rational schemes for a just world government have never made much progress against the love of nation. Justice alone cannot win the battle with love. One form of love can only be challenged by another; for example, familial love can be challenged by love of another individual or by love of the community—and, vice versa, when the familial challenges the political.[10] Yet justice leaves its mark such that we feel the taint of injustice in love. Experiencing love, we do indeed "know" good and evil: we know it as a demand for justice that we fail to meet. Like Adam, we will take the apple from the beloved even when we know it is unjust.

Love reminds us of our prelapsarian state of completeness, but love in this world is never free of moral knowledge. For us, the physical act of sexual union bears much of the weight of this ambiguity: simultaneously a symbol of love and of moral failing. It is both the point of union in which two become one—"they become one flesh"—and the point at which we discover irremediable moral failure. It is the symbol of completeness and of endless desire, of becoming one with another

[9] See H. Frankfurt, *The Reasons of Love* 41–42 (2004).

[10] See, e.g., recent accounts of parents' opposition to military recruitment of their children. D. Cave & L. Cummins, "Growing Problem for Military Recruiters: Parents," *N.Y. Times*, June 3, 2005, at A1.

and of using the other, or transcending the flesh and of being sunk in the flesh. When love expresses itself through sex, it simultaneously recoils from the limits of the body. This is why Aristophanes describes the body as suffering a wound. This is why the original sin of *Genesis* has been linked to the experience of sex, not merely as procreation but as the symbol of love between Adam and Eve. Thus Augustine locates the transmission of original sin in the sexual act, regardless of how loving the couple.

This incommensurability between the sexual act and the meaning it must bear appears as comic in Aristophanes' account of the sexual union of the circle-people. That sex can bear the weight of love is comic; that it cannot is tragic.[11] The aspiration for dissolution of the self symbolized in sexual union always verges on the comic, just as that aspiration always moves toward tragedy as it elides into a symbol of the disappearance of the self in death. In the presence of sex, we are never far from death.[12] Thrown upon the body, the subject inevitably discovers his or her own limits—the fact of his or her own mortality. This is precisely the point of the *Genesis* story, which links sex, labor, and death as the consequences of the sin brought on by love. Unlike Aristophanes' lovers, the lovers of *Genesis* know too much. What they know is that the completeness of love is never fully what it seems, that in this world two cannot quite become one flesh. There is always a remainder of the self apart from love. That remainder is the subject who knows good and evil, and knows it as an aspect of his or her own mortality. Turning to love and only love, the lovers find themselves thrown into a world of labor, justice, and death.[13]

LOVE'S INCOMPLETENESS: SHAME

Two-become-one is a metaphor for the selflessness of love. In a pre-lapsarian world there is nothing sinful in sexual union: "and the man and his wife were both naked, and were not ashamed." There is noth-

---

[11] For an example of the comic, consider *Midsummer Night's Dream*; for the tragic, consider *Othello*.

[12] The French expression for orgasm is "petit mort" or "the little death."

[13] I mean to invoke Heidegger's concept of "thrownness" here. For Heidegger, man is thrown into "projects," just as fallen man "labors." See M. Heidegger, *Being and Time* 219–24 (J. Macquarrie & E. Robinson, trans. 1962).

ing shameful in being naked, as long as one is not observed. Observation requires a separation between subject and object, between the viewer and the viewed. Observation, in this sense, is the condition of all knowledge, including self-knowledge. To be without shame is to be without the separation that is the condition of knowledge; it is to be in love without that excluded remainder. Accordingly, to have knowledge, to have eaten of the tree of knowledge of good and evil, is to experience this separation. We cannot know the world without knowing ourselves as yet another object in the world. Naked, we are just such an object. Knowing the self, we experience shame.[14]

Shame is the emotive state that accompanies self-knowledge. We can understand that shame in two ways, and both figure in the story of the Fall. First, finding oneself limited to a particular body and condemned to death is shameful for a subject who knows him- or herself as an image of God. Before the Fall there is love without shame, because there is not yet knowledge of death. Second, we know the good as a demand beyond our limited capacities. We know it as a demand that we have already failed to meet once we have taken up the burden of labor. I do not appear to myself as just one subject among others. Rather, I appear to myself with a certain urgency: What should I do? Asking that question, I know that I have not done all that I should, nor will I in the future. For that reason, too, we experience shame.

In the Garden there is no shame between man and wife, because there is only the experience of the two-in-one, which is the common world of lovers. We cannot characterize this as self-knowledge but rather as the contentment with being that precedes knowledge—the unity of being and meaning. Their naked union is no more shameful than nakedness between mother and infant. In each case, it is a love beyond—or before—language. If the other does not appear as an object, neither does the self appear as a subject. This love is a forgetting of the self in that union of two. There is shame after the Fall, because now we labor under the conditions of self-knowledge. Lovers may aspire to a forgetting of the self in and through the other, but they find that they cannot achieve that complete love without a remainder. That remainder beyond love is the subject as the object of self-knowledge.

---

[14] See chapter 1 above.

The aspiration for the completeness of love remains, but completeness itself is beyond our grasp because we cannot forget that we will die. Our fate is to be one body alone. The lover is reminded of that not just when he engages in self-regard but equally when he thinks of the death of the beloved. That death, too, leaves him or her alone with the self. Just as the infant grows into self-knowledge, lovers fall apart—not necessarily wholly and completely, but love can never completely overcome loneliness for a self-conscious subject. A subject who can take the self as an object of thought has an unlimited capacity for loneliness that love cannot fully heal.

Shame, then, marks the incompleteness of the union of love. When Adam and Eve feel shame before God, they also feel shame before each other. Covering themselves before God, they cover themselves from each other. Covered they are two, not one. Their separation is characterized simultaneously by moral knowledge and by death. God told Adam that "of the tree of knowledge of good and evil you shall not eat, for in that day that you eat of it you shall die." For a self-conscious being, death is not the singular event marking the end of life. Death characterizes the whole of our lives as the knowledge of our own finitude. Self-consciousness appears in this double form: "I will die; what should I do?" Our mortality raises in compelling form the question of our action. The question of action always raises the question of justice.

We are never fully at one with the beloved because that relationship is marked by the self-consciousness of a finite subject. We act, and we observe ourselves acting. Our capacity for judgment is as broad and deep as our capacity for self-knowledge, that is, we inevitably judge ourselves just as we judge others. To cleave to the other as one flesh is now not just a recovery but also a forgetting. It is no longer only a fulfillment but also a fleeing. It is both comic and tragic. Lovers may forget that they will die, but they can never forget for long. They may forget the demands of justice, but that, too, they will remember.

Nothing in the story of prelapsarian union suggests anything other than fulfillment, an overcoming of loneliness through the two-be-come-one. Sin comes later. The experience of sin is the knowledge of a radical incompleteness and an insatiable longing. For women, the structure of that incompleteness is located in the linking of sexual desire to the pain of childbirth: "your desire shall be for your husband." Sexual union is never complete in itself; it leads to the pain of procreation and thus of separation. Two can no longer be one. Rather, two produce a third. The possibility of union is displaced onto this third, who inevitably both is and is not the parents. The child is the objectification of the promise of love to overcome our loneliness; the child is equally the denial of that very possibility. Indeed, the inevitable independence of the child is a reminder of the incurable loneliness that is individual existence. Procreation is not just physically painful. It is both a symbol of mortality and the thing itself. It points directly back to the creation of Eve out of Adam's rib. But God's procreative act was accomplished while Adam was asleep and led immediately to the uniting of man and woman. Procreation after the Fall always reminds us of the pain of separation. In our children, we see not only our own fulfillment but also our own death. We see again the remainder—the finite self—that is beyond love.

Just as women's labor links sexual union to separation and death, so does God's condemnation of Adam to labor mark a similar fate. Having eaten of the tree of knowledge, what exactly does Adam know? Most simply, his knowledge is of the good. When God judges creation to be good, he is also explaining the goal of his creative act: to bring forth the good. The good remains man's end. As Aristotle says, "The good has rightly been declared to be that at which all things aim."[15] But for a finite creature without the power of creation ex nihilo, knowledge of the good presents itself as the endless demand for labor: man must labor to bring forth the good. Apart from God, knowledge of the good is only possible for a temporally conscious being: one who can look to the future and ask, "What should I do?" This effort at self-government, however, inevitably results in knowledge of death. For when man looks to the future, he sees his own death.[16] Thus the one thing Adam most definitely knows is what God now tells him: "You are dust, and to dust you shall return." This knowledge applies not only to man himself but to all the products of

---

[15] See Aristotle, *Ethics* I, I.
[16] See the discussion of I. Kant, "Speculative Beginning of Human History," in chapter 2 above.

his labor. Nothing he can produce endures in the end. No matter what he achieves, it will not endure. For man, too, the pain of creation is the realization of mortality.[17]

Man's fall is represented as an effort to become like God by gaining the knowledge God possesses. Instead of grasping a timeless identity of being and the good, however, man's knowledge includes an awareness of the nothingness of his own existence. Death is his fate, which no amount of labor can prevent. Man cannot save himself; he cannot give up the knowledge he has, but that knowledge is never enough. It is not sexual desire that ultimately defeats the will to the good—the focus of much Christian moralizing at least since Augustine—it is death, which is why the most urgent message of Christianity is that of overcoming death.

We have no reason to think that the Adam and Eve of Genesis one are immortal, but we have every reason to think that they lack knowledge of their mortality. For them, procreation is not linked to sin. They are not troubled by death. After the Fall, both man and woman take up the task of labor in a condition of shame. No achievement of either—not children, and not the products of man's labor—can overcome this basic fact: we labor in the shadow of death. Nothing man can do, and nothing he can learn, allows him to transcend this existential fact. Knowledge of good and evil is knowledge of the self, and self-knowledge is the knowledge of death. At the core of man's existence is a metaphysical puzzle: death. In myth, the existential condition that expresses this puzzle is shame.

Socrates proclaimed, as the first principle of a full life, "Know thyself." In the Genesis account, that principle has just the opposite moral valence. To know the self is to know that one is dust and will return to dust. To know the self is not to transcend the conditions of mortal existence but to be burdened by those very conditions. Here we find one of the deep tensions between the classical and the biblical worldview: original sin is not a matter of ignorance but a matter of gaining knowledge. For biblical man, knowledge, not ignorance, is the temptation. At the opening of *Metaphysics* Aristotle states, "by nature all men desire to know." In *Genesis*, that desire leads to the Fall. In

---

[17] See H. Arendt, *The Human Condition* 18–19 (1958).

the Judeo-Christian world, only love, not knowledge, holds the promise of locating a meaning adequate to the burden of death.

The Platonic vision of the idea of recovery of the "true self" also
appeals to an idea of a self prior to birth. That self, however, is without
the limits of the body, which means that it is not the self of an individual subject. The experience of longing to overcome the conditions of
life is, for Plato, a longing to be relieved of the burden of being a
subject. To know the Forms is to realize a unity of knowledge and the
object of knowledge.[18] The Genesis myth, on the other hand, reveals
a subject who would overcome the divide not by abandoning but by
expanding the self. Adam and Eve become one flesh; they do not become disembodied selves. They do not overcome their existential loneliness by becoming "nobody at all." They remain particular to each
other, even as each finds the truth of the self in the other. Together they
occupy the point at which subject and object merge, without giving
up either their individual subjectivity or the objectivity of the world.
They are two-in-one, not less than one.

The subject of *Genesis* longs for a condition in which he is a finite
self with an infinite breadth. This would be the completeness of love,
or love without remainder. He or she longs to achieve the infinite
within the finite, to be a subject who is also the whole of creation. The
symbolic realization of this infinite in the finite is Christ, of whom
there is no parallel in classical thought. After the myth of the Fall,
knowledge cannot offer the path out of the burdens of labor. For
Christians, only in Christ are knowledge and love reconciled. Thus
Christ loves without remainder. The absence of a remainder is, in the
domain of the symbolic, the resurrection. The knowledge of death is
experienced as a kind of metaphysical rift, producing a feeling of
shame. Christ is to redeem man from the shame of Adam—the shame
of endless labor, moral failure, naked bodies, and death.

The narrative of Adam and Eve, accordingly, is a mythical account
of that first Copernican revolution, which was the creation of human
self-consciousness. Before the Fall, there is only the unity of being and
meaning that is the creative power of God. God does not know the

---

[18] Of course, the Platonic idea of self-transcendence remains a part of the Western philosophical inheritance.

world as the object of a proposition that could be otherwise. Rather, for God, to know and to create are one and the same. Thus creation is a function of speech itself. Divine omniscience is coterminous with divine omnipresence; both are inseparable from divine omnipotence. The same logic of the sacred is at work in Christology: Christ does not know the Church; rather, the Church is his body. There is further "mythic pressure" to see all of creation as the body of Christ.[19] The two-in-one of Adam and Eve has this same quality of a union of knowing and being. This very quality supports the lovers' lack of need of God, which leads to disobedience in the mythical narrative. For man, accordingly, this unity cannot sustain itself. Wanting to be one with the beloved, we discover instead the loneliness of our own death.

Only a being that knows itself as a particular subject can know the world as an object. Subject and object are created in the same act of knowledge. The self that knows the world is the dying self of *Genesis*. To know the world as other than myself is to acknowledge the possibility of my own death, for I know the object of my knowledge to be quite independent of my own existence. I imagine a world without me; I see myself as the dust I will become. This is the knowledge that love would overcome—if it could. This is the existential condition that grounds the myth.

Copernicus would put natural science in the space that opens up between man's knowledge of himself and of the world. The Genesis myth puts moral knowledge—knowledge of good and evil—into that same space. We experience the alienation of self from world first in a practical form—the labor of production—and only much later in the form of science. Both labor and science are efforts by finite men to establish a new home in the universe. The lost home is represented in three different ways: the unity of meaning and being, the two-in-one of love, and life in the Garden. These are the approaches of philosophy, the romantic imagination, and myth.[20] No one ever makes it back home, for finite man does not have the resources to recover the infinite foundation of his own existence.

---

[19] See, e.g., *Letter to the Colossians* 1, 15–20 ("He is before all things and in him all things hold together").

[20] We could also describe them as stages in the life of man: the old age of the philosopher, the romance of the young adult, and the innocence of youth.

MEMORIES OF EDEN

Man remembers Eden, because he remembers that unity of being and meaning which is the sacred. The break with the sacred is simultaneously the incompleteness of love. Through that gap we quite literally discover a world of objects, one of which is the dying body of the subject. This is also the world of other subjects, each one distinct from ourselves. We orient ourselves in this world by measuring our actions against the standard of justice.

Before the Fall, Adam and Eve's knowledge of each other is inseparable from their being one with each other. Symbolically they are made of the same flesh; they know each other as one hand knows the other. They are bound together not as the result of a practical argument, nor as the consequence of a duty, moral rule, or customary practice. Rather, each knows a self that already includes the other. Propositions are always inadequate to represent this ontologically prior experience of unity. Once we enter into discourse, there is no end to talk. Before that first proposition, before subject is separated from object, man is the point at which being shows itself to itself—yet another meaning of the image of God. This experience of pre-propositional unity is at the opposite pole to the existential loneliness that accompanies the finite knowledge of the subject.

In the Bible sexual union is often called knowledge; we still speak of "carnal knowledge." This graphic expression is more right than wrong: love is a way of knowing that is bound to the flesh and thus inseparable from being. To find the self in the other, to overcome the subject-object divide without doing violence to either the subject or the object, is love. There is nothing abstract about this. This experience is at the heart of every experience of ultimate meaning—familial, political, or religious. In each of these domains, who we are and what we know are one and the same.

The two-in-one of love is always an attachment to the body of the beloved. That beloved might be the lover/spouse, child, or sovereign. If we think of this attachment as a claim on the body, then we will be led to evaluate love under the standard of justice. We will object to commodification; we will demand autonomy and equality. We will measure what each person "gets out of the relationship." But love's claim is not a matter of property at all. Rather, it borrows from the sacred. Because the body bears the meaning of love, the "awesome" character of the body in love overwhelms us. It is more accurate to speak of subjects being possessed than possessing the body of the beloved. This relationship is quite literally incomprehensible, because it is not a thing in the world but at the foundation of a world. Only because we love do we care about the world. We cannot grasp this relationship within the logic of the proposition; we cannot subject it to judgment. Or, if we do try to judge it, we are likely to find judgment ineffectual.[21]

Today we can better understand the phenomenon of meaning at stake in the Genesis myth if we think of the love between parent and child. We tend to locate our deepest experience of love in the child; here we find a kind of lost innocence. The child acts without awareness of death, and thus without that differentiation of self that accompanies the awareness of death. He or she does not yet know good and evil. We imagine childhood as a taste of prelapsarian existence.[22] Loving the child, we experience again something of that lost innocence. This is love without desire. Desire is a quality of a subject who exists in a world that is other than the self. For this reason, desire for another always brings with it the problem of commodification. Like propositional knowledge, desire exists in this gap between subject and object. Desire disappears when the gap is closed.

Familial love is an end in itself; it resists reasoned explanation. Yet it offers a non-propositional answer to the question of the meaning of life. Enthralled by the child, we do not ask what or where is the meaning of our lives. Parent and child constitute a world to themselves, a world that is beyond our ordinary categories of time and space.[23] It is of the body—I love a particular child or children—but it does not require presence. This relationship of love always brings the whole into the present moment: loving the child we experience the fullness

[21] See Kahn, *Law and Love* 7–12 (arguing that *King Lear* opens with an attempt to put love on trial).

[22] This is a distinctly modern view of childhood. See C. Heywood, *History of Childhood in the West from Medieval to Modern Times* (2001). It was, for example, not shared by Augustine, who saw the child as already corrupted and thus never innocent.

[23] This also explains why the representation of romance is often located in the journey.

of the past and the potential of the future. In this way, we are bound to the world in and through the child. I cannot love my child but be indifferent to the world.[24] Of course, because we also have reason, we never find ourselves wholly absorbed by this experience of love. There is a remainder to the self. Standing within that remainder, we can reflect upon the experience. But that reflection is misunderstood if the thought is that love itself requires a justification in some "deeper" source of meaning.

Not too long ago, childhood was seen in just the opposite way.[25] The child, it was thought, lacked internal control and was therefore always vulnerable to temptation. Incapable of exercising reason, the child required outside direction. Parental authority was valued, whereas childhood had no value in and of itself. Childhood was not the moment before the Fall but the moment after. How and why childhood became the privileged site of love is a story of the shifting place of religious authority and the rise of a familial ideal that claims its own ultimate value quite apart from politics and markets. Sociologically, the shift reflects economic developments as well as improvements in childhood survival rates.[26] These changes do not explain the character of love, but they do set the conditions under which subjects are likely to find love.[27]

In a disenchanted world, we remain enchanted by our children. The archetype of "lost innocence" is more important than its location.

[24] Environmental and peace movements often make use of this intergenerational connection to the child.

[25] See Heywood, History of Childhood in the West; P. Ariès, Centuries of Childhood: A Social History of Family Life 365–404 (R. Baldick, trans. 1962). But see L. Pollock, Forgotten Children: Parent-Child Recognition from 1500 to 1900, at 262–71 (1983).

[26] The romantic image of the family, which puts at its center the innocence of the child, is also related to the militarization of the twentieth century. Teenagers were drafted, and millions were to die in the trenches. The innocence of childhood is, in part, a reaction to the politicization of adolescence. Childhood is not just an innocence before the burden of reason but also an innocence that is pre-political. The child exists in a privileged world before the state claims him. The same point is made with the rise of a romanticized nature that stands opposed to the destructive character of modern politics. No longer does the wilderness appear as the domain of danger—the disordered and untamed. Rather, it appears as life without the evil of man. The innocence of childhood is set within this depoliticized, natural world. What could be more natural than the child and the relationship between parent and child?

[27] I suspect that it remains the case that the more religious the family, the less pervasive is the romanticism of childhood.

Innocence lost is the mythical/romantic cost of coming into the possession of knowledge, which always brings a guilty conscience. The innocence of childhood, accordingly, is life before reason; even more so, it is life before a knowledge of death and sex. The relationship to the innocent child represents a kind of sexual unity without sex: to be of one body. This is again symbolic of its prelapsarian character.[28] The infant's longing for the breast is one thing, the sexual longing for the breast is another. But after Freud, of course, we know that this distinction does not hold.

Instead of longing for a return to Eden, Freud tells us that we long for a return to the mother's breast. There is a longing to return to a point prior to knowledge, that is, prior to the differentiation of the subject into a unique, separate being. For Freud, this longing for a return to an infantile condition of nondifferentiation is a source of religion.[29] What myth identifies as Eden, and romance as love, the modern science of the psyche identifies as immaturity. For Freud, the world of innocent union is broken when the child becomes aware of the parents' sexual activity and its own sexual desires. Innocence is shattered not so much by the perception of the father's violence against the mother as by the awareness that the parents may form a unity from which the child is excluded: In the family, which two becomes one? Oedipus, after all, does not just kill his father, he marries his mother.

Genesis points to the shock that procreation is to the two-in-one of the loving couple, but Freud reminds us that there is an equal and opposite shock as the child comes to know his parents. In both directions, there is differentiation of self and other. The child's longing to replace the parent is a longing for recovery of unity. There are two forms of response to this shock: to murder the father or to displace the impulse to murder with the work of civilization. Having fallen out of the innocence of love, we have two choices: evil or civilization.

---

[28] The appropriate characterization of the sexual unity of Adam and Eve, before the Fall, has long puzzled theologians. We must think of sex that is not tainted by desire, of nakedness without shame, and of reproduction without pain. Whether there was sex and whether it was generative are all controversial issues. The problem of interpretation arises, in part, from the very different attitudes toward procreation presented in the two different stories of Adam and Eve.

[29] See S. Freud, *Civilization and Its Discontents* 11–15 (J. Strachey, trans. 1961)

Freud invents a new myth of an original murder that leads to a guilty conscience—shame—which in turn provides the foundation for a moral code of good and evil that allows the work of civilization—labor—to go forward.[30] Like the founding myth of *Genesis*, the Freudian myth is one of lost love, knowledge of good and evil, labor within a world of existential loneliness, and endless longing to recapture the unity of being and meaning.

Whether we think of Eden as garden or as breast, the same experience of longing for unity is at stake.[31] It is a longing for a life without the burden of knowledge, moral judgment, shame, and death. We long for the experience of a free will that is also a complete will: the point at which freedom and necessity coincide.[32] We long for this, and yet we recoil from our own longing. For Freud, we recoil because the cost of fulfillment is murder. We cannot have that unity without giving up civilization itself. In *Genesis*, we recoil because the longing for unity is always matched by the awareness of death. Who succeeds in love seems closely related to who lives and dies. Our own death is linked not just to civilization—labor and justice—but to murder. Love appears to us as simultaneously innocent and irresponsible, as the most important and the most dangerous of pursuits.[33]

Justice is labor's end and the ground of civilization: we work to produce the good. Yet justice cannot explain why we care about the world. Care, I have argued, is a function of love. The action of love always moves from justice to care to self-sacrifice. The sacrifice of the self is a condition of the two-become-one. Self-sacrifice is enacted symbolically in the giving up of the rib; it is reenacted in the procreative economics of the family, and enshrined at the heart of love as romance. Self-sacrifice is the response to the remainder, which always subverts love.

Because self-sacrifice is the action of love, we feel that it is not completely of this world. It cannot be measured in pleasure and pain—the

<hr />

[30] See S. Freud, *Totem and Taboo* 141–44 (J. Strachey, trans. 1950).

[31] Using Jung's terminology, we can say that both are archetypes of innocence embedded deep within the cultural consciousness. See C. G. Jung, "Approaching the Unconscious," in *Man and His Symbols* 1 (C. G. Jung, ed. 1968).

[32] See I. Kant, *The Critique of Judgment* 184–200 (J. Bernard, trans. 1951).

[33] See the discussion of Cain in chapter 1 above.

calculus of desire. If we thought that all value was a consequence of the subject's desires or interests, then self-sacrifice would make no sense.[34] There cannot be a value higher than the source of value. Nor can self-sacrifice be derived from any kind of calculus in the discourse of justice and rights. Rights protect the subject. A willingness to sacrifice the self for the rights of others cannot derive from the substance of the rights alone.[35] Rights are not free-floating; they only attach to subjects. I might be willing to sacrifice myself for the rights of some subjects but not because rights are at issue. I am not willing to sacrifice myself for all similarly situated subjects. I care about my children as an ultimate value but not because they fall within the general category of children, all of whom have certain interests and rights. The same is true of political communities. I may be willing to sacrifice myself to achieve justice within my community but not for other communities with equal claims to justice.[36]

Self-sacrifice never "makes sense." Yet it often seems to be the most sensible thing in the world, for it affirms the world in and through the self. It is a truism that love is beyond words. We cannot explain the qualities of the other that evoke love. If we try to explain, we end up sounding trite. This is because it is not the particular qualities of the other that we love, as if a change in those qualities would undermine our love. Rather, through the particular, we grasp the whole. Love is not really of anything or anybody; rather, it is a way of being in the world. That love leads us to such a unity of the self with the world is the lesson that Socrates tells us, in the *Symposium*, he learned from Diotima.

Love is the sole necessity in a meaningful universe. In and through the beloved, we are literally enthralled by this world. Without love, we would still know good and evil, but we would not care. We cannot help but respond to this world with an endless sympathy, because through love we are always already fully and completely invested in it.

---

[34] Of course, it might make sense as epiphenomenal, as an appearance resting on some other structure of benefit to the individual: the economist's explanation of altruism. Or it might make sense from the perspective of the interests of the group or species: the Darwinist's explanation of altruism.

[35] This is why Hobbes has such trouble with the idea of sacrifice for the state. See M. Walzer, *Obligations: Essays on Disobedience, War and Citizenship* 82–89 (1970).

[36] See Kahn, *Putting Liberalism in Its Place* 239–40.

We cannot hold ourselves apart, as if we are awaiting some alternative universe. Without love, one is literally out of place in the world.

Like Aristophanes' circle-men, who can say nothing once they are united, love cannot speak its own being. Fully invested in the world through love, that world only becomes articulate as the object of reason, which is then subject to the measure of justice. To speak is already to break apart being and knowing. We labor at speech. Seeking to give expression to our "original" experience, we find that our words are never commensurate with that experience. We "remind" ourselves of that experience through ritual; we invoke that experience through the poetic and metaphoric use of language. We appeal to myth. When we try to translate these symbolic forms into the discourse of reason, we inevitably fail. The prelapsarian character of the divine word may be realized only at that quintessential moment of love as speech: the naming of the newborn. Speaking the name—resisting the propositional form—ever after can be a reminder of that moment of realized love.

Love remains a mystery impenetrable to knowledge. Thus we cannot explain love. Like language, we are more a part of it than it is a part of us. Love is timeless and complete, whereas reason operates in time, breaking our experience into discrete propositions. Love is a singular wholeness at the foundation of our relationship to being, but knowledge finds only plurality among subjects and objects. Loving, we feel that we have overcome our limits, but knowledge speaks of the hard reality that is the dying body set among similarly limited objects. Thus one of the most common representations of the relationship between love and speech is the deathbed scene. There, words reach their limits as the subject confronts the death of the beloved whom he or she would embrace in the timelessness of love.[37] The cycle of our experience is from love to knowledge to death, and back to love. Love, we hope, can transcend death; reason never gets beyond the reality of labor and death. Our sin, as *Genesis* describes, is original, which means that it is produced by the very resources that constitute our way of being in the world: love and knowledge.

[37] The ritualistic expression of the move from the speech of reason to the symbolism of instantiation is "extreme unction." In the modern world, extreme unction competes with the love of the familial, because love of family is a firmer foundation for our faith in the ultimate than is religion.

The love of Adam and Eve becomes the labor of work and reproduction. That is the Fall. Even romantic lovers cannot remain locked in each other's embrace, as Aristophanes' circlemen would. The world that love founds becomes the finite world of separation of subject from object, of the limited capacities of labor and production in a world that is inevitably unjust and, equally inevitably, decays. Even the most beloved child grows up. We might try to extend the innocence of childhood, but we cannot do so indefinitely. The child rebels and, with that, breaks apart the complete world of the romantic family. Becoming a unique subject, the child is overwhelmed by a world that is not his own. He now faces that same task of refounding that world on the basis of love.

EVIL AS MURDER

Like love, evil occupies a space of infinite longing and endless failure. It is not a mundane carelessness about others or an excessive concern with the self, both of which can lead to bad or unjust acts. To think of evil as injustice is a metaphysical mistake. Evil's opposite is love, not justice. Evil, too, belongs at the foundation of the world, not among the finite acts and objects of the world. It, too, is constitutive of a way of being in the world. For this reason, the domains of the appearance of evil track those of love. The close bond of love and evil is like that of God and Satan or that of the sacred and the polluted. The genealogical survey of forms of religious evil in chapter 2 demonstrated this: we find evil where we find the sacred. Approaching the mystery of one, we always find ourselves confronting the other.

Love expresses itself in sacrifice of the self; evil expresses itself in murder of the other. The paradigmatic murder—the first murder in the Bible—is that committed by Cain. Cain's murder of his brother shows us evil in the house of love. If we ask why Cain murdered Abel, the myth tells us only that God recognized Abel over Cain. Abel's offering was more pleasing to God. We can never really know why one person is loved and another is not. The two brothers are equally deserving—both make offerings—but love extends to one and not the other. The failure of recognition leads to murder. At first reading, it seems that Cain would recover God's recognition by displacing his brother from God's love. He would substitute himself for the beloved. This is the shape of jealousy, which always has a murderous character even if only metaphoric.

If we leave the interpretation at this point, however, we have not penetrated the narrative form of the myth but have only set forth a conventional critique of jealousy. We have read the myth as simply a variation on Freud's Oedipus myth. Wanting his mother's love, Oedipus murders his father; wanting God's love, Cain murders Abel. God may be a father figure, but he should not be read literally as a father. The appropriate question of interpretation is not "Why did Cain murder Abel?" but what is it about the human condition that turns a person from love to murder. The story of Cain is not simply a morality play concerning brotherly love. The existential condition for which the myth provides a narrative explanation is a pervasive feeling of guilt and loneliness. We find ourselves as if we have already murdered. Murdering Abel, Cain is literally on his own. And so are we all.

The myth does connect murder and recognition, but, once we reject the inclination to moralize the relationship, the connection appears more complex than one of cause and effect.[38] Why this urge to murder? Why this sense that we have already done the deed? Pushing beyond the narrative structure of the myth, we can say that it puts at issue not just Abel's recognition by God but the relationship of recognition between the brothers. Murdering Abel, Cain is not likely to gain his place before God. What he does assure, however, is that there will be no recognition—no love—between himself and his brother. We can further suggest that Cain murders Abel not to gain God's recognition but to avoid recognition by Abel. God's recognition of Abel suggests Abel's capacity for love, which Cain cannot tolerate. To avoid love, he would murder. Nonrecognition is his end and murder the means.[39] But why would Cain recoil from this recognition? Our sense of ourselves as if we have already murdered is rooted not in a jealous desire for recognition but in this partially suppressed fear and rejection of

---

[38] See above, chapter 1 at 28 (on inversion of cause and effect in the Oedipus myth).

[39] See S. Cavell, "The Avoidance of Love: A Reading of *King Lear*," in *Must We Mean What We Say? A Book of Essays* 267–353 (1976). But see Kahn, *Law and Love* 179 n.14 (distinguishing a political psychology from the psychological per se).

recognition. To understand this is to understand the relationship of love to evil.

In the myth of Adam and Eve, recognition of the other and knowledge of death are closely linked. Loving, we discover our own finitude; we find that remainder—the dying body—that is beyond love's capacity for repair. That is the knowledge God gives to Adam—"you are dust"—and under which we all labor. If love forces upon us acknowledgment of our own death, then avoidance of love is avoidance of death. This is the self-knowledge that Cain would put off by murdering Abel. Recognition is precisely what he does not want. Thus murder is not the response to nonrecognition but the flight from recognition. If Cain's is the power of life and death, then he would be immortal. That, at least, is how he would see himself. Cain's punishment is suggestive of this interpretation of the myth. He does achieve a kind of deathlessness, if not exactly immortality: "And the Lord put a mark on Cain, lest anyone who met him should kill him." The mark itself, as a divine sign, suggests that Cain is not to be looked upon by others as yet another finite or dying person. It is a mark of his own power over life and death.

To recognize the other as a subject means to imagine oneself as an object of that person's knowledge.[40] This is an experience as shattering as the loss of love. Truly to appreciate the other as a subject is simultaneously to recognize oneself as a potential object. To that subject I can appear as just one more object in a field of knowledge. This thought is inseparable from the thought of death. Indeed, it is to imagine oneself dead, to recognize that the world will continue without me. The dead are always the object of someone else's gaze. Precisely that transition from subject to object is murder. So Cain murders Abel. Cain would not be an object but only a subject. Abel will not bury Cain; Cain will bury Abel. Cain will be nothing but subject, never object to any other subject. Thus the odd quality of the end of the myth: Cain does not die but has a son and founds a city. Love and evil are reciprocal forms of power: the giving of oneself to the world in the act of sacrifice, on the one hand, and the making of the world as an image of the self in the act of murder, on the other.

[40] See the discussion on self-consciousness as knowledge of oneself as an object in the world in chapter 1 above.

We see this dynamic clearly in the family. Members of a family are bound to one another in love. But, at the same time, family is the most immediate context within which we imagine our own deaths. Each family member, at some point, imagines the others standing over his or her own dead body. This is most especially true of parents; it is part of the meaning of parenting. We love our children, but we also think that they will bury us. If we could love purely, then we would only imagine the self-sacrifice of love. Loving our children, we think there could be nothing worse than our seeing their death. But because there is always a remainder to the self beyond love, we also imagine our own death as end, not fulfillment. Loving my children, I am forced to confront my own death. No one can take hold of that thought for too long. Indeed, there is only a short step—perhaps no step at all—from imagining oneself as dead to imagining oneself as murdered. The Freudian father is in just this situation. Cain shows us the response to this dread: it is murder.

To know the other as a subject is to know oneself as finite. To recognize the other is to acknowledge one's own death. This is the deepest point to which interpretation of the myth can take us in the understanding of evil. It is the point at which the myth of Adam and Eve merges with the myth of Cain and Abel. One is the story of self-sacrificing love, the other of murderous evil. Adam would take up the burden of death out of love for Eve; Cain would flee that burden by murdering Abel. We can overcome shame—the condition of being observed in our nakedness (itself a symbol of death)—either by love or by murder. Love and murder are bound to each other in the symbolic dimension. They are reciprocal ways of overcoming the divide between subject and object that first shows itself in the shame of self-knowledge.[41]

The evil person cannot live with the acknowledgment of his own death that lies implicit in the recognition of the other as a subject. His response to this is murderous. His actions are guided by a Ptolemic psychology that places his own self at the center of the universe. Rather than experience the shame of finitude, he would eliminate the subject before whom he could feel that shame. He deals with his own

[41] In chapter 4 below, I take up a sustained inquiry into the meaning of "shame."

death by eliminating the conditions under which that death is imagined. He looks out upon a world and sees only himself; he never imagines an other looking at him. Not imagining himself as an object, he need not imagine his own death. Of course, the strategy of murder offers only a temporary respite from acknowledgment of one's own death. Shame returns, for indeed we are mortal. Murder is not the cure for mortality. We can put off self-knowledge only for so long.

Because this murder can be metaphorical, it is not always easy to distinguish love from evil. At stake is not necessarily the physical destruction of the other but destruction of the other's capacity to imagine a world without me, the subject. The other's world is to be my world. The evil subject, then, will see only himself when he looks at the other. This is the parent who would see only himself in his child. It is the foundation of that political form in which the ruler would see only himself.[42] His subjects are reduced to images of the ruler; their very being is an occasion for the display of his power. At no point can the other stand apart from, and look back upon, the one in power. The very possibility is the object of murderous intent. This subordination and control is the "murder" of the other as a free subject. Traditionally, political subjects were literally not permitted to look upon the ruler. When observation was unavoidable, it was ritualized as a sacred act.[43] Is the child/citizen, who sees in the parent/ruler her all, experiencing a profound love or victimization? She herself may not even know whether her life is one of self-sacrifice or murder.

A classic, literary example of this close relationship between love and evil—and of evil as a murderous intent aroused by the reminder of one's own death in the recognition of the beloved—is found in Leo Tolstoy's portrayal of the relationship between the old Prince Bolkonsky and Maria, his daughter, in *War and Peace*. Maria puts the love of her father before every other relationship in her life. She turns down suitors in order to take care of him, despite his authoritarian manners. In return, he subjects her to an abusive domestic discipline that is the familial counterpart of the military regime with which he had been

---

[42] *King Lear*'s opening scene combines both forms of evil in the father/king who insists that his adult daughters tell him that he alone—not their husbands—constitutes their world. When Cordelia fails that test, he would destroy her.

[43] See L. Marin, *Portrait of the King* (M. Houle, trans. 1988).

familiar. Still, she extends to him an infinite Christian sympathy, excusing all his abuse and willingly making herself the suffering subject. Her love expresses itself as an ethic of care and self-sacrifice. The self-sacrifice is all the more poignant because she appears to us as a victim. There is no good reason for her to stay; her brother, Prince Andre, leaves. There is only her love of her father, which is not reasonable at all. Justice has nothing to do with this relationship. The old prince's abuse undermines any claim of right he may have had on his daughter. Yet she loves him still.

The old prince turns from abusively authoritarian to genuinely evil, when Maria turns down her suitor and announces she will live for no man except her father. His behavior is no longer just a misplaced militarism but is palpably evil. In her explicit avowal of self-sacrifice, he receives what he most feared he would lose: the love of his daughter. Yet he panics as he considers that she might actually have accepted the proposal of marriage. Marriage, after all, remains a possibility; self-sacrifice may have limits. His panic is not unconscious. He knows that he has an infinite need for his daughter, that he longs for her to stay with him, to tell him exactly what she does: that no man matters to her except him alone. He knows this but cannot acknowledge it.

His reaction to this knowledge about himself is to attack her dreadfully. All her care he labels treachery. He knows precisely how to cause her the most pain possible, by taking advantage of the vulnerabilities created by her love for him. Most painful of all is to pretend a loving attachment to her companion, Mme Bourienne. This not only turns her sole friend against her but at the same time sends her the message that her father can form loving attachments elsewhere. It is a murderous act: to meet the proclamation that "you are my all" with the statement, "you are nothing to me," is a kind of spiritual murder.

We are horrified by the penetration of evil deep into this familial domain of love. Yet surely we recognize the phenomenon. The old prince occupies that familiar place of longing for love and revulsion at himself for that longing. His reaction is not to turn away from the object of his love. In no way does he want to live without the loving support of his daughter. His abuse always has the dual aim of maintaining his daughter by his side and rejecting her from that position. He does not turn her out but only acts as if he will. He wants to see the continual affirmation of her love for him even as he abuses her. That endurance is, for him, the true measure of her sacrifice and thus of her love. He must be her all, even as he makes that position one of utmost pain for her. He would be complete in himself, the only subject in his world. The test of that completeness is his capacity to reject love. Is he strong enough to murder the object of his love? Behind all this is the simple fact that the old prince cannot recognize Maria as a subject without acknowledging his own death. He would murder her before he would acknowledge that.

The old prince's evil is rooted, therefore, in a refusal to recognize his own vulnerability and finitude, that is, his own mortality.[44] He will not allow his loving daughter to exist as a subject who can consider him an object. His actions are to fill her world: she will see only him, and he will not see her at all. He makes an infinite claim for recognition upon his daughter while at the same time completely rejecting her. He cannot live without her recognition, but he cannot live with the knowledge which that recognition implies. He would live completely within the familial, but he would create the conditions under which his entire family is nothing but an expression of his own power. He can form no relationships that are not projections of his own self, and thus he abuses all who come in contact with him.

Yet, of course, he dies. The prince's strategy of avoiding the shame of death is no more successful than that of Cain. Refusing to recognize death, it nevertheless recognizes him. Rage as we might, death works at is own pace. Only at the moment of his death is he able to recognize the possibility of his death. With that recognition, the existential fear that fuels the furor of evil disappears. All that is left is love. We see, therefore, the paradigmatic deathbed confession of love. A confession that must be speechless—he has already lost his voice—because it is beyond propositions. But it is already known by Maria, and therefore speech is not needed. Only when he has become the literal embodiment of death can he allow her the possibility of viewing him as object. Now her failure to attend the dying body, her failure to sit vigil as he

---

[44] He acts out his immortality by taking up the activities of youth, claiming to find a new lover in Mme Bourienne. Because this relationship rests on nothing more than a denial of death and a paralyzing fear of love, it strikes us as both comic and evil.

dies—a consequence of her fear of him—is a blow to his love. In death, Tolstoy tells us, the remainder that is the subject alone disappears: only the love that founds the world remains.

Just as love is something greater and deeper than bodily desire, so, too, is evil. Both negotiate the relationship between the infinite and the finite. Because both love and evil are about the foundation of meaning in the world, the two-in-one that is love can easily become the one-in-two that is evil. Evil is, as Auden says, "to love the self alone." The cost of that love is murder. Love sees the infinite in the finite; evil sees the finite in the infinite. Neither love nor evil can be understood within a discourse limited to the body itself, but neither can be understood apart from the body. Moral judgments, too, miss the domain of meaning at issue here: love is often unjust, and evil can be perfectly just. The claim of the king to be the body of the state is a model of evil, even if he is a just king.[45] Yet the belief that Christ is the body of the Church is a model of love. Love and evil are not about good and bad, but about being in the world.

Reason can never explain the world-destroying sense the lover feels upon learning of the beloved's betrayal. No matter what we say about respecting the autonomy of the other, despite how we reason about the distinction between the body's pleasures and the emotional commitments we make, the words ring entirely hollow. The betrayed lover is in the same position as the religiously devout who comes to believe that his religious rituals were mere illusions, not a showing forth of the divine at all. One feels simultaneously the dissolution of the world and the shame of one's own being. In place of the sacred, there is nothing at all; in place of the subject there is only the experience of the self as negation. What had been love looks dangerously like evil,[46] for in the turning away of the beloved, there is an imitation of murder: where once one had been a subject, one now feels only the shame of being an object in the gaze of an other. It is as if one were dead.

This shock is as deep and disturbing as the Freudian shock of discovering the father with the mother. It is, indeed, the same shock. At

[45] See chapter 5 below.
[46] See chapter 2 above (discussing idolatry as the power of negation). Perhaps the idea that marriage is a sacrament and cannot be dissolved has its origins in the sense of the world creating/destroying power at issue.

the moment it occurs, the world collapses into the self alone. It was through the two-become-one of the lover and the beloved that a universe of meaning was revealed. The thought of the beloved with another always invokes shame: the shame of self-knowledge, of knowing that one is nothing but dust and will return to dust. This, indeed, is a world without divine presence. The body of the beloved bears the weight of the entire world, and when the beloved turns away, that world is destroyed.

Because the turning away produces an experience of death, it is imperceptibly close to an act of evil. Still, we do not think that falling in love with another is evil, although its consequences may be tragic. If we are speaking of children turning away from familial love toward new objects of erotic attachment, it is not evil at all—painful as it may be to the parents. Lover and beloved share a world, but, in doing so, each is necessarily vulnerable to the other. Thus the death of a child or parent is often experienced as the end of the world. We are thrown back on the self and experience quite literally that remainder, which always escapes love and constitutes the dying body. The beloved has died, but in that death we experience a kind of murder of the self.

In love, we place our lives in the hands of another. If we cannot bear that knowledge, there will be an impulse to murder. Thus evil arises when we refuse to make ourselves vulnerable to this world-destroying power. The fear of destruction of the self and of one's own world leads to the destruction of all worlds but one's own. Because love always contains the risk of betrayal, the only way to accomplish this end is murder. Evil is failed love.

Lover and beloved have a claim upon each other, for each is the foundation of a common world. Each always has the power to destroy the other's world. It is as simple as turning to another. This is why the first concern of love is always care and why the action of love is self-sacrifice. To affirm one world, the subject must give up the possibility of others. For lovers, care is more important than justice or truth. This insight is as old as the biblical description of God as "choosing" the nation of Israel, but it is lost to the rational moralists of the Enlightenment and to their liberal successors. Truth and justice do support each other, but, as I have explained, love and justice are always in tension. Lovers do not want to hear the truth if it is that we are dust and will return to dust; the lover's claim to care is not the assertion of a right. The lover has no right to demand of the beloved that she not turn away, that she not fall in love with another. When love ends, the pain the lover suffers is the shame of finitude. He dies, we might say, but he is not murdered.

Our lives in their symbolic dimension are as vulnerable as our biological lives. Worlds fall apart, even when founded on love. *Genesis* speaks of the original failure of love: every child falls out of the unity of familial love. The child must leave the parents' home and love another. This is not evil, although the parents may experience it with a world-destroying sense of shame. A parent's response to this shame can be the symbolic murder of the child. When Cordelia refuses to proclaim her love for her father alone, Lear responds: "we / Have no such daughter, nor shall ever see / That face of hers again; therefore be gone / Without our grace, our love, our benison."[47] Lear would have Cordelia be "nothing." This is a symbolic act of murder that follows from the child's refusal to see the father as the only subject. The opening scene of *King Lear* may look like a father arranging his bequests, but it is really about a father refusing to die.

Conversely, the child may leave the parents' home carrying the burden of shame, when he or she feels their love to be a demand to recognize them alone. Unable to satisfy that demand, the child may feel that he or she has murdered the parents. The child, Freud tells us, bears the guilt of what seems an unavoidable evil. Cordelia, it has long been noticed, is not quite an innocent. Her father asks for little—a small rhetorical display—but, in insisting upon truth, she sets in motion Lear's experience of a kind of royal death. For this, she feels shame. Thus, when she returns to England to fight on behalf of her father, she asks his benediction.[48]

The contemporary phenomenon of the suicide bomber provides an example of this tight connection of love and evil. As a self-sacrificing martyr, the terrorist appeals to love; as the murderer of innocent individuals, he or she engages in evil. The point is not that love and evil are just a matter of one's point of view, as if "one man's terrorist is

---

[47] *King Lear* I, I, 261–64.
[48] *King Lear* IV, vii, 44–58.

another's freedom fighter." Both love and evil occupy the point at which the finite intersects with the infinite, the point at which the finite subject realizes an ultimate value. For love, the finite subject becomes the point at which the macrocosm shows itself of ultimate value. Love affirms a world in and through the sacrifice of the self. The suicide bomber engages in just such a ritual of self-sacrifice, making a statement that he acts out of love for family, religion, and community. To sacrifice the self, however, simultaneously entails the murder of an other.[49] The subject destroys a world that leaves him with only a sense of shame and death. He acts with murderous rage toward that world that has produced the shame of his own being. When we view his act from the perspective of love, we see it as an affirmation of ultimate value. When we look at it from the vantage point of evil, we see the exclusionary and destructive character of this claim to realize the infinite. Evil would see the self in all that is, while love would bring forth the whole of the world through the sacrifice of the self.[50]

The suicide bomber shows us that love and evil can exist simultaneously in the same subject and even in the same act. But why not? My interpretation of Cain and Abel in chapter 1 already suggested this possibility. Was this not also true of the absolute ruler of early modern Europe? Does it not remain true of many charismatic leaders? That the sacred and the polluted can occupy the same site is hardly surprising to the mythical mind. Nor is this idea unusual to anyone who has thought about the complicated world-creating and world-destroying character of the family. Indeed, it is a contemporary commonplace for the media to show us the affirmation of familial love surrounding the suicide bomber. Even a loving family can be a dangerous force in the world—a lesson we continually relearn from Shakespeare. Is this not the same lesson we have been retaught by contemporary forms of ethnic nationalism in the remnants of the Soviet Empire? In the final chapter I argue that it is no less true of our own liberal state.

[49] The symbolic dynamic of killing and being killed is at the center of my analysis of political evil in chapter 5 below.

[50] That the suicide bomber is usually a young adult suggests a deeper psychological point: the murderous rage directed outward, while affirming familial and communal love, may well be a displacement of the murder of the parent that is implicit in the young adult turning toward a new object of his love.

This is not to suggest that evil is located in the failure to treat the other as a subject. Indeed, evil must implicitly acknowledge the victim as subject, for it is the rage at the possibility of appearing as an object to the subject that leads to evil. Treating someone as a means, rather than an end, is an ordinary failing. It may be injustice, but it is not evil. We are all guilty of this failing most of the time. To treat the other as a means is not to attempt his or her elimination. It does not make us murderers, metaphoric or actual. Evil lies in the ambition to murder these subjects, not in order to use them as means to some other end but because of the shame we experience in our own character as finite objects in the world.

Just as the murder at the heart of evil need not be a literal killing, not every killing expresses evil. Of course, we can use the term in that way, making it synonymous with serious crime, but then evil is a sociological, not a metaphysical, issue.[51] The murder that is evil is present wherever a subject denies the other the capacity to take a perspective in which he (the subject) would appear as an object. Evil arises when the subject says that "knowing me, you are to see only your own death—never mine." This murderous intent is the outward expression of a claim to personal immortality.[52] For a mortal creature, such a claim can only lead to more desperate acts of murder. In the final chapter I argue that the immortality of the political sovereign is linked to this power to take life. Politics makes visible the symbolic structure of love and evil, but individual subjects, no less than polities, live within this structure.[53]

Evil is a response to understanding that the other *is* a subject. A world of plural subjects is only naïvely thought to be a dialogic community—a mistake of much contemporary political theory. It is also a world in which I imagine my own absence, that is, my own death. To affirm that possibility as the maintenance of the world is the self-sacrifice of love. To refuse to imagine my own death is the beginning of evil.

[51] See, e.g., E. Becker, *The Structure of Evil* (1968).

[52] We often hear reports that the contemporary Islamic terrorist believes that his suicidal act will lead directly to an immortal heavenly life—one that is filled with the pleasures of the body.

[53] On the city as an enlarged image of the individual see Plato, *The Republic* II, 368D–369A.

To respond to evil by insisting that the actor treat others as subjects is exactly the wrong response, for if others are subjects, then he—the evil actor—is potentially an object. Recognition of this is beyond his imaginative possibilities. Justice cannot cure evil any more than justice can bring love. We can tell pathological parents to treat their children justly, but at stake is an entire world of meaning. People do not commit evil acts because they fail to understand what justice requires. They do so because it gives expression to the only world they are willing to see, one where they will continue indefinitely. Of course, evil actors could do otherwise—they are free actors—and worlds do change. But worlds do not change in response to a moral directive. We cannot legislate evil out of existence.

The response to evil is not justice but love. Judeo-Christian culture has always placed this conflict between love and evil—not that between justice and injustice—at the center of man's normative experience. The conflict over justice is central to the political debate internal to particular communities, but those communities are themselves founded on love.[54] The drama of the family, as of every other group that claims an ultimate meaning, is that of love against evil. That does not mean that families have an excuse to maintain injustice among their members. The virtue of justice does not disappear. Rather, justice is secondary to love—and to evil—in the family. We love in spite of injustice; we fall into evil despite justice. We are bound together "for better and for worse."

Arguments about justice and injustice are played out in the court of reason. They are arguments about what one subject owes another subject. Subjects do not owe each other love. They cannot reason themselves to love; rather, they find themselves in love. Neither do subjects reason themselves to evil. Accordingly, we never can make sense—that is, offer an adequate explanation of the causes—of the murderous rage of evil. We cannot say why Cain murdered Abel any more than we can explain why the Nazis murdered the Jews or the Hutus murdered the Tutsis. We can describe the conditions which led to the event—God favored Abel—but we cannot say why evil followed. Such actions always defy reason, including the reasons of-

[54] See Kahn, *Putting Liberalism in Its Place* 226–41.

fered by those carrying out the murders. Evil, like love, appears as if from nowhere.

Markets and market behavior, justice and injustice, can generally be understood on their own terms. This is why economics and political theory are such powerful tools. We can explain why one market either is or is not pareto-superior to another; we can write a legal code and explain what one person owes another. We cannot, however, explain love and evil in the analytic structures of reason or interest. When we attempt to do so with respect to love, we get only parody, as if love were mere desire or the aspiration for universal justice. When we do so with respect to evil, we are likely to sound trite or prejudiced. Genocide, for example, is not the result of an error of judgment. The Germans did not lack an adequate theory of justice; nor did they want anything from the Jews. Our ordinary understanding will always leave us unprepared for the outbreak of either love or evil. Both come as a surprise to the reasonable mind. But while the surprise of love is something we can relish as a recovery of meaning, the shock of evil leaves us devastated and uncertain about the very value of existence.

Accordingly, evil is not injustice, nor is it banal.[55] Like love, evil is metaphysical before it is psychological. It is a way of being in the world, of locating an ultimate meaning, for a finite subject. Neither the lover nor the evil person can live with the knowledge of his or her own separation from others. Both love and evil are responses to shame, which is the experience of finitude in a subject with aspirations for the infinite. The lover responds to shame by seeking a return to that state of innocence that precedes knowledge: the mythical moment of two-in-one. The evil person responds to shame by murder. There is no shame if one is not observed. Both would overcome the separation of the self from the other that characterizes finite knowledge and finite desire. Both seek that unity of being and knowing that founds a world of meaning.

Love and evil are speechless, not because they are somehow brute facts but because their symbolic structure is not propositional. Thus the reasons offered for evil actions are never commensurate with the

---

[55] Compare H. Arendt, *Eichmann in Jerusalem: A Report on the Banality of Evil* (1963), discussed in the conclusion below.

actions themselves. First comes the murderous act; only later do we seek to articulate a difference to justify that act. But justification is not interpretation, and this language will fail. It is the same problem as that of the lover seeking to justify the "choice" of the beloved: he or she will speak of beauty or character or individuality, but these justifications will also fail. Political evil generates ideologies as easily as religious faith generates theology, but we do not have faith for theological reasons. Injustice does not provide an account of evil any more than justice provides an account of love. The incommensurability in both instances is between our reasons and our consciousness of ourselves as meaningful subjects in the world.

The failures of justification of love and evil are no different from the traditional problems of understanding myths as causal explanations. For centuries, reasonable people theorized over how Adam's sin could burden future generations or what exactly about Cain's offering accounts for God's rejection. The sociologist's or the political theorist's approach to evil today is different in technique but not in ambition. Both are trying to locate the causal conditions of that which is without causal explanation. We can better approach the truth of love and evil through fiction and poetry. Shakespeare is a better guide than sociology, and so is the Bible as myth, not history. We must strip away the reasons which theory offers and confront, as well as we can, the fundamental structure of our experience as subjects who exist with the simultaneous awareness of a meaningful world and of our own death, of our connection to the infinite and of the fact of our own finitude.

We find evil then, as we find love, where individuals act in a symbolic dimension that has neither the abstractness of reason nor the particularity of desire. Love and evil exist where the word has become flesh, where meaning shows itself in the body. Toward that symbolic body, we have two fundamental attitudes: self-sacrifice and murder. Each is a way of making the body bear the meaning of the world. In the West, the domains of the symbolism of the body have most prominently been those of family, state, and religion. Accordingly, here is where we find love and evil.

To understand love and evil we must remain within the domain of the symbolic. We cannot go too far in either the dimension of the body itself—its pleasures and pains—or in the dimension of reason itself. A life of pleasure will fail to be meaningful, as will a life of reason. We cannot say of a life of love, however, that it failed to be meaningful. Neither can we say that of a life of evil, although we may put ourselves at war with that set of meanings given life through evil.

CONCLUSION

There is an old idea in the West, dating at least to Saint Paul, that associates sin with sex and love with asceticism. On this view, the problem of sin is that of substituting the fulfillment of the body for the fulfillment of grace; it is to mistake pleasure for meaning. My argument rejects this view, for man, even when he does evil, never lives within the terms of the body alone; he never lives merely for pleasure. It is a conceit of reason that its opposition comes only from the animal nature of the body. Opposed to reason is the entire dimension of the symbolic, of the word become flesh. The deepest problems for justice—that is, for the norms of reason—arise not from desire but from love and evil.

Reason will never show us this truth about ourselves. Reason will move immediately from the discourse of justice to the discourse of bodily need, from the categorical imperative (binding all rational subjects, whether human or not) to utilitarianism (measuring all pleasure and pain, whether human or not). But ours is a human world that lies always between reason and the body's pains or pleasures. It is a world of meaning located in the body but not reduced to the body. Ours is a world of birth and death, of families and nations. It is a world to which we are tied by love and which we would destroy by evil.

Today we live in a largely disenchanted world. We seek to deploy reason in the place of mythical narrative. Reason, however, reaches its limit in the loving body. If the sexual body is taken as just another object of reason, subject to the modern techniques of social construction, we react with a kind of horror. This was the project of eugenics in the early twentieth century; it is the threat some see in contemporary experiments with cloning.[56] At stake in the sexual body is love. With-

---

[56] Consider not just European eugenics—in particular, German—but American efforts as well. See D. Kevles, *In the Name of Eugenics: Genetics and the Use of Human Heredity* (1995).

out love, we are back in that state of existential loneliness that characterized the second Genesis story.

We may no longer live in a world of the sacred, but we continue to live in one where we are very much aware of the threat of that existential loneliness that was Adam's fate before Eve. We no longer know how to speak of this world. Still, we have no better cure for this loneliness than the two-become-one of love. And, as is already clear from the myth, not even this is enough, for love cannot save us from knowledge of our own death. When we demand this of love, we become evil.

CHAPTER FOUR

■　■　■　■

POLITICAL EVIL: SLAVERY AND
THE SHAME OF NATURE

In the last chapter I offered an interpretation of the Adam and Eve myth which puts at its center the loneliness of a subject who knows he will die. Refusing to acknowledge his finitude, the subject murders those who are in a position to recognize his death. Evil is less about a moral demand for recognition of the other as an autonomous subject—the concern of justice—than it is about the refusal to imagine the self as an object, that is, the dead body that is no longer subject but only object. Evil produces unjust acts, but to understand the source and power of evil we must turn from the demand of the other for equality to the subject's flight from death. The evil person may know he is acting unjustly, but justice is not an answer to the problem of death. The same is true of the lover: he, too, may act unjustly for the sake of the objects of his love. Adam knows he should not eat of the apple, but he chooses love even at the cost of death. If evil arises out of the flight from death, the possibility of accepting death remains bound to love. That love makes death possible—that is, acceptable to the imagination—is an old thought. This is implicit in the argument I offered that self-sacrifice is the action of love.

Evil can appear within the same domain as love, because the subject before whom we refuse to appear as a dying body is often someone to whom we are already bound: friends, lovers, family. These are the relationships within which one imagines one's future, and that future inevitably ends in death. These relationships constitute what we might think of as the ordinary boundaries of the testamentary imagination—the subjects who will appear in my will. These are the people to whom I am closely bound through love. In the previous chapter my concern was with love in its intimate, familial forms. Eros, however, is not exhausted in these forms of intimacy. In this chapter and the next I pursue the forms of evil as it appears in Western political experience. Here, again, we find a close relationship between evil, love, and the knowledge of death. In politics, too, injustice is not a sufficiently expansive or rich concept to capture what is at stake in evil.

In the personal life of the family, evil takes the form of murder, but this is largely metaphoric killing. In politics, murder is not metaphorical at all. Can we understand the character of political evil as a kind of enlargement or projection of the same familial dynamic of love and hatred—this time, however, resulting in actual murder? Is the evil of politics a murderous response to the recognition of finitude? There are certainly some grounds for thinking that the analogy holds. After all, the history of many Western states was once tied to the history of particular families. We do not have to read *King Lear* to understand that political and familial pathologies have often been linked. Still today political communities rely upon bonds of affection among citizens. Similarly, states continue to cultivate sentiments of patriotism and nationalism, which are surely kinds of love. In politics, unlike families, however, love and killing are more often aligned than opposed. Love of the state has often taken the form of a willingness to battle its enemies.

Regardless of what Western political theory has written about safety and justice as the ends of the political community, Western politics has, in fact, been characterized by the reciprocal phenomena of citizen sacrifice and killing of the enemy. The sovereign nation-state is distinguished from other forms of association by virtue of its capacity to deploy force. It has, in the familiar Weberian phrase, "a monopoly of the legitimate use of physical force within a given territory."[1] This capacity is ordinarily a function of its ability to call upon its own citizens to sacrifice themselves. That willingness is not a function of justice alone: individuals are rarely willing to sacrifice for a state that is not their own, regardless of how just its cause. Conversely, they can remain willing to sacrifice for their own state even if they believe a particular government policy is unjust—although there are likely to

---

[1] M. Weber, "Politics as a Vocation," in *From Max Weber: Essays in Sociology* 77–78 (H. H. Gerth & C. Wright Mills, eds. and trans. 1946).

be limits on how much injustice they will tolerate. What needs explanation is the bond to the political community which precedes these judgments of justice and injustice. True, that bond commits the individual to an interest in making this *particular* community just. Nevertheless, the state's unique ability to demand sacrifice and the citizen's willingness to sacrifice are the fundamental political phenomena that theory must explain.[2]

We need not celebrate the violence of politics, but we must recognize the possibility of violence that attaches essentially, not accidentally, to the experience of the political. The state, and only the state, has the power to conscript. To understand oneself as a citizen in the modern nation-state has been to recognize the possibility that one can be legitimately called upon to sacrifice in defense of the state. Even today, when conscription is out of fashion, we recognize that political identity carries deadly risks as well as rewards. We can be the target of violence for no other reason than we are citizens of a particular state. Of course, we argue about the conditions under which sacrifice can be legitimately demanded. We want the state to fight only just wars. But from the beginning of any such argument, we acknowledge the possibility that those conditions can be met. The just wars of this state, and of no other, are ours to fight.

Still, the question is whether the killing we find in politics is a form of the evil of murder analyzed in the last chapter. Is the political phenomenon of war, for example, a kind of mass expression of individual citizens' flight from the recognition of the possibility of their own death? On its face, this claim seems implausible, since there is no killing in politics that does not involve a reciprocal risk of death. Violent political conflict is a kind of reciprocity of self-sacrifice: to threaten the enemy is to be threatened in turn. Here, killing the other brings us closer to the fact of our own death. It is a turning toward, not a turning away, from death.

Because politics is a field of potential killing and being killed, the killing of another loses its character as a marker of evil. Consider the paradigmatic political phenomenon of battle: Is the field of battle the scene of virtue or evil? To be in battle is to accept a reciprocity of risk,

---

[2] This is the fundamental theme of P. Kahn, *Putting Liberalism in Its Place* (2005).

which means that battle relies substantially on a willing self-sacrifice on both sides. We know that the field of battle, violent as it is, is also a field of love, as individual soldiers sacrifice themselves for friend, comrades, units, and ultimately the nation. Under these circumstances, killing can be a mark of personal heroism or courage, as well as of communal commitment. Killing cannot be condemned as universally evil without rewriting the moral and historical imagination of the state and its citizens. They will not ordinarily judge their own efforts of self-sacrifice as evil, even if others see those same acts as murderous. Political evil, however, is not simply a matter of one's point of view, as if the other side is always evil. Evil is a pathology of politics that is just as likely to appear in one's own political culture as in another.

To understand political evil, we must take up a specifically political point of view, that is, the form of self-understanding that creates and maintains political power. Politics, Aristotle noted, begins with speech—not, however, just any speech. We have politics only when individuals take up as a topic of ongoing discussion the meanings for which they are willing to exercise their collective, coercive capacity. In part, this is a matter of internal regulation, of the laws and practices that govern the community; it is also partly a matter of external self-expression, of how the community shows itself to the rest of the world. In both these respects, the political community stands for something; it is a product of ideas as much as of material resources. Members may disagree over the character of these ideas, but such disagreements, unless they break the community apart, are like arguments over the meaning of a common text. They affirm, rather than undermine, the representational character of political life. Politics is sustained by this debate over who we are. Were the members to find that the community stands for nothing or nothing important to them, politics might be replaced by mere administration—bureaucratic efficiency would replace political debate.

Political power is the capacity to give substantial form and material embodiment to one set of ideas over another. Ideas have political power only insofar as members of the community are willing to defend them.[3] Too much emphasis on politics as discourse misses the critical fact that at some point discussion ends and the act follows: campaigns end with the vote, jury deliberations end with a verdict, legislative debate ends with enactment, and foreign policy debate ends with the threat or use of force. Talk can go on forever. Politics is not academic debate, because its discourse is cabined by the act. Politics is about the coercive power of ideas, but that power arises in the first insistence from citizens' willingness to sacrifice for the sake of the political community. A regime that sustains itself only through the deployment of force by "outsiders" may express the political life of that other community, but it represents a failure of the political in the community over which it rules. Politics, in this case, is reborn in resistance.

A political idea for which no one is willing to sacrifice himself lacks power; it is a mere abstraction. It might be a good idea, but it does not belong to any particular community. For its sake, no one is prepared to give up anything. To understand political evil, then, we need to understand the pathologies that arise in the relationship of an idea to its political embodiment. Here a religious conception, transubstantiation, can help us: this is the mystery by which an idea of the sacred takes on a material form. Politics is just such a process of transubstantiation: it links ideas to action, voice to force. Thus, where we find politics, we find rhetoric—debate—and armies.[4] Political evil appears when something goes deeply wrong in the process of transubstantiation.

Instead of looking at politics through the prism of murder—the pathology of love—we need to take up the problems of slavery and killing. I treat slavery in this chapter, and killing in the next. In each instance, I show how the particular practice—slavery or killing—offers a paradigm through which to view a wider category of political evil. Together, they cover the ground of much of what we ordinarily consider the evils of politics, including subordination, physical abuse, unjust war, and genocide.

[3] See R. Cover, "The Supreme Court, 1982 Term—Foreword: Nomos and Narrative" 97 Harv. L. Rev. 4 (1983).

[4] By "armies," I mean all the instruments of coercive power, including police.

The paradigm of slavery is at stake whenever the merely natural element of man's character is projected on to an other. The slave is what we are not: nature without culture. If the slave is pure nature, the master is not a product of nature at all. He creates himself by embodying an idea. To embody an idea in politics is to express a willingness to sacrifice for it. Not accidentally, the same American culture that practiced slavery was also one which thought of itself as particularly committed to the military virtues of honor and sacrifice.

When the rituals of sacrifice fail and we are left with only the pain of the suffering body, we are in the domain of torture. This will be my most controversial claim: when politics loses its power of transubstantiation, it becomes torture. On this view, the soldier at the front who loses his faith and confronts only the possibility of his own destruction for an idea in which he sees nothing at all is in the same position as the torture victim, who suffers in the secret cell of the authoritarian regime. Through self-sacrifice we seek to transcend death by becoming the embodiment of the idea of the nation. If we no longer believe that is possible, then the suffering of political life literally makes no sense to us. Both soldier and victim, then, anticipate death and mutilation for the sake of an idea that they view as making no claim upon them at all. Both might overcome this perception of torture by thinking of themselves as martyrs sacrificing themselves for the truth of some other idea. Both may reject entirely the claim of self-transcendence through suffering. In that case, their suffering becomes mere torture. Again, the place to begin is with a reading of Adam and Eve, for no less than in our personal lives, this myth has informed our deepest imaginings of the political.

MAN AS AN IMAGE OF GOD: NATURE AND LABOR

In the first Genesis account, man is created in the image of God. He does not represent the divine because of what he can achieve; labor comes later, in the second narrative. Rather, as created, he already manifests a sacred quality. Before the Fall, the natural self inspires awe, not shame. We know this phenomenon today, for example, in the experience of wilderness or in the presence of the newborn. Both can leave us with a sense of awe at the majesty of life before it is shaped by convention. That awe points in two directions at once—to the majesty of the natural and the wonder of the human. We cannot separate the two, for man is the point at which nature gains consciousness of itself.

After the Fall, however, there is nothing awesome about nature. It is that against which we labor. Nature, we say, must be "tamed." We clothe the self not just to hide our participation in the natural but literally to do away with it. Our nature is no longer to be a part of nature; rather, our nature is to be unnatural. The natural is now the less than human. It is that which must be given a human form—made to serve human goals—through labor. We cannot see through the clothes to the natural man, and we do not want to. When we are forced to view the naked body, we are reminded of the ultimate corruption of the flesh. Man is fully himself only in a world of human convention. That is the world that puts off the ultimate shame of nature—that we die.

The shame of nature spoken of in the myth is not just the shame of actual nakedness but the shame of being reminded that there is a naked body beneath the clothes. We carry this shame forward even when we are fully clothed. We feel shame at others' nakedness, as much as at our own, because we cannot see the former without being reminded of the latter. We avert our eyes, wanting to see nothing but the clothed subject. We want to live in a fully clothed society, that is, a world given shape by human agency. We get confused on this point if we imagine the other as the model of beauty. Even here, outside the boundaries of art, we are likely to feel shame, as much as fascination, with the naked body portrayed, for example, in pornography.[5] But first of all and most of the time, the naked body is that of the aging and the old, the injured and the out of shape—that is, life in all its commonplace forms, which include ourselves. The nude that is the object of beauty in art is not the shameful, naked body of Genesis two. It may indeed be the divine image of Genesis one. Nevertheless, from the perspective of the Fall, recovery of that image is the product of the labor of culture.

[5] On the double character of the pornographic, see Kahn, *Putting Liberalism in Its Place* 183–227.

Genesis one and two capture a fundamental ambiguity in our attitudes toward our "natural self" and our place in nature. Is the naked self the source of shame because it is less than human—the fallen condition that we begin to transcend only through the act of clothing the body—or is it the point at which we affirm our connection with a sacred nature? Is man's nature something to be achieved by his own labor, guided by his own knowledge of good and evil, or is it something given, perhaps to be recovered as we might recover the wilderness from the encroaching civilization? Do we claim to be an image of God because we are the end point of divine creation or because we have the capacity to create our own world? Are we an image of God as created objects or as creative subjects? Becoming like God was exactly what the serpent promised when he tempted Eve with the fruit of the tree of knowledge, but, according to the first myth, she already was an image of God.

These are not antinomies that can be resolved, which is just why the Adam and Eve myth appears both as a story of the sacred character of the truth of our nature and as a story of the burden of self-creation. At least, the antinomy cannot be resolved on its own terms. In Christianity, the resolution is the appearance of Christ, whose naked, suffering body—literally, a divine body—takes on the shame of nature for all men. His pain becomes the point of universal redemption, allowing believers to remain clothed even in death. Nakedness may characterize Hell but not those resurrected to God's presence. There is no going back to the Garden.

Whatever one may believe about Christology, man finds himself located in the antinomy of the unclothed and the clothed. Man is always a part of nature and always apart from nature. He can always appeal to nature to attack the artificial character of conventionality. Conversely, he can appeal to convention to condemn the merely natural as base and shameful. Choosing to locate the truth of his character in one direction always exposes him to criticism from the other. Failing to exercise knowledge and will—labor—he will experience shame; exercising those faculties, he will experience sin. He is caught between the shame of his nakedness and the sin of his knowledge.

Because this dualism is fundamental, it informs our everyday experience of ourselves and others. We use it to sort out preferences and identify character types. The myths of *Genesis*, for example, describe two different personalities: those who find self-realization in a stripping away of convention and those who find it in the projects of culture. Some flee the city to find the truth of themselves in nature; others flee from nature to the city. Some believe that the truth of the self is to be discovered; others believe that the self is a project for construction. Each is likely to see the other as profoundly mistaken, as failing to see the fundamental source of the possibility of a full and meaningful life. Similarly, the myths describe two different philosophical approaches: Do we look for the truth of the human condition in an unsullied conscience or pure reason, on the one hand, or in the cultivation of civilization or character, on the other?

As in all such antinomies, the terms themselves do not have a particular content. The categories shape a debate, the content of which depends on the circumstances. Because of this, their applications are easily reversible.[6] In the abstract, we can never say what is natural and what is conventional. Any particular context can be described as natural or conventional; we cannot know which it is in advance of a particular argumentative situation. The most conventional of social arrangements can be criticized as nothing but a manifestation of nature. Justice in the city, Thrasymachus already argued in the *Republic*, is only the interest of the stronger. The social order can always be criticized as nothing but a manifestation of an unjust nature, for the stronger interests always dominate the weaker. In this sense, politics replicates the natural world of animals; it is, accordingly, shameful. Such beliefs can lead to revolutionary efforts at reconstruction or to a turning away from politics as inevitably an expression of man's fallen nature. That same social order, however, can be criticized as mere convention that does not do justice to man's nature. Rousseau's project was to align the political and the natural equality of man. Nietzsche turned Thrasymachus around and argued that justice was only the unnatural victory of the interests of the weaker. From one perspective, nature is shameful and must be civilized; from the other, nature sets forth the norm, whether of Rousseauian equality or Nietzschean in-

---

[6] See, e.g., J. Culler, *On Deconstruction: Theory and Criticism after Structuralism* 139–50 (1982); J. Derrida, *Of Grammatology* 62–63 (1976).

equality. Even the most apparently conventional context—for example, a cityscape—can be portrayed by the artist as an exemplar of nature. Conversely, wilderness can be deconstructed to show that it is nothing but a particular cultural manifestation.[7] This conceptual indeterminacy is the contemporary version of *Genesis*, which tells us that naked man is both an image of the divine and shameful.

Despite this indeterminacy, certain patterns of argument emerge in the way the Western political imagination uses the double myths of *Genesis*. We use the myth of man as an image of God to speak of fundamental rights that attach to all men everywhere. This is the Lockean state of nature. Jefferson appealed to this myth to give expression to the moral foundation upon which American nationhood was to stand: "All men are created equal, endowed by their creator with certain inalienable rights." Even as he is created, man already has these rights. All men have these rights, regardless of their conventional circumstances. We feel no shame in our common humanity but appeal to it as the source of norms and principles that precede and measure the work of political construction. Jefferson hardly invented this use of Genesis one, and its use remains vitally present.

This is the mythic source of the strong egalitarian strand of Western political culture. We are all equal, because we are all created beings standing in just the same relationship to God.[8] We find the same divine imprint in each and every person. No person falls below this level; each is a subject with moral rights; each should have the same legal rights. We are to see in the poor and the naked not the shame of nature but the bearers of rights. Each can demand, and is entitled to, equal recognition. Accordingly, rights are not an achievement of man's labor in the production of political culture; rather, they are a recovery of that nature which is there from the beginning. To offend against this equality is to offend God by disrespecting the product of his creative act. Respecting that divine presence is the demand that "natural law"

---

[7] What we mean by "wilderness" is hardly the way that other peoples have seen nature; where we see promise, they may have seen only threat. See, e.g., W. Cronan, "The Trouble with Wilderness, or Getting Back to the Wrong Nature," in *id., Uncommon Ground: Toward Reinventing Nature* 69–90 (1995); R. Nash, *Wilderness and the American Imagination* 1, 273 (1973).

[8] See G. Fletcher, "In God's Image: The Religious Imperative of Equality under Law," 99 Col. L. Rev. 1608 (1999).

makes upon any political order. Governments are put into place, Jefferson and Locke tell us, to enforce the rights we have by nature. When they fail to do so, they should be replaced.

This myth continually fuels a strand of antipolitical politics in the West. The aim of the political, on this conception, is to realize the natural. A perfect politics would be one that was invisible, allowing man's true nature to show itself fully. This is the attraction of the idea of the withering away of the state, of visions of utopian simplicity— for example, of yeoman farmers—and of a general skepticism about government. On this view, the virtues of politics are not those of the labor of self-creation but of recovery and preservation. Of course, the divine character of natural man can be interpreted in many different ways, and there are many different utopian visions in the history of the West. The myth will not tell us whether we should locate the natural self that politics is to recover in the operation of free markets or in the preservation of the environment. It may not even tell us about the place of hierarchy, since nature in *Genesis* already includes a hierarchy of man over beast and, arguably, of man over woman.

This belief in nature as the measure of political convention continues in contemporary human rights discourse. Imagining natural man as an image of God, however, must be juxtaposed to one of the sharpest lessons of modernity: the possibility of a political rage directed at the merely natural man. In the concentration camps of the twentieth century man was indeed stripped naked, reduced to nothing but the natural thing itself: "a bare forked animal." Everywhere the response was the same—not sympathy and not respect for the natural man but revulsion before the shameful spectacle of natural man.[9] Too often, out of this revulsion emerged organized, systematic murder. If all that man can rely on before political power is his claim to be naturally an image of God, then he may indeed be doomed.[10] In the camps of the twentieth century we find a reminder of the moral economy of that form of slavery which was brought to an end less than one hundred years earlier. We find natural man as the shame of nature.

[9] American experience in Iraq—particularly the scandal of Abu Ghraib prison—are a recent reminder of this phenomenon.

[10] See H. Arendt, *The Origins of Totalitarianism* 300 (1973) ("It seems that a man who is nothing but a man has lost the very qualities which make it possible for other people to treat him as a fellow man").

The human rights community has too often assumed that it is enough to defend the naked man as the bearer of natural rights. But this lesson of equal rights has never been absent in the West. It was, we might say, there at creation. The problem has been that it has not been enough, for it is countered by the second moment of the mythical narrative in which nature is the source of shame. In American history we do not have to look far to find this second element operating alongside the first. Jefferson, who wrote eloquently of the equality of all men, lived in a slave society and himself maintained a large number of slaves. Reconciling the ideals of the Declaration of Independence with the reality of a slave society has been a perennial problem in understanding the American, revolutionary mind.[11] The double character of the myths of *Genesis* helps at just this point.

GENESIS TWO: THE SHAME OF NATURE

Slavery may have been inconsistent with the first moment of the Genesis myth, but it gave visual embodiment to the second.[12] The slave was the natural man, the man stripped of even his clothing. In this image of man, the slave-holding society recognized the shame of nature. This does not mean that it was ashamed of itself for treating men as less than images of God, although some men, including Jefferson, certainly did feel such shame.[13] Just the opposite. To be a slave was shameful; slavery was not. For many, slavery seemed the appropriate response to the shameful condition of the slave. The slave is a reminder of the Fall—of naked man before the beginning of that recovery that is the

[11] See, e.g., J. Ellis, *Founding Brothers* 81–119 (2000); J. Ellis, *His Excellency: George Washington* 258–65 (2004); R. Wilkins, *Jefferson's Pillow: The Founding Fathers and the Dilemma of Black Patriotism* (2001); G. Wills, "*Negro President*": *Jefferson and the Slave Power* (2003).

[12] My argument here is not directed at slavery whenever and wherever it has appeared, for example, in classical Greece or among Muslim nations. I am concerned in particular with American slavery, but much of what I argue extends back more broadly to the European attitude toward indigenous populations and forward to continuing manifestations of racism. For Europeans and Americans, the problem is that of reconciling Christian ideas of equality and dignity with the practice of subordination.

[13] Jefferson's most eloquent expression of his own sense of shame before the unnaturalness of slavery is found in the famous passage from *Notes on Virginia*: "I tremble for my country when I reflect that God is just: that his justice cannot sleep forever." Query XVIII, at 163 (W. Peden, ed. 1982).

product of labor. The blackness of the slave served as a kind of natural marker of this state not just of difference but of shame. The slave's nature was to display shame. If his being is shameful, his value is as pure labor. Apart from labor, the slave exists only as a negative. In the slave, there is a perfect match of shame and labor.

Linking shame and labor, the slave is a reminder of the fragility of labor's achievements. That fragility is apparent in three dimensions: existential, cultural, and political. Existentially, we know we are no less connected to the dying body than is the slave; culturally, we know that our finest achievements can never overcome the burden of historical decay; politically, we know that we are always vulnerable to the contingencies of war. The slave reminds us of all three: death, forgetting, and defeat.

Man feels shame when that nature he shares with animals intrudes into the human world—when he sees himself as if he has not yet "made something of himself." He feels shame, because he knows that he is ontologically incapable of making something of himself. He is no less doomed to the corruption of the flesh, despite the achievements of culture and polity, than those who preceded him. He is no less vulnerable to the vicissitudes of political power. If covering up nakedness is movement from the merely natural world to the fully human, then, conversely, stripping off clothing is movement in the opposite direction. The slave reminds each of us that the nakedness we cover up we also reveal in our daily routines with our own bodies—from eating to sleeping, and most especially, in this context, sex. Each of us is as much a slave "by nature" as we are a master, for each of us stands within an imagination framed by the double myths: man is both the image of God and the shame of nature.

This imaginative state is critical to understanding the status of the slave. It is not enough to say that the slave was considered property—a mere object—rather than a legal subject. That legal categorization was the end point of a certain way of seeing the slave; it was the product of a "social imaginary." Slavery was, moreover, always a contested category. From very early on in the age of exploration and colonization, there were some who would extend the first Genesis myth of moral equality to the indigenous populations discovered outside Europe. Those populations did not simply appear under the category of slave. While it would be anachronistic to speak of a kind of multicultural imagination that respected foreign civilizations for their own achievements, Christianity was a religion of universal aspirations. Christianity proved itself compatible with slavery, but the resources were always there to contest the practice. It was not unimaginable to see the indigenous as populations open to the Christian mission of spreading the gospel and saving souls; it was not impossible to see these populations as equal to others before God and entitled to the respect that comes with equality.[14] This proselytizing mission was never abandoned. The indigenous, too, could share in the body of Christ; they could be seen as the image of God.

While the indigenous populations could be seen through the framework of the Genesis myth of equality, for the most part they were not. Instead, they were seen through an appeal to the second element of the Genesis myth, for the slave powerfully presented the shame of man's nature. Because his condition was shameful—merely natural, not yet fully human—he could be treated as less than a subject. He was seen through a prism of negation: the slave was not what the master was. He lacked culture or civilization along the only dimension the master was willing to see: that of the West. The explorers themselves were often struck by the cultural achievements of the peoples they met; their cities, social organizations, and means of production are noted with wonder.[15] Simultaneously they were accused of "uncivilized" behavior, meaning cannibalism, human sacrifice, nakedness, and sexual licentiousness. The issue is not what the slave was but what he represented. The space of negation—the shame of nature—represented by the slave is not an objective quality but a way of seeing that the Europeans and Americans were prepared to adopt.

Undoubtedly, the fact of forceful subjugation of the slave was known by the members of the slave-owning society. Some knew of the indigenous cultures that had been destroyed. All knew that slaves could be taught to read and to participate in civil society—even if there were doubts about the capacity for full political participation.

[14] See, e.g., B. Las Casas, *A Short Account of the Destruction of the Indies* (N. Griffin, trans. 1992) [1552].

[15] See, e.g., B. Diaz, *The Conquest of New Spain* 216–19 (J. Cohen, trans. 1963); S. Greenblatt, *Marvelous Possessions: The Wonder of the New World* 75–79 (1991).

Laws making it illegal to educate slaves are themselves testimony to the slaves' capacity to learn. All knew that slaves were taught religion; they had families; and, of course, they occupied diverse roles within the economy of production. Certainly, political and economic power went a long way toward sustaining the institution of slavery, despite Jefferson's and the nation's invocation of the first myth of Genesis in the Declaration of Independence. Still, the moral complexity here goes beyond mere hypocrisy. Those who sustained slavery may have feared a just God, but they also had to provide a moral narrative to themselves.

In his role as political revolutionary, Jefferson projected the evil of slavery onto King George. It was the king who had attacked African societies, enslaved their members, and shipped them to America. This is a specific charge in his original draft of the Declaration of Independence:

> He has waged cruel war against human nature itself, violating its most sacred rights of life & liberty in the persons of a distant people, who never offended him, captivating and carrying them into slavery in another hemisphere, or to incur miserable death in their transportation tither. This piratical warfare, the opprobrium of *infidel* powers, is the warfare of the *Christian* king of Great Britain.[16]

Whatever the injustice of bringing the slave trade to the colonies, by the time of the Revolution, slavery within the colonies was a well-established practice, creating a set of moral and political dilemmas quite different from those of the slave trade itself. This moral difference is reflected in the constitutional response. The international slave trade was to be gradually eliminated over twenty years; slavery as a domestic institution was protected.[17] At the edge of the moral and political imagination of the postrevolutionary world was the possibility of repatriation of the slaves.[18] As that disappeared as a practical

---

[16] The passage was eliminated from the final draft. The original text was recorded by Jefferson in the autobiography he composed in 1821.

[17] See U.S. Constitution amend. I, sec. 9, cl. 1; amend. IV, sec. 2, cl. 3.

[18] Some slaves who fought with the British in the Revolution, for the promise of their freedom, were relocated to the Canadian maritime provinces and from there to Liberia shortly after its founding in 1821.

solution, the dilemma of what to do about the slaves overwhelmed the practical imagination. Even Lincoln, before the Civil War, could not imagine more than limiting the spread of slavery—and hoping that it would die out of its own in the southern states. Of emancipated slaves, he still entertained vague hopes for repatriation to Africa.[19]

Some, like Washington, released their slaves upon their own deaths. But death is the moment at which the practical, political calculus is replaced by the moral calculus of eternity—or, at least, the calculus of lasting fame.[20] Putting off release until death is itself an admission of the failure of the political imagination. What changes at death is not the practical possibility of imagining a multiracial society but the need to take responsibility for living in and administering such a society. It is a bit like living a luxurious life and then using one's estate to buy indulgences.

We only approach the moral complexity of the Jeffersonian position when we examine not just the fear of divine justice but, more immediate, the fear of rebellion. Like all those around him, Jefferson feared a slave rebellion: in *Notes on Virginia*, he worried that if emancipation did not come "with the consent of the masters," it could well come "by their extirpation." His draft of the Declaration accused the king of "exciting [slaves] to rise in arms among us, and to purchase liberty . . . by murdering the people on whom [the king] also obtruded them." To rebel is to take up the task of political construction. One does not fear the rebellion of one's property. Subjects rebel when they react to their present state as shameful. Then, they take up the labor of creating a proper human order for themselves.

To acknowledge the possibility of a slave rebellion is implicitly to recognize the slave's humanity. This knowledge, however, appears not as a fact but as an element in a normative field: it contributes to the structure of the moral imagination. Recognizing the potential for rebellion did not push the slave owner to substitute the Genesis image of man as an image of God for that of the shame of nature. It is not plausible to believe that Jefferson, Madison, and the other founders

---

[19] On Lincoln's ideas of repatriation even during the war, see his speech to a group of free Negroes on August 14, 1862. 5 *Collected Works of Abraham Lincoln* 370–75 (R. Basler, ed. 1953).

[20] See Ellis, *His Excellency: George Washington* 263–64.

who failed to characterize slavery as a violation of their own principles were simply hypocrites. Rather, they lived within the moral universe of the Fall, which sees shame in nature. On this view, the slaves' failure to take up that task of rebellion is morally shameful. In that failure, the slave confirms his own nature as less than human or as merely natural. Thus there were two sides to the moral tension. Jefferson clearly understood that slavery violated the Declaration's principles:

> What a stupendous, what an incomprehensible, machine is man who can endure toil, famine, stripes, imprisonment, and death itself in vindication of his *own* liberty, and the next moment be deaf to all those motives whose power supported him through his trial, and inflict on his fellow-man a bondage, one hour of which is fraught with more misery than ages of that which he rose in rebellion to oppose.[21]

Yet, strikingly, the slaves did not rise in rebellion against their condition.

The white population—whether slave owners or not—could say that they themselves would not have tolerated the conditions of slavery but would have rebelled. They could be confident in this judgment because they understood themselves to have rebelled against that condition of slavery to which the British Crown had tried to reduce the colonies.[22] Revolution as a rebellion against slavery is a constant rhetorical form for the founding generation, endlessly repeated in political tracts, sermons, and public speeches.[23] A popular ballad, sung by the Sons of Liberty, repeated the line, "Parliament's voice has condemned us by law to be slaves." Jefferson's description of King George as "tyrannical" echoed Patrick Henry's earlier speech of March 23, 1775, in which he asked, "Is life so dear and peace so sweet as to be

[21] Quoted in D. Post " 'Words Fitly Spoken': Thomas Jefferson, Slavery and Sally Hemings," *available at* http://www.temple.edu/lawschool/dpost/slavery.PDF (last visited Oct. 17, 2005).

[22] There is an interesting connection in this respect between Jefferson's role in the revolution and his decision to wage war against the Barbary Pirates as president. It had been the practice of the Barbary states to take prisoners who would be released for ransom or sold into slavery. This "white slavery" was again intolerable to the American self-image. See A. Shipple, *To the Shores of Tripoli: The Birth of the U.S. Navy and Marines* (1991).

[23] See A. Burstein, *Sentimental Democracy: The Evolution of America's Romantic Self-Image* 52–82 (1999).

purchased at the price of chains and slavery?"[24] Political independence had its moral foundation not only in the positive idea of freedom as self-government but equally in the negative idea that the colonists would not be slaves.

Using the language of resistance to slavery to justify their own rebellion suggests a moral distinction between their own intolerance of shame and the slave's tolerance. This is already implicit in Jefferson's observation of the American moral contradiction: the issue is not only how the revolutionaries could tolerate slavery but how the slaves could fail to rebel. Indeed, the worse the master class made the conditions of slavery, the more reassurance they had of the slave's moral failings; that is, as the conditions of servitude became more intolerable, the failure to rebel marked a greater moral failure. It was thus a reassuring, vicious circle of belief.

The moral pattern here is a kind of reverse image of Hegel's master-slave relationship. Hegel's master wins the battle for recognition with the slave but then finds that the very conditions of victory deprive him of that which he most wants: recognition from an equal subject. Hegel's myth is a story of the move from equality to inequality; it establishes, as a theoretical matter, the instability of inequality. The early Americans found themselves with an existing social practice of inequality—slavery—that needed legitimation. They found themselves already having slaves, just as individuals find themselves already having families or religious practices. Of course, these are social constructions that can be changed. First of all, however, they are social practices that require a moral narrative of legitimacy, if they are to make sense to their participants—especially to the most thoughtful among them. The master class in a slave society needed to explain and confirm this asymmetry. The narrative of revolution—or, more specifically, of a failure to revolt—operated to link political history to moral and religious belief. Rebellion would be the condition in which the slave demanded political and moral equality. The failure to rebel is read as the justification for maintaining those very conditions which, from the perspective of an autonomous subject, would justify a rebellion.

---

[24] P. Henry, Speech at the Virginia House of Delegates (March 23, 1775), reprinted in 2 Annals of America 1755–1783, at 321 (1968).

This is a recurring political pattern: one confirms the moral failure of one's enemies—domestic or foreign—by treating them as less than human. One knows that Jews, for example, are less than human, because one can see the inhumane conditions of the concentration camp. The intolerable supports a practice of intolerance. Of course, there is always the implicit knowledge that the circle can be broken. At some point there may be a rebellion. A slave-owning society always exists with this fear. The pattern here is no different from that within familial life: women and children confirm their subordinate condition by accepting the conditions which maintain that subordination. Here, too, we know that rebellion is possible. Freud bases a theory of the emergence of civilization on just such a myth of subordination and rebellion of the children against the tyrannical patriarch. Until they rebel, they are not equal.[25]

This does not mean that rebellion will be welcomed as a sign of a new-found equality. After all, the narrative has already legitimated inequality: rebellion against this natural inequality appears now as "unnatural." This self-confirming myth of inequality is not a matter of logic but of move and counter-move. Nevertheless, we do know that sometimes the logic of rebellion does convince. The black regiments of the Civil War did help to move the nation toward emancipation; similarly, black soldiers of the Second World War helped to bring on the second Civil Rights movement. This is the larger pattern of the postwar decolonization movement: rebellion is the condition for recognition of political equality.

This fear of rebellion distinguishes American slavery from other forms of hierarchy. Aristotle thought some people natural slaves. The appropriate response to such a hierarchy was not fear but action for the sake of the slave. Hierarchies often recognize pedagogical concerns, for example teacher to student or parent to child. Frequently, hierarchies are fluid and circumstantial, depending on temporary relationships, for example, employer to employee; others are understood to be directly beneficial, such as priest to penitent; and still others rest

---

[25] See S. Freud, *Totem and Taboo* 141–43 (J. Strachey, trans. 1950). The traditional tendency to see the rape victim as the shame of nature was a product of the same mythic line of thought.

on knowledge, for example, doctor to patient. American slavery was marked not just by the permanence of its inequality but by the way it created and maintained a structural condition of fear to support that inequality.

The fear of slave rebellion took a double form: fear of murder of the master and fear of rape of white women—precisely the story Freud tells of the origins of civilization.[26] In the American slave society, the myth of murder and rape was used not to explain a feeling of guilt that is the Freudian precondition of one's own self-subordination to law but rather to relieve the potential guilt of the master class. It was used, that is, to overcome the Jeffersonian guilt present in the implicit recognition of the injustice of slavery. These fears were an exact objectification of the moral imagination that supports slavery. Murdering the master, what Jefferson called "extirpation," is the act of political rebellion: the assertion of equal humanity by effectively going to war against the conditions of slave subordination. The master demands this rebellion by the slave as a condition of recognition and respect. Nevertheless, at the same time he fears it and acts to suppress the threat by denying the slave's humanity. But if the slave's position is a function of his nature rather than his misfortune, then he reemerges as a sexual threat. The naked body of the slave, which represents the shame of nature, was inevitably read as the sexual body. The naked body of *Genesis* is, after all, the body that also labors in reproduction. Fear of rape, accordingly, expresses the imagination of the merely natural, that which the slave showed himself to be in his failure to revolt.[27]

Just this fantasy of rape tells us that we are within the world of the second Genesis myth. For the sexual act bears the aggregated weight of millennia of emotional, symbolic, and mythic thought about man's fallen state. Regulating sexual access is the first object of man's labor, the very condition for the emergence of a world of work after the

---

[26] See S. Freud, *Civilization and Its Discontents* 78–80 (J. Strachey, trans. 1961).

[27] Corresponding to the fear of rape was a fear that the white subject would "go natural," that he or she would find the truth of his own existence in the nature revealed by the slave. Access to female slaves was an element of the hidden self-knowledge of the master class. Master and slave are always reciprocal images of the suppressed truth of the other. Jefferson has much to teach us here as well.

Fall.[28] Violation of that ground norm is symbolic of the destruction of civilization itself. For some, sex is the point of transmission of original sin; more broadly, sexual desire reminds us that we are never all that far from the naked body. We remain tied to the body, and thus to the threat that the labor of culture can disappear in that meeting of bodies which is a necessary condition for the species to continue. When we distance ourselves from the carnal knowledge of ourselves—when we regulate sexual contact through law, morality, and social structure—that knowledge comes back at us as a fear of rape.

The slave is an object of sexual temptation—real or imagined. He or she reflects the shame of nature that extends to the slave-owner society. We know that slave women were very much the object of sexual temptation for white men. Is not the fear of rape of white women, in part, a fear that, after the Fall, women no less than men are sexual beings? If men are tempted by the slave body, why not women? Indeed, women's relationship to the sins of the body are believed to be more immediate, complex, and deeper in much of the Christian tradition. A patriarchal, slave society labors to maintain a social and political hierarchy; it does so by "naturalizing" the position of subordination. But if women are closer to nature, they are also closer to the slave. The fear of a violation of the lines of sexual access easily becomes a fear of sexual communion between the white woman and the black slave. Thus the fear of rebellion and of rape is also a fear that rebellion and rape could constitute joint action of the subordinated—women and slaves—against a slave-owning, patriarchal class.

One had to fear either the humanity of the slave or his bestiality. These correspond to the fear of murderous rebellion and rape. Either way, the fear reflected less about the genuine danger of violent rebellion and more about the self-understanding of the dominant class. At stake is the shame of nature, not the slave's but the master's. The slave who is imagined to threaten rape and murder exposes the vulnerability of the body, and thus the vulnerability of the cultural construction that would turn away from the body. Increasing the distance from the slave

---

[28] Again, for Freud, it is the origin of the incest taboo. For an alternative view linking taboo to transgression, see G. Bataille, *Eroticism: Death and Sensuality* 63–65 (M. Dalwood, trans. 1986).

by subjecting him to the intolerable is the analogue of the hatred directed at the beloved described in the previous chapter.

Thus the shame of the slave has a twofold root. More precisely, racism takes a double form, for the social imagination that sustained slavery continues, even after slavery's formal demise. This racism rests on the one hand, on the belief that the black man is a part of nature, not fully human, and on the other, on the belief that his shameful character is a result of his own moral failure. He brings it on himself by failing to take up the task of creating culture, the first object of which would be rebellion. Thus the status of the slave is both a fact of nature and a moral condition.[29] These two propositions are mutually supportive: failing to rebel, the slave shows himself to be naturally inferior. He is stripped naked, reduced to a sexual being, and then negated quite literally in a ritual of desecration that establishes an unbridgeable distance between the civilized and the shame of nature.

The danger of rape was only a fantasy projected on the victim, just as the fear of rebellion was largely only a projection. The fantasy of rape, nevertheless, often functioned as a justification for the torturous mutilation of black men, which is a pure expression of rage at the shame of nature.[30] It is the point where political and sexual power merge. The mutilated, lynched black man is, most especially, not that image of suffering martyrdom that defines the white man's civilization: Christ. For the master class, the black victim is at the opposite extreme. While Christ transcends the body through his suffering, the lynch victim is reduced to nothing but the naked, shameful body. He is what we might even call an "anti-Christ": nothing but the shame of nature.[31]

Slaves who did rebel by fleeing proved their own humanity in that very act—at least some would read their act this way. In fleeing, they distinguished themselves from those who remained. This, for example, was the moral narrative of escape, rebellion, and moral equality sym-

---

[29] Much the same combination of fact and failing is used to characterize the black underclass today. See, e.g., R. Hernstein & C. Murray, *The Bell Curve: Intelligence and Class Structure in American Life* (1995).

[30] See chapter 5 below on torture.

[31] This, of course, does not tell us how that victim was seen by the slave class. For them, the analogy to Christ was indeed available. See, e.g., L. Hughes, "Christ in Alabama" (1931) in *The Collected Poems of Langston Hughes* 143 (A. Rampersad, ed. 1994); C. Cullen, "The Black Christ" (1929) in C. Cullen, *The Black Christ and Other Poems* (1929).

bolized by Frederick Douglass. They had freely acted, separating themselves by that action from the shame of nature. If one accepted this moral reading of flight, then the most offensive political act would be to return the escaped slave to a condition of slavery. This would change the character of slavery from a moral hierarchy to a political act of war, in which the general class of black people were declared the enemy. This moral narrative of freedom won was just the target of *Dred Scott*, which held that no black person could be a citizen of the United States regardless of his or her personal achievements. For the *Dred Scott* Court, blackness was itself a stigma beyond the capacity for repair or recovery. It marked a natural man outside the political community: "The unhappy black race were separated from the white by indelible marks, and laws long before established, and were never thought of or spoken of except as property, and when the claims of the owner or the profit of the trader were supposed to need protection."[32]

The master class was in the ideologically difficult position of having to deploy that narrative of rebellion but at the same time undermine its application in instances of actual rebellion, including flight. To do so it deployed another traditional tool of ideological construction: the claim that slave rebellion was caused by "outside agitators." The threat of slave rebellion could not be seen as an expression of self-liberation but only of third-party intervention.[33] Because slaves were merely natural, they were easily misled or tempted. What might appear as rebellion could really be only an aggressive political act by those outside the immediate community. Thus the South engaged in a massive effort to suppress and expel abolitionists and even abolitionist literature.[34] Secession, when it came, would be seen not as the initiation of war but as a continuation of a war already engaged.[35]

---

[32] *Dred Scott v. Sanford*, 60 U.S. 393, 410 (1856).

[33] One example of this rejection of third-party intervention was the gag rule in the House of Representatives that prohibited consideration of the thousands of antislavery petitions sponsored by the American Anti-Slavery Society from 1836 to 1844.

[34] See, e.g., C. Eaton, *The Freedom-of-Thought Struggle in the Old South* (1964); W. Savage, *The Controversy over the Distribution of Abolition Literature 1830–1860* (1938). Southern states also tried to prohibit the presence of free blacks. See P. Finkelman, "Race and Domestic International Law in the United States," 17 Nat'l. Black L. J. 25, 41 (2003) ("By 1860 every southern state prohibited the migration of free blacks").

[35] See, e.g., the Georgia Declaration of Secession which accuses the non–slave-holding states of ten years of hostile action, which "has placed the two sections of the Union for many years past in the condition of a virtual civil war."

An individual can respond to the shame of the slave in two different ways. He can cover up the nakedness of the other or he can hold himself apart, projecting the shame of nature wholly onto the naked slave. In other words, he can extend the human world built through labor or he can narrow it. What he cannot easily do is rely on the idea that man is an image of God to counter what is perceived to be the shame of nature. Once we see that shame, there is no going back to the innocence of Eden. For this reason, the discourse of human rights, which relies on the ideal of equality, often seems curiously detached from the real world of power, hierarchy, and subordination. This moral ideal alone is not enough to deny the distinction between master and slave, autonomous subject and shame of nature. To think that it is sufficient is to fail to recognize the Jeffersonian dilemma, which begins precisely with the acknowledgment of both. Knowledge of a fundamental human equality is never completely absent; rather, it is just the starting point of the dilemma presented by the inequalities within which we find ourselves.

A three-termed state of the moral imagination characterizes a slave-owning society: first, the slave is stripped down to the merely natural; second, he is recognized as a fully human threat; and, third, he is denigrated for his moral failure to take up his own humanity. The human must be dehumanized. Suffering that dehumanization is then taken as proof of a less-than-human—a shameful—quality. Together, these three steps reconcile the two elements of *Genesis*: equality and inequality; man's divinity and his shameful nature.

This is the moral imagination not just of slavery but more broadly of racism and colonialism. We find, for example, the same imaginative construction of the other in the earliest reports of the Spanish interaction with the indigenous populations in their American possessions. These populations are first described as a part of the discovery of a new world. They are like the geography, the flora, and the fauna. They can be treated as mere objects, collected as curiosities.[36] Quickly they become not just curiosities but productive assets. Their existing worlds can be ignored as they are turned into beasts of labor for the material

---

[36] On Columbus's return from his first voyage, he already took back to Spain a number of Tainos along with a cargo of a variety of plant and animal species.

interests of the colonists. Yet they are not merely beasts. They are seen to have their own families, polities, and civilizations. They have their own gods, their own rulers, their own social structures. Most important, they have their own capacity for resistance. They have armies with their own loyalties and, in some instances, loyalties they are willing to betray. This combination leads the Spaniards to commit mass atrocities on this population. These atrocities are only inhumane if these are human subjects. That they are not is confirmed by their very suffering. Not the defeat but the humiliation constitutes the natural shame of the indigenous.

These actions are misunderstood if interpreted only as a practice of treating the natives as if they were mere objects upon which the Spanish could test the sharpness of their swords. Killing is not mere sport; torture and murder are designed to send a message. One does not send a message to merely natural objects. Like all atrocities since, these actions were meant to be witnessed by potential victims as well as by other victimizers. They are designed to tell the victims that it is *as if* they are mere possessions of the Spaniards, to be disposed of as they wish. At the same time the Spanish are telling one another that the indigenous peoples are not subjects. They are not subjects because "we, the Spanish, can do this to them." Master and slave are reciprocally constructed in the act of humiliation. As the conditions of repression become worse, the failure to rebel becomes greater evidence of moral failure and thus of the shame of nature. *We* never could live like that.

The pattern has remained the same with the modern terror of authoritarian regimes: terror does not just defeat, it humiliates. The subordinated are understood to affirm their position by accepting the humiliation. When they do rebel—with outside assistance or not—the construction of political inequality often collapses very quickly.[37] That is because the construction of the inequality of slavery just barely suppresses a recognition of equality.

[37] This pattern creates substantial dangers for the liberator, as the United States is learning in Iraq, for with liberation comes a need to overcome years of humiliation, that is, to overcome the shame of nature. A liberated population is more likely to be rebellious than a politically repressed population. See F. Fanon, *The Wretched of the Earth* (C. Farrington, trans. 1976); A. Memmi, *The Colonizer and the Colonized* (H. Greenfield, trans. 1965).

The resource of Genesis one and the idea of moral equality can always be used to question the inequalities that support the idea of the shame of nature. Once that ambiguity is opened up, it is possible to invert the practices of hierarchy and subordination. This move is not an innovation of the abolitionists of the nineteenth century but has always been a possibility in the West. If the native is denigrated as merely natural because he lacks the signs of civilization, does the colonizer's action not demonstrate the same capacity for uncivilized, merely natural behavior?[38] Already in the early 1500s Las Casas fully worked the transformation of values, labeling the conquistadors evil and the indigenous the suffering innocent.[39] This is the same message that Conrad portrays in *The Heart of Darkness*, in which the colonizer "goes native," revealing the truth of the colonial enterprise to be the shame of nature. From the beginning, labor is tainted with sin.

The politics of slavery or racism erects a symbolic order that would suppress the appearance of the natural man. Metaphorically, man covers his natural self in clothes.[40] In actual political life, man is clothed with uniforms and insignia of rank, on the one hand, and with the expressions of fashion, on the other. The substantially impenetrable character of the symbolic world of the political is seen in its transformation of those sites that might otherwise most vividly express the natural self. Birth becomes the origin of political identity, if not political rank. Death becomes honorable sacrifice. Fighting becomes the expression of political strength, the construction of history, and the display of political virtue. There is no world of nature to be found within this polity. In every direction we see only more of the symbolic order, for it would be shameful were any of these activities to become merely the expression of nature. We prevent this emergence of the shame of nature in our own activities by projecting that shame completely upon an other. That other is the scapegoat, the slave, the native, the black, the enemy who threatens to remind us that beneath the

---

[38] See above at 151–52 on the instability of the terms "nature" and "culture."

[39] See Las Casas, *A Short Account of the Deconstruction of the Indies*.

[40] In *Genesis*, the paradigmatic "covering up" is that performed by Noah's sons, Shem and Japheth, when they carefully avoid observing their father's nakedness. Ham, who sees too much and is too much of the body, suffers his father's curse of his own son, Canaan, who will be "the lowest of slaves."

world of class, power, patriotism, and culture remains the shame of our own nature: we are born like every other animal, and we die just the same.

Corresponding to the construction of the slave as the shame of nature is the construction of a master characterized by fear and guilt. He cannot fear rebellion without implicitly acknowledging his own guilt. Evil arises as fear dominates the guilt, producing an ever-increasing repression and dehumanization. The greater the distance between master and slave, the more the master's world seems to depend on exclusion of the slave. The fear of the slave rebellion is a fear that this world will collapse. The slave states of the South claimed for themselves an especially "high" culture of honor, dignity, and tradition.

We always fear that the world in which we have invested our labor and found our meaning will be exposed as nothing but a manifestation of the Fall. We fear we will be exposed as worshiping idols, that is, as nothing at all. This fear is deeply embedded in the Adam and Eve myth. There the product of man's labor is not spoken of with the pride of achievement. This is not Hobbes describing the creation of the Leviathan, or Burke describing the cumulative labor of generations to create and maintain a civilization. Rather, it is the fear that all that we build will fall apart. Civilization is no less mortal than the subject who labors. The shame of our nature is not a condition that we leave but only one that we cover up. It remains a constant accusation that we are dust and to dust we will return.

CONCLUSION: REVOLUTION AND SLAVERY

Revolution, as Jefferson taught, is always the throwing off of those who would treat us as slaves. Ideas prove their power in a community by creating this distance from the merely natural. Jefferson and his cosigners pledge to one another "our Lives, our Fortunes, and our sacred Honor." There is nothing natural—and so nothing shameful—about this body that bears an idea. This is the sacrificial act that founds the political order; it remains a constant possibility carried forward by the citizen's self-identification with that founding sacrifice.[41] The

---

[41] On the concept of the popular sovereign as the symbolic vehicle for this identification see chapter 5.

slave is imagined as failing to take this first step of political foundation. He is not an embodied idea at all; he remains, therefore, a part of nature.

A world built on symbols is simultaneously the strongest and the weakest of constructions, for it both founds a universe and can disappear in an instant. When we maintain that world by projecting outward the threat that nature poses to the symbolic, we create the conditions for evil, for just then we defend our own humanity by making the other less than human. We are not him. He lives a life of shame; we live a life of culture. His life has no meaning; our life is one of ultimate meaning. He is slave; we are masters. His life is bound always to that wasting asset, which is the body. Our life may not be free of death—that would claim too much—but does transform death itself into an expression of an idea. Death becomes sacrifice for honor, love, family, or nation. The master freely "pledges his life," which is exactly the moment at which he shows himself to have overcome the shame of nature. This much Hegel got right.

This form of evil appears whenever the social order sustains its own humanity by dehumanizing the other. The more precarious a society's own symbolic system, the more likely it is to seek support by projecting nature outside itself. Reciprocally, the more it does so, the more it places itself at risk from rebellion. Thus colonial regimes were particularly brutal. Evil feeds upon itself but not without reason. There was every reason to fear that a slave rebellion, were it to come, would indeed be a very destructive affair. Revolutionary violence, when it comes, may speak the language of universal equality, but frequently it merely inverts the locus of the shame of nature. Now the old order is recast as the shame of nature. The king must be killed to prove that he is merely human: humiliation is his due.

Thus, Louis XVI is stripped of his place in the symbolic order of the state and becomes merely citizen Louis Capet. Only in part is this an expression of political equality in the new order, for Louis, along with his spouse, Marie Antoinette, is vilified in ways that directly suggest the shame of nature. Both are the objects of pornographic representations; they are accused of crimes arising from uncontrolled desire; they are charged with showing a kind of primitive fear in their flight.[42] Court society is no longer the expression of culture but is recast as the natural life of predation, of the abuse of power for the ends of interest, and of uncontrolled sexuality. To cut off the head of the king is to confirm the belief that he is not just another man sharing our world. Rather, he is nothing but the shame of nature, to be expelled from the new political order. The transformation of Louis from the symbolic center of the state to the shame of nature shows the fluidity of a symbolic order structured around the antinomy of culture and nature. Louis ends his life as slave, enemy, scapegoat. He moves from Christ to Antichrist. So must every slave master have feared the rebellion of the slave, just as every tyrant fears the rebellion of the repressed. They fear, because they "know" they are guilty.

The problem, moreover, is not just one for tyrants. Louis XVI, after all, was a reformist king, and many a colonialist had the best of intentions. The shame of nature is an imaginative space, not a substantive category against which we can measure behavior.[43] The need to defend the symbolic order against the shame of nature works in just the same way for those who oppose revolutionary change. The conservative defense of the state is cast as an opposition to the merely natural man who would destroy civilization. Rebellion is rarely seen on its own terms as a demand for equality. It is not seen as such, for civilization itself seems to turn on maintenance of the inequality. Popular forces are denigrated as the "mob," which is driven by passion rather than reason. Instead of proving a common humanity, rebellion is cast as undeserving greed. The fear of rape is never far behind.

Such transformations of the locus of the shame of nature are characteristic of the revolutions that follow the French revolutionary example for the next two hundred years. Revolution is not understood as political disagreement—a clash of political ideals—but rather as a confrontation between political truth and a state of nature characterized

---

[42] See, e.g., R. Danton, *The Forbidden Best-Sellers of Pre-Revolutionary France* 225–26 (1996); M. Walzer, *Regicide and Revolution: Speeches at the Trial of Louis XVI* (1993).

[43] President Clinton's impeachment and vilification—also involving allegations of sex and interest—was a modern version of Louis XVI's humiliation. Surely there were those who wanted his head. Fortunately it was a less revolutionary time.

by the predation of the ruling class. The source of that "political truth" can be an appeal to an alternative conception of nature—Genesis one remains a vibrant resource. But my point here is about the political uses of Genesis two in order to legitimate inequality and subordination. Revolutionaries strip naked the old political leadership—often the aristocracy—to reveal the hidden truth, which is that their behavior has been only the shame of nature. There is an acting out of just the vulnerability of the symbolic order that the revolutionary relies upon, yet fears. He is right to fear it, for if the traditional order can be shown to be nothing but the shame of nature, then the revolutionary order can be subject to the same charge. It remains precarious, and revolutionaries often end up victims of the violence they cultivate. The Terror becomes the shame of the Revolution. The American Revolution, for the most part, avoided the Terror. It may, however, have purchased moderation by limiting its reach. Slavery remained, and when finally it did go, the means for its removal were no less terrifying.

In American history, of course, the end of slavery hardly marks the end of this conception of the shame of nature against which the political and social order must protect itself. In the South, slavery is succeeded by Jim Crow. The Fuller Court at the turn of the century has a deep fear of rebellion by the working class.[44] This pattern of thought is not limited to political conservatives. Those who would lead the proletariat revolution of the twentieth century had no trouble identifying the aristocracy or the capitalists or both with the shame of nature. Surprisingly, we see the same conceptual form deployed by Hannah Arendt, when she writes that the people's pursuit of the "social question"—the demand for material necessities—destroys the possibility of politics.[45] This is only another version of the shame of nature. The merely natural man is always just one step away from being treated as the slave, for slavery is the institutional expression that confirms the difference between us and them, between satisfaction with a world of symbolic meaning and the fear that that world is so intangible as to be nothing at all.[46]

[44] See O. Fiss, *Troubled Beginnings of the Modern State, 1888–1910* at 53–74 (1999).

[45] See H. Arendt, *On Revolution* 22–24 (1965).

[46] David Cannadine's recent book, *Ornamentalism: How the British Saw Their Empire* (2001), describes the peculiar character of the British imagination of their empire. In the face of the social question at home—the "naturalization" of domestic politics by the rise of

The lines along which the distinction between the shame of nature and the achievement of political culture will be drawn are not predictable in the abstract. Their substantive character is the product of their deployment. We can say, however, that the deeper the faith in a symbolic order—whether revolutionary or conservative—the more its supporters will defend it against the shame of nature. This is partly a matter of drawing on the willingness of members of a community to sacrifice themselves—a pattern of belief explored in the next chapter. It is also partially a matter of making a meaningful world unimaginable apart from the continuation of this belief system. The alternative is seen as nothing but the shame of nature. This form of reasoning reaches right back to that of the slave master who is confident that he would choose death before he would be a slave.

There remains a kind of primal fear of returning to nature. Political communities combat that fear by projecting nature onto the enemy, the destruction of which will be the affirmation of their own non-natural life. Nature is not the friend of politics but its enemy. A liberal political movement that understands the end of the state to be the health and welfare of its citizens—their material well-being—is dangerously close to slipping into the mythic formation of the shame of nature.[47] The place of evil in the contemporary politics of well-being is the subject of the next chapter. The politics of well-being may have overcome the shame of nature that was the slave's, but it has left us with just as challenging a form of evil: killing for the state. Slavery and killing are two ways of driving out the shame of nature, two ways of founding the ultimate meaning of politics by denying our own finite character.

---

an industrial, urban, working class—an immense amount of political energy was invested in the symbolic reconstruction of indigenous societies in the colonies. Those societies were imagined as aristocratic, hierarchical, and rural, just as England had once been. There one would find the maintenance of the truth of politics, while England was succumbing to the shame of nature. Rather than constructing the indigenous populations along the lines of race—a category of natural inferiority—they were understood within the categories of class. Class can be determined by birth, but just at that moment it can displace the merely natural from the imagination. Not even at birth—or death—is the shame of nature allowed to penetrate the symbolic order.

[47] This was Carl Schmitt's complaint against liberalism. See C. Schmitt, *The Concept of the Political* 60–61, 69–70 (G. Schwab, trans. 1996); see also G. Agamben, *Homo Sacer: Sovereign Power and Bare Life* (D. Heller-Boazen, trans. 1998).

CHAPTER FIVE

■ ■ ■ ■

POLITICAL EVIL: KILLING, SACRIFICE, AND THE IMAGE OF GOD

Within modern, liberal states one generally finds belief in a narrative of political progress. That narrative has three central elements. First, there has been a transition from personal to democratic forms of power—from kingdoms to republics. The people are the sole source of legitimate power today. Expression of that power takes the form of law. Second, there has been progress in the character and operation of the law. This is a story of movement from a world of torture to one of procedure, from the spectacle of the scaffold to the science of penology. The ambition of modern law extends to the care of every citizen, even to those who violate its proscriptions. The democratic, people's republic is, in this way, simultaneously the republic of law. Third, there has been a humanization of war. This is, in part, a claim for battlefield discrimination such that the intent directly to injure is limited to combatants.[1] Perhaps more important, war itself is increasingly displaced by law—international law and transnational institutions of adjudication are to resolve disputes among nations. War, we tell ourselves, is an anachronism in the modern age.

Each aspect of this narrative of political progress appeals, then, to law. Indeed, the rule of law is the dominant theme of the entire narrative. There is no space, within or without the modern state, that is not to be regulated by law. This includes both democratic political processes and the deployment of force, both internal self-regulation and relationships to others. In the modern, liberal state, politics and

---

[1] Even among combatants, the means of warfare are not unlimited. See Hague Convention IV, Annex, sec. II, art. 22 ("The right of belligerents to adopt means of injuring the enemy is not unlimited").

law are to be coterminous normatively and factually. Wherever there is politics, there must be the rule of law.

The rule of law plays this central role in the narrative of progress, because law is imagined as the realization of reason within the space of political life. Thus the larger framework of the progressive narrative is one that moves from a politics driven by the personal interests of a privileged class to a politics of justice for all. Justice is the normative claim of reason, and the aim of law is the realization of justice—on this, both our jurisprudence and popular political ideals agree.[2] This political narrative is modeled on other forms of progressive narratives: nature is tamed, sciences are purged of false belief, and economic production is rationalized. In all these narratives, the issue is not historical accuracy. Rather, they are ways of imagining the past (and the future) from the perspective of contemporary values. In fact, politics never lacked a conception of justice; science never lacked a conception of truth. Nevertheless, the past is recast as a story leading to the present, just as the future is cast as the space for the realization of contemporary projects—a space for the realization of reason's ends.

The political narrative of progress, then, is yet another version of the story of the triumph of reason. The modern state appears as an endless project of reform: every institution and arrangement is subject to critique and improvement on the basis of reason. The rule of law always includes deliberate mechanisms for the reform of law.[3] An irrational law, let alone an unjust law, is always an appropriate object of critique. Critique is always the predicate for reform. Reform and reason, however, to what end? Just like the myth of nature, the claim of reason represents an imaginative possibility, not a substantive position.[4] Reason is not self-defining. Not so long ago reason took the form of theology: understanding the mind of God as it shows itself in and through creation. Stripped of the sacred, a humbled reason today is more likely to offer us a politics of well-being.

---

[2] See, e.g., R. Dworkin, *Law's Empire* (1986); J. Rawls, *A Theory of Justice* (1971); O. Fiss, "The Supreme Court 1978 Term—Foreword: The Forms of Justice," 93 Harv. L. Rev. 1 (1979).

[3] See H. L. A. Hart, *The Concept of Law* 92 (1961) (on secondary rules that allow for revision of laws).

[4] See above at 151.

The theological project had no particular connection to the body's well-being. Indeed, reason's ambition, from within this earlier perspective, was better understood as seeking to understand pain as part of the divine plan.[5] In the contemporary liberal state, however, the edifice of reason is tightly bound to the health and well-being of the body of the citizen—not the advancement of the interests of a particular group but the well-being of all. The liberal state does not generally tell its citizens where or how they can realize their own ideas of a good life. But it does assume that all such ideas include bodily well-being—health, freedom from pain or want, and, of course, life itself. These are necessary, although hardly sufficient, conditions of every reasonable idea of the good.

The well-being of the individual, understood quite literally as the health of the body, is assumed to be the unproblematic foundation for public policy. This is related to, but not the same as, the satisfaction of interests that drives the economic order. Economic outcomes are measured against citizen well-being in this more basic sense. Despite its economic success, the United States, for example, is not only deeply criticized for its failure to assure universal access to high-quality health care but is itself in a kind of unending policy crisis over how to advance toward this goal.[6] Government cannot proclaim its indifference to citizen well-being. It cannot define care of the body as private—not a public concern—even if it is committed to the use of private institutions to achieve that well-being. That does not mean that governments are always successful, only that they will be measured by their success or failure to improve the health and well-being of their citizens.

Health care is not different, in this respect, from general economic performance. Both are fundamental public concerns quite apart from the use of private institutions to advance these interests. Morbidity rates stand right next to, if not above, the gross domestic product as the ultimate measure of progress. A democratic politics is thought "naturally" to pursue these ends: How could government by and for

---

[5] See S. Neiman, *Evil in Modern Thought* (2002) (arguing that modern philosophy can best be understood as driven by the problem of theodicy).

[6] Health care reform has been at the center of the domestic policy agenda of the most recent Democratic and Republican administrations.

the people fail to seek the health and well-being of its citizens? We conclude the general narrative of progress, then, with a contrast between contemporary biopolitics, the end of which is the minimization of the body's pain and the maximization of its health, and the premodern state in which the end of the state seemed often to be the production of pain, whether as punishment or warfare.[7]

Reason turns to the body's well-being in an effort to ground what would otherwise be an abstract discourse of progress. Nevertheless, this grounding can only be partially successful. Neither formal reason nor material well-being tell us anything about our relationship to the particular communities of which we are members. Both fail to set forth a history that is ours or a destiny about which we should care. Progress in the development of reason—including the medical and productive sciences—is a common possession of mankind. In the concern for well-being, all individuals are the same. No one has a stronger claim than anyone else for health or well-being. We see the impulse toward the universal, for example, in utilitarianism, which theorizes the application of reason to well-being. Indeed, the logic of utilitarianism not only transcends particular communities but moves beyond man himself to a concern for the well-being of other species.[8]

This progressive narrative has not gone unchallenged. The modern era has generated a counternarrative as well. In this account, the state remains deeply invested in the production of pain. This is the narrative that begins not in the hospital but in the concentration camps; that registers a gap between the reformist ambition of penal science and the practice of incarceration; that notes the deployment of weapons of mass destruction threatening entire populations; that perceives the disappearance of the spectacle of the scaffold but sees in its place the rise of mass armies. This narrative takes as its reference points the trench warfare of the First World War, the mass bombings of the Second World War, the terrorizing tactics of the wars of decolonization, the recurrent outbreaks of civil war, and the proliferating threats from weapons of mass destruction. The liberal state, no less than the non-

---

[7] The word "biopolitics" is derived from Foucault's concept of "biopower." He uses it to identify a politics directed at the maintenance of populations. See M. Foucault, *History of Sexuality* vol. 1, at 143 (R. Hurley, trans. 1980).

[8] See P. Singer, *Animal Liberation* (1975).

liberal state, has been intimately involved in these phenomena. The United States, for example, imprisons well over two million men—a portion of its population equivalent to that of South Africa under apartheid.[9] It maintains armed forces of roughly similar size.[10] Until recently, the history of modern Europe was one of concentration camps and confrontations between mass armies, not to speak of the European involvement in colonial and neocolonial efforts. Leading liberal states have not seen a problem with their own possession of weapons of mass destruction.[11] In this counternarrative, the symbol of political power remains the body in pain, and the measure of power is the capacity to produce pain. Not surprisingly, the contemporary threat of terrorism makes a claim to political power based on its ability to inflict bodily pain.

The modern nation-state may understand itself as caring for the body, but it is not clear that we have become generally safer as a result of modern political developments. This was self-evident during the Cold War, with its imminent threat of mutual assured destruction. It took only twelve years after the end of the Cold War for the specter of mass destruction to again haunt the political imagination. Political identity in the contemporary world remains a source of deadly danger. This is true not just in those states struggling with civil war but in Western liberal states as well. We are potential targets because we are Americans—or British or Spanish—and we respond to that perceived threat through our own deployments of force. The United States never disarmed after the Cold War. Today Europeans debate the need to create a military capability coordinate with the changing character of the European Union and the contemporary perceptions of threat.

This counternarrative of pain is a bounded narrative. Well-being points to the universal, but pain particularizes.[12] Pain always seems

---

[9] See U.S. Department of Justice, Bureau of Justice Statistics Bulletin, July 2003.

[10] As of September 30, 2004, there were 1.5 million active-duty military, with another 1.2 million national guard and reservists. See Department of Defense, Selected Manpower Statistics, Fiscal Year 2004.

[11] Despite the formal obligation set forth in the Nuclear Nonproliferation Treaty to move toward a world free of nuclear weapons, no nuclear state has ever expressed a real interest in giving up its weapons—apart from some remnants of the Soviet Union.

[12] Tolstoy starts *Anna Karenina* with the line: "All happy families are alike but an unhappy family is unhappy after its own fashion" (R. Edmunds, trans. 1978).

exceptional. It intrudes into our lives, stopping our ordinary progress and concerns. In the first instance, suffering pain makes us aware of ourselves in a way that excludes others.[13] We feel quite literally that others cannot share our pain. Pain makes us lonely. While well-being leads us out into the world, pain tends to focus attention inwardly. As the intensity of pain increases, the boundaries of our world tend to contract. Pain is not just a metaphor for death but a part of the very substance of death. Just as my death is my own, so is my pain. Extreme pain is often thought to be worse than death. Moderns argue about whether suicide is a justified response to pain; premoderns represented Hell as a place of perpetual pain.

An overwhelming pain may close off the world entirely, limiting the self to the boundaries of the body. It is hard to pursue the well-being of others when suffering one's own pain. This is true not just of individuals but of societies as well. A society suffering economically or physically—from whatever source—will focus on itself to the exclusion of others. While pain may cause the world of the sufferer to shrink into the self, pain does not remove the sufferer from our common, human world. I may not see others through my physical pain, but others surely see me. When a child, friend, or lover suffers pain, his or her pain can constitute our world. If love is a disinterested caring for the success and well-being of the beloved, then we cannot help but suffer the pain of the object of our love. We do not simply "carry on" or go about our usual business in the face of such pain.

Pain, accordingly, is a phenomenon of human meaning; it is an especially powerful source of political meanings. It marks the borders of a community of care. At the foundation of the Christian myth is the claim that Christ suffered for all of us; he has taken on our pain through a universal love.[14] To show equal care for all pain is to constitute a universal community—the aspiration of the Church. Unlike Christ, we do not take up the pain of all others. For us, a community of pain is a bounded community, just as love is always for a particular individual or community. The boundaries of pain are the boundaries

[13] See E. Scarry, *The Body in Pain: The Making and Unmaking of the World* 4–5 (1985).

[14] For this reason, however, Christian martyrs are often represented as not suffering pain at all. Theirs is a beatific experience.

of love, for I suffer the pain of those I love. Indeed, it is not too much to say that one cares about one's own pain because of a love of the self.[15] Indifference to the pain of those one loves is unimaginable, except as that form of evil which was the subject of my argument in chapter 3: the flight from that recognition of death—and pain—that necessarily accompanies love.

A state, like an individual, organizes its history around pain. It is a story of battles fought, of war and threats of war, of disasters—natural and man-made—overcome. When we commemorate loss, we acknowledge that the pain is ours. It tells us who we are: we are the people who have suffered this pain—others have not.[16] When we lose the memory of that pain, we lose the connection to that earlier community. Its experiences strike us in the same way as those of any other foreign community: subjects about which we may learn and to which we may extend sympathy, but about which we do not care.

This counternarrative of pain is surely not the only history that is or can be written; it is not even the favored form of professional history today. Nevertheless, even in the modern state, the counternarrative is encountered as a story of past sacrifice. It provides the foundation for a patriotic identification with the community—love of nation. It provides the national myth. Thus the counternarrative of democratic pain succeeds the narrative of royal succession. That, too, was a narrative of life and death, focused, however, on the body of the king. The move from the monarch as sovereign to the people as sovereign relocates the suffering body that bears the state. It does not abandon what I have called the counternarrative of suffering for that of well-being but locates that suffering in every citizen.

The popular sovereign truly emerges when all members of the polity can experience the pain of politics. This is not a matter of extending the franchise but of a revolution in the political imagination. All citizens are equal, when all read the same history of suffering as their pain, and all stand equally before the threat of future pain—sacrifice—for the state. Institutionally, this demand for an equality of suffering

---

[15] See H. Frankfurt, *The Reasons of Love* 79–80 (2004).

[16] At the center of the Jewish Passover service is a line that always puzzles children but which they repeat yearly in the formulation of the counternarrative: "It is because of this that the Lord did *for me when I left Egypt.*"

expresses itself in the extension of military service to groups previously excluded: participation in the military expresses equal dignity within a democratic state. Groups excluded will not see in that exclusion good fortune but a stigma of shame.

Implicit in the imagination of the democratic state is a deep rejection of that ideal of modern humanitarian law, which insists upon a distinction between combatants and noncombatants. That is an aristocratic ideal in tension with the democracy of pain that founds the modern state in the revolutionary action of the popular sovereign. At the heart of this state, accordingly, we find a commitment not to the principle of discrimination on the battlefield but to the willing sacrifice of all the national resources—human and material—for the purpose of preserving the state. All can be called upon to sacrifice—to suffer—for the maintenance of the state.[17] Nuclear weapons are the perfect expression of democratic pain. A policy of mutual assured destruction is the endpoint of the counternarrative.[18] Just as the narrative ends in a vision of well-being under the regime of reason, the counternarrative ends in a vision of universal self-sacrifice founded on a love of nation.

The attachment of politics to pain, accordingly, is not simply a premodern phenomenon. At the core of modern political belief has been the imagination of violence: the Western idea of democratic citizenship entails the possibility of killing and being killed for the state.[19] Nothing is easier to describe than the horror of the battlefield. Yet, despite our knowledge of that horror, we celebrate a political history of achievement on the battlefield.[20] The West not only experienced the destruction of a generation of young men in the First World War, it pursued the Second World War to the point of genocide and the destruction of European material wealth and civil society. My point is not that all the participants in these wars are to be judged equally accountable, that all violated moral norms, or that we cannot make normative dis-

---

[17] This is linked to the demand for unconditional surrender: all the resources of the enemy state must be emptied of their political meaning.

[18] See P. Kahn, "Nuclear Weapons and the Rule of Law," 31 NYU J. Int'l. L & P. 349 (1999).

[19] On the history of the citizen as soldier, see V. Hanson, *Carnage and Culture: Landmark Battles in the Rise of Western Power* (2001).

[20] For a recent reflection on this phenomenon, see C. Hedges, *War Is a Force That Gives Us Meaning* (2002).

tinctions between the politics of the different nations. Rather, it is that the imaginative connection of politics to violence remains vibrant. My own generation has lived its entire life under the threat of mutual assured destruction. The ordinary background condition of our lives has been the constant possibility that we will die for the sake of our political identity: where and how are accidents of circumstance. This willingness to hold an entire population hostage to political meanings is now celebrated as victory in the Cold War. More than anything else, the Cold War should have taught us that modern political identity extends to everybody the possibility of pain and the demand for sacrifice. If we missed that lesson then, surely the contemporary war on terror is teaching it again.

The narrative and counternarrative of the modern state, accordingly, exist in deep tension. The former links reason to well-being; the latter links love to pain. Pain is the enemy of reason but not of love. The narrative leads toward the universal; the counternarrative celebrates the particular. The former generates law; the latter, sacrifice. Advancing the interests of the individual in his or her own well-being, the narrative imagines the state as nothing more than a transitional point in the progressive development of a universal legal order in which the well-being of every individual will be of equal concern. The counternarrative focuses on the special character of the particular state to is own citizens. It speaks of friends and enemies, not universal care. This counternarrative commemorates past pain and speaks of future sacrifice. Narrative and counternarrative are literally at war with each other, and often at war in the single individual. One appeals to well-being, the other to pain; one imagines a universal order, the other a bounded community; one appeals to reason, the other to will.

From the perspective of the narrative, the counternarrative represents the pathology of politics. The counternarrative offers a politics of killing and being killed as the history of the state. It takes only a slight shift of perspective—the shift from sacrifice to well-being—to see in this the great evil of the modern era. Thus contemporary liberal theorists are likely to see the idea of sovereignty not as the foundation of political meaning but as a threat to a rational politics. What can be rational about the celebration and willing suffering of pain? The narrative rejects a politics of pain as nothing more than a failure of reason. It links the development of human rights law, which seeks to prevent torture, to the development of humanitarian law, which seeks to minimize the suffering attendant to warfare.[21] In both cases, the ambition is to secure a politics of reasonableness—that is, a politics that no longer expresses itself through the infliction and suffering of pain. It finds here the face of evil in modern politics.[22]

This may be the greatest puzzle in the inquiry into evil: Has the Western nation-state itself become so bound up with the production of pain that we must condemn the entire history of that political form as an expression of evil? While we need to distinguish between good and bad among these political regimes—democracies are not the moral equivalent of totalitarian regimes—these distinctions may themselves occur within a domain of profound evil. A state that simultaneously devotes its resources to health care and weapons of mass destruction can never decide whether it is founded on the narrative or the counternarrative. Somehow the two narratives have become tightly bound to each other. Had the politics of sovereignty produced a nuclear exchange—a threat not yet gone—could we take any other position than to condemn this politics as the greatest of evils, regardless of whether the bombs were launched in the "defense of freedom"? To make sense of the evil of political violence, we need to return again to *Genesis*, for the Genesis myth tell us that even the best we can do in the world of labor will never be enough to escape our fallen condition. Is this not precisely the political condition within which we find ourselves?

POLITICAL LABOR

To be expelled from the Garden is to fall into the space for human construction—the world of labor. That construction is possible because man now knows the good. He knows it, however, as idea, not material fact. The material nature upon which he labors is, in itself,

[21] See, e.g., T. Meron, "The Convergence between Human Rights and Humanitarian Law," in *Human Rights and Humanitarian Laws: The Quest for Universality* (D. Werner, ed. 1997).

[22] In a new book, Christopher Hedges describes this evil—that is, a willingness to sacrifice for the state—as a form of "idolatry," just the form of argument I describe in chapter 2 above—the worship of nothing at all. See C. Hedges, *Losing Moses on the Freeway: America's Broken Covenant with the Ten Commandments* (2005); see also M. Howard, *Wars and the Liberal Conscience* (1978).

devoid of any meaning. Man goes from a paradise in which being and the good are identical to a space in which being and the good are linked only through the mediation of his own labor. Without labor, the world will produce nothing. It remains "dust." It confronts man as the ontological emptiness that is death. Thus to dust man will return. After the Fall, all life occurs in the shadow of death. As soon as his labor stops, man dies, and his world falls apart. Whatever meaning the world has, it is the meaning that has been put there by man's labor, not by God's creative act.

A world that we are to understand as meaningful must therefore be a fully human world. The point, however, is not that man is free to judge the good however he pleases, rather, every event, object, and person we find in our world appears to us as an idea given material form through our own labor. When we understand the world, we understand the ideas that founded that world. Absent those ideas that inform our labor, the world would be literally nothing at all. Labor may appear as punishment for eating of the forbidden tree, but the knowledge produced by that mythical act of consumption is a necessary condition of labor. We see this clearly when we come across an artifact of another culture, of which we cannot make sense. We do not know it as a thing. Instead, we apprehend it only as a question. We say, "What is it?" or, "What purpose did it serve?" We understand objects in the world when we can read them as representations of ideas.[23] This is not merely a condition of the artifact. Dropped into an unknown place, we ask, "Where are we?" We answer that question by setting this space in relation to all the other spaces we know—those are spaces that have been shaped by human labor. We place ourselves within a geography of cultural and emotional space. Similarly, we ask of a stranger, "Who is he?" And, with that, we invite entry into a world of relations, friends, and known others. A person with no such connections is not just a stranger but rather represents the pathology of a person who has "forgotten" his identity; he is no one at all.

Ideas may seem the most ephemeral of things, but, given material form, our ideas far outlast us. A person may long for immortality, but

[23] Compare R. Barthes, "The Death of Author," in *Image, Music, Text* (S. Heath, trans. & ed. 1977).

his body is a rapidly wasting asset. When he gives material shape to his ideas, however, he puts himself into the world in a way that endures. We find the pot shard in the streets of Athens. We know that it was the product of a particular subject, who held it in his hands and gave it shape. He is forgotten, but the artifact that is the product of his ideas endures. What is true of a pot shard is all the more true of our great works of art, from cathedrals to books to symphonies. We impress our ideas upon the world, and they endure. Labor makes a world that is our own. The ancients understood this well. When they attacked an enemy, they aimed to destroy this material instantiation of the will. They razed the city, killed the men, and sold the women and children into slavery. This is what it means to destroy a world: to leave no artifact or person that can be read as an expression of the idea of that world.

This fully human world does not maintain itself; there is no day of rest. Man spends his entire life laboring to shape and sustain a meaningful world. Because the material of the world does not take form easily, labor entails violence. This is equally true in politics: it requires a good deal of labor to shape a resistant population into the representation of an idea. Political violence is never the molding of the merely natural into the human world of order, for there is no "natural" in the domain of politics. The violence of politics cannot be understood as if it were a lack or an absence of something else, a mere negation without a meaning of its own. Violence is not a forgetting of ourselves. Rather, to create our polity, we may have to destroy someone else's. To sustain one set of political meanings, we have to defeat alternative possibilities. The nation's history is a story of suffering for the sake of political ideas. Any particular narrative is only as secure as the victory it records.

This is the lesson that Thucydides conveys in his description of the Athenian expedition against the Melians. Not only is ours a fully human world, but it is already a fully occupied world. From the Athenian perspective, there were only two possibilities for the Melians: either they were part of the world of Sparta or that of Athens. If they chose Sparta, then the Athenians were prepared to make them into nothing at all. Athenian power existed in its opposition to Spartan power.[24] Of course, had the Melians had sufficient power, they could have constructed their own world as neither that of Sparta nor that of Athens. To do so, they would have had to fight both Athens and Sparta. What they could not do was to express that idea of themselves without the power to make it real. Ideas become real through the application of force—labor—to build and sustain a world. The destruction of the Melians was all about an idea: the Athenian idea that if you are not part of our world, then you will not be at all. There is no empty space, no unclaimed peoples, no *terre nulla*, as the expression went in classic international law. This ancient conflict was, in this respect, not very different from the modern conflict over spheres of influence in the Cold War.[25] Today we see the test of an American political idea in Iraq. We cannot know in advance whether the United States and its allies have the power to give sustained material reality to that idea. It may very well be that Americans are not willing to suffer or cause much pain for this idea in this place at this time.

The ideology of nineteenth-century colonization teaches us something here as well. The Europeans often understood their colonial populations as not yet fully civilized. They were like children, requiring further formation fully to realize the truth of their own being.[26] If they had been seen as a fully formed other, then the imperial attitude would have been that of Athens toward Sparta: the destruction of the meaning of that otherness. In this sense, recognition of the other may be more dangerous than the paternalism of quasi-recognition. My point is not to justify European colonialism but to see the connection between destruction and construction, between violence and pedagogy. In politics, they are inseparable.[27] At stake is the construction of a human world—our world, not someone else's. Colonization always

[24] See Thucydides, *History of the Peloponnesian War*, Book V, ch. 17.

[25] Or, for that matter, President Bush's description of the obligations of other nations in the war on terror: "You're either with us or against us in the fight against terror." See S. Tay, "Perspectives on Terrorism from Asia, the United States and the Middle East," 28 Fletcher Forum of World Affairs 113, 117 (2004) (quoting Bush from Nov. 6, 2001).

[26] See R. Jackson, *Quasi States: Sovereignty, International Relations and the Third World* (1990).

[27] Indeed, much of postmodern political theory has explored the violence implicit in the constructive project of modern politics. See, e.g., M. Foucault, *Discipline and Punish: The Birth of the Prison* (A. Sheridan, trans. 1977).

had this double track of military violence and civic construction. When a state gave up the latter, it became merely another form of imperial occupation.[28]

The extension of one's own world inevitably appears as a good thing. Symbolic orders are complete: they make sense of an entire world. The market wants to go global, just as information "wants to be free." For most nineteenth-century Europeans, it was not conceivable that the truth of Christianity should not be relevant everywhere: at stake was "civilization." Today we are more likely to speak of multiculturalism and respect for the other, but this is hardly a concession to the boundaries of symbolic forms. Contemporary discourses of universality speak of markets, rights, and democracies. Our respect for the other is an affirmation of our own value of tolerance. A pressing question for many today is whether we—the United States and other modern, Western states—are willing to use force to extend this world.

In its ordinary appearance, then, political violence is a form of labor. It is an expression of the will by which a political order extends itself by forming the beliefs of those subject to the authority of the state. When we approach political life in this way, we view violence as we do other forms of labor: as a means to an end. We speak of casualities as costs to be measured against gains. We hope to keep the casualty count low as we set about extending our own political authority. We hope to exercise coercion in more efficient ways. We think that the point of the violence is not to eliminate its immediate targets but to "break the will"—change the beliefs—of those who survive. This is true whether we apply violence internally as criminal punishment or externally as war. The destruction of the Melians had as its point not mere destruction but impressing Athenian power upon other allies who might have contemplated breaking out of the alliance. The same spectacle of violence can be witnessed today in the American intervention in Iraq. As von Clausewitz pronounced, "War is the continuation of politics by other means."[29]

If political violence were only a means to an end, then there would be reason to think that we could pursue a program of reform to mini-

[28] The classic example is the Belgian rule in the Congo, but consider also the early Spanish occupation of South and Central America, and the Japanese occupation of China.

[29] C. von Clausewitz, *On War* 605 (M. Howard & P. Paret, eds. & trans. 1976).

mize its costs. This is always the ideal of labor: to reduce the burden of work. We dream of accomplishing our end of fully investing the world with meaning without exhausting our limited resources. In the domain of political meanings, that dream often takes the form of law, which is to be a "machine that will go of itself." Just as we seek to replace domestic violence with law enforcement and adjudication, we hope we can replace war with international law and courts. The spread of Western ideas in the era of colonization was as much a matter of proselytizing, pedagogy, and institutional construction as of brute violence. Today we compare the effectiveness of "soft" power with that of "hard."[30] These are all elements of the narrative of progress. Suffering from political violence, on this view, is not exactly the pathology of politics, but still it is pure cost. Past political history is tainted by this pain. A liberal politics is progressively moving toward a politics of pedagogy in place of painful coercion. The critique of liberal politics is often an effort to show just how coercive and painful politics remains for its intended beneficiaries. In this respect, the critique, too, remains within the boundaries of the imagination of labor, for, no less than the narrative, it believes that labor's end is bodily well-being.

If political violence is a form of labor, it is bad but not evil. We may, of course, do terrible things in the course of political labor. This is just what the Athenians told the Melians; the same thing has been repeated ever since. Politics is a labor of violence and suffering. Individuals will be injured and die, but they do so as well in every form of labor. Nineteenth-century industrialization probably produced as much injury as nineteenth-century politics.[31] Stalin's economic policies were no less brutal than his politics. Application of criminal punishment is not evil, even if we would prefer a world in which it was not necessary. War is no different in this respect: we regret the losses, but we believe the benefits exceed the costs. Of course, from the perspective of the individual victim, suffering is a terrible thing. But suffering in all forms—disease, poverty, injury, back-breaking labor—is terrible. If

[30] See J. Nye, *Soft Power: The Means to Success in World Politics* (2004).

[31] See J. Witt, *The Accidental Republic: Crippled Workmen, Destitute Widows, and the Remaking of American Law* (2004).

the labor of politics produces more suffering than necessary, it should certainly be condemned as misguided and wrong. Under many conditions, we may properly regard it as unjust.

Nevertheless, we cannot take the production of pain as the measure of evil in politics without losing hold of the special threat of evil. The evil of twentieth-century political violence—and now that of the twenty-first century—is misunderstood if approached merely as the cost of labor. As labor it makes little sense: wars generally extract costs far greater than their possible benefits. Wars can be fought over claims to quite unproductive territory; they are fought over conflicting ideas, beliefs, or historical claims. Viewed from the perspective of the well-being of each individual, all would be better off if disputes were settled by arbitration or if those groups that hold different beliefs accepted a modus vivendi practice of political tolerance. If the body's well-being is the end of politics, then war makes no sense, and criminal punishment should be replaced by rehabilitation and remediation. Well-meaning individuals are always ready to suggest alternative forms of labor that are not only more humane but more efficient. But politics is not merely a matter of social engineering, because pain is not simply a cost.

POLITICAL SACRIFICE

Political violence is more than labor when it occupies a space of unmediated meaning. Violence can be the point at which politics sets itself against the desacralization of the world. This is no longer violence as a means of impressing the will upon the world. It is violence as self-sacrifice, not as labor. There are not more or less efficient ways to engage in sacrifice. There are no finite measures available as we approach the sacred. Sacrifice and labor both work in a medium of pain, but they are not the same. Labor's end is to alleviate pain, to minimize resistance to production. The end of sacrifice is not to alleviate the pain of labor but to transcend the conditions of labor. This is the fundamental tension that produces the contemporary conflict in the liberal state between the narrative and the counternarrative, for pain appears in the counternarrative as the testimony of self-sacrifice.

Hobbes claimed that in creating the Leviathan man was acting in the image of God—he, too, becomes a maker of a world. This idea of creation is the project of labor that characterizes man after the Fall. Politics, however, is not just about labor. It is equally about recovery of a prelapsarian experience of the unity of being and meaning. The political name for that experience is sovereignty. Hobbes got the name right, but he never offered an adequate explanation of that one power that characterizes the sovereign: the power to claim the life of the citizen. Hobbes could not do so because he thought the whole point of the labor of politics was to put off the moment of death, that is, to pursue the well-being of the body. If so, for politics to require the citizen's death is a logical contradiction. Yet this is exactly what we find. Hobbes's Leviathan may shift the field of killing from civil to international war—although often not even that shift occurs—but there is no reason to think that an international field of battle offers the Hobbesian individual a life any less nasty, brutish, or short than that from which he fled in the state of nature. If sovereignty is a power over life and death, then, we cannot understand politics simply as the labor of fallen man.

For the individual, the difference between the Hobbesian state of nature and the organized state is not the difference between violence and peace, or death and life, but between the fight for survival and sacrifice for the polity. The struggle for survival is always a form of labor. Laboring, man hopes to come to feel at home in the world that he creates. This is the end of a politics of well-being.[32] No matter how successful an individual is in this task of construction, man can never fully overcome the separation between himself as subject and the world as object. The permanence of that separation is realized in the thought of his own death: when he dies, the world goes on without him.

A politics of well-being can put off death, but it cannot overcome the very thing it would avoid. Contrary to Hobbes's claim, we do not find ourselves to be an image of God as laborers, for labor ties us to

---

[32] This is why contemporary game theorists are so interested in Hobbes: politics for them is an answer to a problem of labor. See, e.g., D. Gauthier, *The Logic of Leviathan* (1969); G. Kavka, *Hobbesian Moral and Political Theory* (1986).

death. Adam cannot save himself no matter how well he performs the task of labor. He can do no more than pass on this task to the next generation. The sacred is literally not of this world. Yet the sacred is where man knows he belongs, for he knows that he is an image of God. Only through sacrifice does the separation of subject from object collapse: only in this act are being and meaning one and the same. The sacrificed object is not re-formed but sanctified. It becomes a point for the showing forth of the sacred. Ultimately the object of sacrifice must be man himself, for it is man who must realize an ultimate meaning.

Just as the Genesis myth grounds an idea of political labor, it provides a source for the Western idea of sovereignty that can support a practice of political sacrifice. According to the myth, man's role in the Garden includes the naming of creation: "whatever the man called every living creature, that was its name." God speaks the world into existence. Naming creation, man gives words to the text that is creation. Naming creation is a kind of reading of the text authored by God. This process of naming/reading constitutes a kind of reverse image of God speaking. To name is to possess in a representational form. The prelapsarian world of Adam, accordingly, has an inner and an outer form. Outwardly Adam occupies a place in a created world— the Garden. Inwardly he doesn't occupy a single place but possesses the whole of that world. Naming creation, Adam is more than a part; he is the point at which the whole is present to itself. The implicit dangers of language, which is always an image of the divine power of creation, are fully realized in the story of the Tower of Babel: a second story of the Fall.

Man is an image of God, because he symbolically reproduces all of creation. Before the Fall, the truth of a proposition is not separate from the act of speech. God's speech creates its own truth—and so does man's. We cannot ask whether a name is true or false. Naming, like creation itself, is a performative utterance. If creation is good in itself, then the symbolic doubling of creation has that same quality. After the Fall, there is no longer a necessary correspondence between being and representation. Just as man must struggle to produce the object of his labor, he must struggle to understand the object of his representations. Not only does labor take time but so, too, does speech. Just as labor can go wrong, so, too, can the proposition. A fallen world is one in which error is not only possible but is expected.

Accordingly, the gap between subject and object appears in both labor and language. The existential loneliness of finite man is rooted in this separation from his world. We experience that separation most intensely in our foreknowledge of our own death. Ironically, death is one of the few certainties among our beliefs. That very knowledge, however, renders all else that we know uncertain. Because we will die, we know that we will never complete the projects of labor or knowledge. We know, moreover, that the objects of our labor are as tenuous as the propositions we construct. Both may outlast us, but neither escapes the decay that is the material world. Today we know as scientific fact what had been metaphysical fear: history itself will come to an end. Our end is followed by the end of all. It does not matter how far away the end is, for the eschatological imagination spans all time. The modern biopolitics of health represents one form of response to the limitations of labor: we aim to conquer death by endlessly putting it off. But death delayed can never answer the metaphysical demand for death transcended.

Bound to labor and death, we nevertheless have an idea of ourselves as subjects of infinite value, not bound to labor at all. This is the prelapsarian subject who is an image of God. This is the subject who has named all of creation, and thus possesses the whole before any task of labor even begins. This subject knows himself as an endless resource that is always more than any finite project of labor. He has a memory of the self as the point at which being and consciousness are identical. This subject can never find himself fully in the world that is the product of labor, for labor cannot encompass the infinite character of the subject.

Death literally makes no sense to a subject who knows himself as infinitely more than the world he occupies. In myth, it is not immortality that needs to be explained, but death, for death is a contradiction to the soul's self-knowledge. The subject longs for immortality but not as an endless task of labor and speech. He longs for immortality as recovery of the subject he knows himself already to be, not the product of labor but the foundation of a world of meaning that labor and language seek to elaborate. The myth of recovery is always a myth of overcoming this separation of subject and object. In politics we express that recovery as sovereignty, which is always imagined as complete in and of itself.[33]

Prior to the age of revolution, it certainly was not true that all men were created equal. Difference was not just material and political. There was a metaphysical gap between sovereign and subject. *Genesis* was a cultural resource of immense symbolic value in providing an understanding of difference, just as it has more recently informed an understanding of equality. In both instances, however, it provided a resource for interpretation, not a particular plan for political or religious action.

For the sovereign to be close to God, he had to take up Adam's position. Accordingly, the central symbolism of the Western conception of the sovereign invokes the idea of a "new Adam, the successor to Christ."[34] The sovereign recovers what fallen man has lost: an intimate relationship between the finite and the infinite. Thus the sovereign exists in different dimensions of time and space from ordinary people: the sovereign is the point of showing forth of the infinite. His body is not what it seems but is fully invested in the symbolic dimension. His true being is as the "mystical corpus of the state." His body is coextensive with the state, not as a map but as a presence. Just as the sovereign is omnipresent, he is timeless: the sovereign never dies, even as particular manifestations of the sovereign come and go. His knowledge is as complete as his presence, not because he can put his knowledge in propositional form but because, for him, being and knowing are one and the same. He is omniscient but not encyclopedic. Just as the body of Christ is the Church, the body of the sovereign is the state.

The sovereign does not labor because he is already metaphysically complete. If he does not die, there can be no shame connected to his body.[35] Rather than turning from the body in shame, there is a ritualis-

---

[33] See Kahn, *Putting Liberalism in Its Place* 259–79 (on completeness of sovereignty). Whether this conception of sovereignty is actually realized in the material reality of state-to-state relations is quite a different question. To ask that question is like asking whether the completeness of God is actually realized in the world. On the failure of sovereign realization, see S. Krasner, *Organized Hypocrisy* (1999).

[34] See C. Lefort, "The Permanence of the Theological Political?" in *Democracy and Political Theory* 213, 250 (D. Macey, trans. 1988).

[35] See chapter 4.

194 · CHAPTER FIVE

tic celebration of the king's body.[36] His private functions become matters of public concern. To be close to that body is to be in the presence of the sacred. Furthermore, he can do no wrong, because there is no gap between idea and act. In him, as in God, word and deed are one and the same. Thus his word is law; the courts of law speak in his name.[37] He is not subject to the law because he is the law—a position Christ claimed as well. His judgment decides the fate of the individual and thus literally creates its own truth. Guilt or innocence, friend or enemy, life or death are expressions of the sovereign voice. For the sovereign, *is* and *ought* are one and the same. The sovereign thereby claims recovery of that power originally granted to man: the power to name being. This is the ultimate meaning of a politics of sovereignty: citizens hold property and even life itself only as an expression of the sovereign voice.

Wherever we achieve an immediate relationship between the idea and its material presence—a relationship unmediated by labor—we are in the presence of the sacred. This is the structure of the miraculous and the magical; it is also the structure of sovereignty. Thus a king who could create political reality by his word alone could also cure the sick by his touch alone: a common practice right up to the age of revolution.[38] Once Louis XVI is seen as citizen Louis Capet, however, he has neither the power to speak the law nor to heal the sick.

That kings have lost their power to instantiate the sacred does not mean that we live our political lives in a wholly desacralized world. The same immediacy in the relationship between idea and reality is present in the popular sovereign. Thus the popular sovereign has the capacity to speak a world into being: this, for example, is the ground of the American Constitution. The Constitution speaks in the sover-

---

[36] See, e.g., L. Marin, *Portrait of the King* (M. Houle, trans. 1988). Even modern states retain elements of the "king's body." Citizens seek to be in the presence of the president, who operates within a ritualized, protected space. Mussolini's body was treated by many as if it "enjoyed semi-divine status," until it lost its sacredness in an execution reminiscent of that of deposed kings. See N. Farrell, *Mussolini: A New Life* 225–30 (2003).

[37] See W. Blackstone, *Commentaries on the Law of England*, Bk. 3, chap. 17, at 255 (1768). Hitler builds on this ancient idea when the German state proclaims that "the Führer's word is law."

[38] See M. Walzer, introduction to *Regicide and Revolution: Speeches at the Trial of Louis XVI* (1993).

eign voice—"We the People"—which is our voice. As citizens, we are bound to the constitutional order because we are a part of the body of the popular sovereign. To understand the transtemporal character of that relationship—how it is that we as individuals can be bound by past acts—we cannot dispense with the idea of the mystical corpus of the sovereign, which spans history and space. Theories of individual consent—a form of labor—are never adequate to this relationship, just as theories of majoritarianism are never adequate to explain the authority of the popular sovereign.[39] The popular sovereign is never just a contemporary majority. The act of the popular sovereign founds the world of the nation-state as the making present of an infinite source of meaning that will be elaborated through that labor which is the nation's history. The nation's sovereignty is never adequately captured by its past or present, as if it were a finite set of actions or the meeting of certain procedural conditions. Thus we are still working out the inexhaustible meaning of the American founding.

The word "sovereignty" is irreducibly religious in origin and meaning.[40] Over time, the locus of the sovereign subject changes but not its transcendent character. The sovereignty of God becomes the sovereignty of kings, which becomes the sovereignty of nations and ends with the sovereignty of man. The claim of sovereignty expresses a sense of the deathless soul of man now made real in the fallen world. It is the reification of this experience of the infinite quality of the self. We may start with the idea of man as the image of God, but we end with the knowledge that God is the image of man. Absent sovereignty, man is doomed to labor and death. Labor, however, proves too much for man. He must believe, and he finds in himself a capacity for faith.

In substantial part, it has been as a metaphysical promise that politics appeals to us. Every member of the body politic is an aspect of the sovereign's body. As part of that mystical corpus, the subject participates in the sacred doubling that is man. He finds himself bound to labor, but he maintains a faith that he is a part of the deathless and omnipresent sovereign. The royal "we" worked in both directions of

[39] See Kahn, *The Reign of Law* 200–201.
[40] See C. Schmitt, *Political Theology: Four Chapters on the Concept of Sovereignty* 36 (G. Schwab, trans. 1985).

the hierarchy of power. It expressed the extended corpus of the sovereign, as well as the political identity of the subject. Still today, the citizen reads his own political order—historically and geographically—as the work of a plural subject. That subject is no longer the king but the popular sovereign. The citizen remains embedded in this "we," when he reads the national history of sacrifice as his own. The Revolution is "our" struggle for freedom; the Constitution is the product of "We the People"; and the Civil War was the test of "our" commitment to the popular sovereign. The citizen knows where he stands in history, because he views that history through the narrative of the popular sovereign. The state's history is our history; its territory is our space; and its future is ours as well.[41] These are the elements of the counternarrative. There is no movement toward the universal, no sense of suffering as a cost, and no idea that the end of the nation is nothing more than individual well-being.

Modern states killed the king, but they certainly did not kill the sovereign. Instead, there has been a democratization of the king's body. The mystical corpus of the state is now the popular sovereign, which maintains just that character of timelessness, omnipresence, and omnipotence that characterized the king. While the popular sovereign has no existence apart from the bodies of its members, those members do not constitute the sovereign in the aggregate. The sovereign is not the product of the social contract. Rather, the citizen is the product of the popular sovereign. The sovereign always precedes and overflows the aggregate of individuals. Hobbes had it backward: actual nation-states—as well as their citizens—have found the ground of their historical presence not in the narrative but in the counternarrative.

The idea of sovereignty is that of an ultimate meaning that is never exhausted in any finite form—that is, in the products of labor. The ultimate value of sovereignty is incalculable. Only so can it make a total claim on an individual's life. There is no value of the profane when measured against the sacred. Once put at issue, the sacred quality of sovereignty will demand war without compromise, even if that

---

[41] The challenge of multiculturalism to this "we" is an important aspect of the rise of the postmodern state.

means consumption of the entire polity. Thus the continued existence of the United States is not one end among many for its citizens. For them, that existence gives meaning to history; it is not a part of a larger historical narrative but the very foundation of that history. We do not measure the defense of sovereignty against citizen well-being. The sovereign has a nonnegotiable claim on all the resources of the state, including the lives of its citizens. We are not yet done with a politics of manifest destiny, even if we mean to abandon efforts at neocolonialism. The nuclear threat implicit in American politics perfectly expresses the ultimate value of that politics: better the destruction of the world than the failure of the United States. Nuclear policy also shows us that killing and being killed are reciprocal political phenomena. We cannot threaten the enemy without suffering the threat in return. We are relearning this lesson from the contemporary war on terrorism.

An understanding of politics must draw on a conception of sovereignty that works outside the categories of labor and representation. We need, instead, the categories of transubstantiation, of the mystical corpus, and of the sacred. Central to the mystery of the politics of sovereignty is the experience of sacrifice: that which is sacrificed becomes sacred. Sacrifice does not appease an angry god; it creates and maintains that god. Sovereign and sacrifice are linked as subject and verb. The sovereign exists as long as citizens are willing to sacrifice for the maintenance of the sovereign. Both sacrifice and sovereignty point us beyond labor and thus beyond death. The finite body must be destroyed, if one is to recover that unity of being and meaning, of the infinite in the finite, that was Adam's but was lost in the Fall. Lincoln captures this when he speaks of the dead at Gettysburg "consecrating" the land. In the presence of such citizen sacrifice, one is within the domain of the sacred. Sovereignty, we can say, is God's political form.

Sacrifice is an act of transubstantiation by which a "mere" thing loses its finite character and becomes a site for the manifestation of the sacred. Thus one participates in the sovereign not through consent but through self-sacrifice. Without a willingness to suffer pain and even to give up one's life, there is no participation in the sovereign. There can be a politics of rights, a politics of management of the economic order and of the body's well-being, but there is nothing in this that rises beyond the horizon of the body's own finite character.

The aspiration for the infinite does not in itself entail a rejection of labor. The politics of sovereignty is not suicidal. Citizens do not literally want to die for the state, although there have been moments of a romantic longing for such sacrifice. But a politics of sovereignty only exists as long as the imaginative possibility of self-sacrifice remains real for citizens. Oliver Wendell Holmes wrote, "No society ever admitted that it could not sacrifice individual welfare to its own existence. If conscripts are necessary for its army, it seizes them, and marches them, with bayonets in their rear to death."[42] A polity that has no power to call on its citizens for sacrifice lacks sovereignty. Indeed, it is hard even to call such an organization a state. Such a polity may understand itself as advancing individual well-being; it may see itself as an adjunct to markets. It is not its role, however, to take citizens beyond their individual interests.

An account of political life that ignores the metaphysics of sovereignty will never confront the actual experience of life and death within the state. It will reduce the political to law, law to reason, and reason to well-being. If it conceives sovereignty at all, it will be as the reified object of a constructive contract. Sovereignty in this sense adds nothing to a politics of rights. The sovereign that moves citizens to acts of sacrifice, however, is not of this world at all. Sovereignty signifies the sacred foundation of the community. The citizen understands that for the sake of the sovereign he can be asked to suffer pain, and that under some circumstances the state can make an unanswerable demand upon his or her life—unanswerable because it is beyond the capacity of any proposition to comprehend. Argument ends, but the act remains. So it is with all faith in an ultimate meaning. Today, in the West, only politics can make that claim upon a life. As long as it can do so, we are in the presence of a sovereign power.

The willingness to sacrifice for the creation and maintenance of political meanings always appears inconceivable to those outside the community. We find it incomprehensible that Palestinians would be willing to blow themselves up for the maintenance of a political identity. But the suicide bomber is not different in kind from the Israeli soldier. Both know that political identity is a matter of life and death.

[42] O. Holmes, *The Common Law* 43 (1923) [1881].

Both sides in this conflict wonder at the capacity of the other to kill and be killed. Both sides try to apply a moral measure to the behavior of the other. In this, they each suffer from the same misunderstanding. Citizens sacrifice themselves and their children not because it is morally correct but because it is politically necessary. This a necessity, however, that can be measured only from within the political world of meaning.

We have the same reaction to the sacrificial politics of others as we do to those who believe in different gods, rituals, and sacred texts. It literally makes no sense to us; it appears "crazy." How, we wonder, can anyone believe that the gods appeared in that object or that place? Why would anyone think that wine can be the blood of Christ or that God would perform miracles for an enslaved people? This shock of difference, however, usually does not cause us to doubt our own beliefs. We think others strange, but that does not unmoor us from our own sacred rituals. The same is true of our own political meanings. We cannot understand how anyone could believe in the sacred character of a king, but this does not lead us to question the way in which the sacred operates in our relationship to an atemporal, ubiquitous popular sovereign. It does not do so, because we have little choice in the matter. There is not some other, nonsymbolic world in which we can choose to live, once we learn that others live by meanings different from our own. There is not a truth of the matter that we have somehow missed.

None of this means that every time the state demands sacrifice from its citizens it will be forthcoming. We live in multiple symbolic orders: the demands of politics can be displaced by those of morality, and vice versa. Moreover, political meanings are contested and can themselves fail. The Russian effort in the First World War collapsed when the Russian soldier no longer thought the state an appropriate object of sacrifice. This happened again in the Soviet Union and Eastern Europe seventy-five years later. Wars end when armies go home. When the symbolic order of sovereignty comes to seem as foreign to its own citizens as that of a distant state, the capacity of the state to maintain itself in and through the bodies of its citizens disappears. The experience of revolution in the West tells us that this collapse of a symbolic order can happen incredibly quickly. The change, however, can be in the opposite direction as well. The Argentine experience with the invasion of the Malvinas teaches us this lesson, as does the recent mobilization of American power in pursuit of the war on terrorism.

We cannot know in advance which meanings—political, moral, or familial—will dominate in any particular situation. However, even if political sacrifice has been resisted at particular moments or for particular causes, the idea of self-sacrifice has not been resisted in the modern nation-state. Citizens have lived with the knowledge that, under some set of possible circumstances, the state could demand sacrifice and there would be no grounds of objection. The unique quality of the political reveals itself in imagining this moment of "exceptionality," which always appears to us as simultaneously familiar and strange.[43] This combination of the most natural and the most unnatural points us in the right direction: sacrifice is ritual, not labor. Americans, in particular, are not yet done with the magic of political life. The Constitution, we say, is the product of an act of popular sovereignty. For the Constitution, individuals will sacrifice themselves and they can be conscripted. For its sake, the entire population is put at risk.

Man's capacity for sacrifice expresses his aspiration to transcend the conditions of labor. Labor is always a burden. It takes time and effort; it is never guaranteed success. We labor only to fail in the end. We are overwhelmed by the recalcitrance of the material which we would shape to embody our ideas; we are defeated by circumstance; we are let down by the weakness of the body and the failure of the will. We labor until we die, and still we are not done, for the world always threatens to return to disorder. The same limits attach to knowledge. We seek to learn until we die, and still we are not done, for our knowledge is never commensurate with the world. Sacrifice, on the other hand, is perfect, complete, and done in a moment.

To sacrifice is to enact an ultimate meaning, not as yet another project but as an irreducible fact. Sacrifice is a ritual of instantiation that literally takes the subject outside the limits of time and space, and

---

[43] Carl Schmitt was right to focus on the exception as a moment beyond law. He was wrong, however, to look to the exercise of authority instead of looking to the sacrificial act of the citizen. See Schmitt, *Political Theology* 5.

beyond the structure of the proposition. Meaning is present not as a goal or an ambition to be achieved but as an infinite presence. The body is fully absorbed in and by the symbolic. The Islamic martyr, we are told, believes that on death he will find himself immediately in the presence of Allah, satisfied in every way. This is the mythic expression of completeness outside the domain of labor. We can reject the literalism of the myth, but we cannot deny the experience of an infinite meaning in the extraordinary act.

Sacrifice, accordingly, is that form of meaning which stands in opposition to labor. Labor always deploys the process of craft. Every craft takes up discrete projects; each one follows a plan. Every plan has a beginning, a middle, and an end. This is no less true of the labor of politics. Labor is not, however, the only way we relate to a world of symbolic meanings. Meaning enters the world through the magic of transubstantiation. Participation in sacrifice is participation in the very foundation of the world. This is the sacred quality of violence. To fail to see this is to see only a suffering carpenter on the Cross.

This opposition of sacrifice and labor is not one between distinct kinds of acts. The same act can be both. Sacrifice and labor refer to forms of meaning, not instances of behavior. Indeed, an individual can see a single act in both dimensions: self-sacrifice for the state is always labor as well. This is just the way we view the virtues and costs of battle: an expression of sacrifice but also a labor of death. It is, we might say, "a sacred project." Nor should we expect victims to celebrate acts of sacrifice. Knowing that my political identity makes me a potential target of a terrorist attack does not lead me to celebrate the possibility of that sacrifice for the state. The terrorist and his victims are, in a sense, out of sync. The terrorist may celebrate the symbolic act of self-sacrifice; the victim finds the threat of death intruding into his or her ordinary world of labor—a world directed at putting off death. Conventional wars between nation-states were efforts to synchronize a politics of sacrifice.

Every symbolic order, I suspect, has a rhythm that moves between transubstantiation and labor. Freud spoke of an "oceanic feeling"; others speak of the flash of creative genius or the presence of grace. I would speak of the experience of love. Like politics, love is sustained through labor: for example, the labor of creating and maintaining the family. But also like politics, the labor of love is founded on an experience of transubstantiation. That is an experience of realizing wholly and completely an ultimate meaning that does not exist in space and time. This is love as infinite—not fulfilled in time but timeless. At these moments we know the whole immediately and completely. This is love as a force that destroys the finite boundaries of the body, as the subject expands through the beloved to a unity with all that is meaningful in the world.[44] We can no more wholly separate these moments of transubstantiation and labor than we can separate the morally free act from the causally determined one. Rather, these are different ways of understanding experience. No meaningful act is wholly one or the other, although the way that we understand ourselves may emphasize one over the other. I can see my life as labor for my family's well-being, but I can see those same acts as infused with a self-sacrificing love that binds me to them—and to the world through them—as an ultimate value. We move back and forth between the divine image of Genesis one and the finite laborer of Genesis two.

We experience ourselves as more than laborers on a symbolic field; we know the world to be fully and completely ours. In biblical terms, the world is ours to name. This is the sacred quality of man and the foundation of human dignity. Politics shares this rhythm and projects it upon the world. In politics, however, the metaphysics of sacrifice—the complete transparency of the self to an infinite meaning—takes the form of literal violent destruction of the finite self. The violent, sacrificial character of politics is not simply a function of its importance—an entire world can be at stake. Every symbolic form puts an entire world at stake. Few are willing to die for the sake of art or even science; even fewer are willing to kill. Galileo recanted, and one would hope that most great scientists and artists would have done the same. Yet Western religion was, and Western politics remains, different in this respect. Christianity is founded on a cult of martyrdom; citizens who recant too early are considered political traitors—itself a capital offense. Self-sacrifice is built into the structure of these beliefs. It is not correct to say that religion and politics are "more important" than science or art. Nor can we say that the former are capable of constitut-

---

[44] See P. Kahn, *Law and Love: The Trials of King Lear* 141 (2000).

ing individual identity in a way that the latter are not. Every symbolic form constitutes identity from a particular point of view. We cannot say which among these multiple worlds will be particularly compelling to an individual subject.

Every symbolic form is capable of a comprehensive reach: we can see science aesthetically; we can understand all that we do from the perspective of religious faith. The politics of sovereignty is no different in this respect. It can attach at any point; it has the fluidity of the sacred. Any object can become an icon, any point a site of pilgrimage. The sovereign shares the ubiquity of Mary, who has been sighted in trees, pastures, and office buildings. So, too, with the dizzying appearance of a politics of ultimate meaning, can the death of one man be made into a national cause that can bring about the sacrifice of millions or find, in the "affront to national honor," a cause for war. Viewed from the perspective of labor, none of this makes any sense. Except that, without the sacred, labor itself lacks a ground adequate to overcome man's sense of himself as fallen.

Carl Schmitt makes an important point here about politics.[45] We cannot say in the abstract what the content of political belief will be. Politics can attach to any cultural production or set of distinctions, including such "natural" categories as territory, race, or ethnicity. Political understandings, for example, can attach to science and art, even if we say that, considered in themselves, they are not political. They can also attach to moral ideals: justice or equality, for example. Surely, an element of a European political consciousness—and still an aspect of Western self-understanding—has been that ours is a "civilized" world, by which we refer, in part, to science and art and, in part, to moral and religious norms. The Western way of war goes so far as to protect great works of art.[46] According to Schmitt, politics adds a dimension of intensity to other beliefs. It places those beliefs—from whatever source—at the center of a world of ultimate meanings to be defended through the medium of violence and sacrifice.

The willingness to kill and be killed distinguishes the political as a distinct symbolic domain. The objects that call forth the reciprocal

---

[45] C. Schmitt, *The Concept of the Political* 37–38 (G. Schwab, trans. 1996).
[46] 1954 Hague Convention for the Protection of Cultural Property in the Event of Armed Conflict art. 1(a), 249 U.N.T.S. 240–88, entry into force August 7, 1956.

violence of sacrifice are as arbitrary as the objects in which the premoderns located the sacred. This does not mean that we should be
indifferent to differences between these objects but only that there is
no neutral position from which we can assess their political meanings.
Neutrality is no more possible here than it is with respect to sacred
objects or practices. Political beliefs speak to a particular community;
they do not offer a universal, normative measure. Friends and enemies
speak the same language, but the referents of their words are entirely
different. In this sense, they speak right past one another.

We cannot predict in advance where the sacred will appear; we cannot foresee what will come to represent the sacred quality of our politics. Even the most mundane act or object can come to be seen as an
element of the "American way of life." To understand a person or
thing as sacred is not a matter of giving it "added value." Value in this
quantitative sense is always an attribute of labor. The sacred does not
exist in the dimension of comparative value and capital preservation.
Just the opposite: the sacred is always at the edge of its own destruction. The *mysterium tremendum* terrifies as it sanctifies. We know the
person as a saint when he sacrifices his own life. We know the sovereign as an ultimate value when sovereignty threatens to consume the
entire well-being of the state. In this dimension, destruction is not
labor lost but labor transcended. This is what the counternarrative
preserves as living memory.

In the West we are never far from the story of the Fall, but neither
are we far from the story of recovery. The model of recovery is the
sacrifice of Isaac, a story not simply of religious faith but of political
foundations. The test of Abraham's faith was belief in the paradox
that, in order to found a nation, he had to sacrifice his only legitimate son. There would be no nation until and unless the divine appeared. That appearance of the divine, however, would consume
the very being of the profane, that is, the son. The nation becomes
possible not as a familial project of labor in either of its generative
senses. A nation begins only with a sacred foundation—just what
fallen man cannot give himself. That is the meaning of sacrifice—a
making sacred through destruction of finite form. This is the paradox
of the sacred: we must destroy to create, die to live. Our politics has

followed this paradox from the beginning: we maintain the nation by sacrificing the sons.[47]

The demand for sacrifice tests our faith in the ultimate meaning—the sovereignty—of the polity, just as Abraham was tested. In fact, we cannot learn that we have this faith until we are tested. That test is not proof to a third party but constitutive for the subject. Fortunately or not, Western citizens have had no trouble passing this test in their relationship to the nation-state. Surely this should not surprise us: we live in a culture that begins with the twin sacrifices of Isaac and Jesus as moments in recovery from the Fall. In politics, as in religion, through death is life.

Labor can preserve but it cannot found the world. Paradoxically, to bring into being a meaning that is worth living for, one must first be willing to engage in an act of self-sacrifice. We know this intuitively in our everyday life. A person unwilling to sacrifice is a person without love. Such persons can see no further than their own interests. They live in a world without objective value. There is nothing against which they measure themselves or which they can claim should be of value to others.

Political violence, then, is not simply a form of labor but is the answer to man's condition as symbolic laborer. Political violence is about redemption from a life of labor. This is why the act of political violence shows us a perfect match of destruction and construction. They are one and the same. Terrible as war may be, we find repeatedly that the experience stands out in people's lives as the point at which they knew a kind of perfection of meaning.[48] This can be equally true of victims as well as victimizers. Once suffering becomes sacrifice, it transcends its own finite conditions. It is constitutive of an identity that can ground or re-ground a life. At the moment of sacrifice, the individual

---

[47] Wilfred Owen makes the direct connection of the war to Abraham, who now rejects the ram in place of his son: "But the old man would not so, but slew his son. / And half of the seed of Europe, one by one." W. Owen, "The Parable of the Old Man and the Young," in *The Collected Poems of Wilfred Owen* 42 (1965). Modernity has largely overcome the gendered character of political experience, first by extending the domain of destruction—that is, sacrifice—to the entire population and, more recently, by allowing women to enter the battlefield itself.

[48] See J. Gray, *The Warriors: Reflections on Men in Battle* (1973); Hedges, *War Is the Force That Gives Us Meaning* (2002).

knows exactly who he or she is and knows the value of life. Labor, on the other hand, never escapes doubt, for labor is never commensurate with death. It is death put off, which is never enough for man.

Terrible as sacrifice may be, it is the point to which reference is made in understanding all that happens thereafter. This is true not only for individuals but for entire societies. The ages of American political life are marked by the violence that founds the meaning of this world: the Revolution, the Civil War, World War II, the Cold War, and perhaps now the war on terror. It is also true of internal wars, even when they take the form of terror and repression. The imaginary construction of political sacrifice means that those who carry out these violent acts have to believe that the nation is at risk and that they, too, are willing to sacrifice themselves. Political killing is always the reciprocal side of a willingness to be killed. Without that reciprocity, killing is just crime and personal pathology—of which there is no doubt plenty—passing for the political. Under conditions of belief in reciprocity, however, even repressive violence can appear as a form of sacred violence. For this reason, those involved will always try to resurrect the moment as foundational in their own lives and in the history of the nation. Argentine dirty warriors want recognition for their victory; Pinochet and his supporters remain unrepentant; Milosevic still believes he embodied the Serb nation.

These views can change, just as religious beliefs can fail. Nevertheless, we cannot manage the movement from one set of beliefs to another. Even punishment can be seen within the prism of sacrifice: what we call justice may be seen as only the politics of war continued by other means.[49] Nor are truth commissions or any other innovative form of "transitional justice" likely to shake these beliefs, at least in the short term.[50] These beliefs are a matter of faith, not evidence. The creationist is not moved by the evidence of evolution. Those who believe in their own sacrificial identification with the sovereign will not be moved by the evidence of their victims' suffering.

---

[49] Those Japanese convicted of war crimes after the Second World War, for example, quickly came to be seen as sacrificial victims of a process that was only victors' justice, that is, the final playing out of the war itself. See J. Dower, *Embracing Defeat* (1999).

[50] See N. Meredith, *Coming to Terms: South Africa's Search for Truth* 314–19 (1999).

CONCLUSION: POLITICAL EVIL

Because the character of political violence as both labor and sacrifice is so obscured by our willful belief in the narrative of the modern state, I have focused particular attention on the deeper rhythm of the symbolic form. Only within this matrix of belief do we get to the heart of evil in modernity. The evil of modern politics is an inverse of the dynamic of the shame of nature represented by the slave, which I described in the previous chapter. The evil of slavery arises out of the desire to localize and expel the merely natural from the symbolic order of the society. If the body is only the shame of nature, it is no longer the site of the passion of Christ; it is not the object of sacrifice or the material proof of faith. A slave-owning class is quick to show its own willingness to sacrifice, to show that it is not bound to the body but fully invested in an idea. This was the language of revolution and thus of popular sovereignty to which Jefferson and the founders appealed.[51] But if the paradigmatic political evil is not slavery but the tortured and destroyed body, then the victim of evil can as easily be the master, who appears now as the citizen-soldier. He becomes the victim of his own imagination. If the master would not be a slave, he would willingly assume the place of Christ. Suffering is proof of his faith in an ultimate meaning. Suffering becomes torture at the moment faith fails.

To the outsider, the ritual infliction of pain—even if willingly assumed in an act of self-sacrifice—will always appear evil. It will appear as a form of that oldest paradigm of evil, idolatry, for the outsider does not see the transubstantiation of the flesh but only the pain. He sees a false promise of redemption, a worship of nothing but an empty idol for whose sake suffering is inflicted and pain endured. This was the reaction of the European colonizers to the sacrificial rites of the indigenous Americans. Outside the faith, other explanations are offered for this suffering: coercion, false consciousness, fear, ideology, or the Devil. To see another culture's rituals of sacrifice as evil, one need not believe all such rituals to be idolatrous. One need only believe

[51] The lingering attachment of southern society to the duel suggests the same distancing from the idea of the body as merely natural. J. Williams, *Dueling in the Old South: Vignettes of Social History* 26–27 (1980).

that this particular practice fails. In place of recovery from finitude it offers only a false path of flight from death.

The experience of "seeing through" sacrifice to a world of pain and death is not, however, only the experience of the outsider. The insider can become the outsider when faith fails. One's own practices of sacrifice can come to be seen as empty. Every ritual of sacrifice stands just at the edge of failure. Even Christ suffered doubt. The failure of faith is as familiar an experience as the fullness of faith. When we lose faith, we no longer see the transcendence of death but only a futile flight from death in which we have become victims. We see pain in place of life.

For the sake of the deathless sovereign, politics creates a world of killing and being killed, of reciprocal acts of sacrifice. This is a world of ultimate meaning as compelling as those of any religious faith. But precisely because it is a violent world, the line between sacrifice and coercion can dissolve for the actor himself. Practically, we see this in the institution of conscription: conscription is not exactly coercion— it is not the same as impressment in a foreign service—but it becomes increasingly coercive as faith in the transcendent meaning of the polity fails. The ultimate failure is when the conscript sees himself as just another victim of state violence. From the perspective of this victim, the conditions of warfare collapse into those of torture. The victim knows that he may be brought to suffer terrible pain or death, that his body will be forced to bear a political meaning he neither agrees with nor has faith in. In politics, killing is always linked to the perception of a threat of being killed. That means that every participant can appear to himself as a victim. Without faith in the sovereign, sacrifice becomes victimhood and injury becomes torture. The war-wounded veteran is likely to resist this reading of his own body. He will insist that the missing leg is a mark of his own participation in the sovereign. But that faith is vulnerable, and when it collapses he becomes, in his own eyes, another victim.[52]

---

[52] The 2004 election showed that American conflict over Vietnam continues to play itself out in this contrast between victimhood and sacrifice. Something similar has been happening in Germany with respect to participation in the Second World War: a dispute over who the victims are.

The experience in the trenches of the First World War, for example, comes to appear to many as nothing other than a torturous mauling and destruction of bodies—a task well beyond the capacity of labor to justify or repair. For the soldier who has lost faith in the sovereign character of a politics of sacrifice, war becomes a scene of horrendous torture: broken bodies, pain, and death.[53] Once a family loses this faith in the sovereign, it will see only the state conscripting and killing its loved ones. This is an entirely familiar phenomenon. The sacred loses its power, and we are left with the tortured body—a residue of politics when faith in the sovereign has disappeared. Wilfred Owen captures this residue of the dying body when he writes: "What passing-bells for those who die as cattle?"[54] Not sacrifice but slaughter; not the transcendence of the merely human but the evil of human loss. To those who do not hear God, Abraham's action must have looked like a bizarre torture of his son.

A secular age looks back at the wars of religion and sees in them a great evil: bodies were destroyed for "no real reason." All the suffering and destruction to what end? Similarly, we look at the tortured destruction of witches and heretics as a kind of madness producing great evil. Once faith is gone, we are left with only tortured and maimed bodies. We are beginning to see our own political past in this way. We see not political martyrs but senseless suffering. No longer understanding the sacred character of the political, we see only the victims' tortured bodies. We can no longer distinguish clearly between friends and enemies among those broken bodies. Do we not all die the same death? We see a field of arbitrary death and destruction that contributes nothing to the well-being that we would place at the heart of the contemporary political narrative. Our customs of war—humanitarian law—may harden us to some forms of destruction over others. But once we lose faith in the ultimate value of politics, there is no particular reason to prefer the killing of young men over others. Nor is there any reason to prefer death by the modern technology of war over the primitive methods of the terrorist or the dirty warrior. To the politics of well-

---

[53] The greatest fictional representation of the tortured quality of the battlefield may be E. Remarque, *All Quiet on the Western Front* (A. Wheen, trans. 1956).

[54] W. Owen, "Anthem for Doomed Youth," in *The Collected Poems*, 44.

being, these are senseless distinctions. If there is no difference between the tortured body and the sacrificed body—both are victims of an idolatrous belief—the debate about the technology of warfare is an argument with the Devil. In a world with no ambition beyond well-being, a politics of sovereignty that leads us to the edge of total destruction in a nuclear Armageddon must be condemned as the greatest evil.

Or, I should say, this is what we might begin to see—or even hope to see—but still not quite yet. The politics of the sublime, of the sacred character of the nation, recedes but is not yet gone. The counternarrative persists. The popular sovereign remains a brooding presence capable of enthralling the nation. It remains a hungry god, and we remain willing to feed it our children. We react in only half-forgotten ways to the attack of September 11. We appeal again to the old language of sacrifice. We fail to see the tortured bodies of the victims of our actions as we pursue the Western politics of sacrifice, of killing and being killed, first in Afghanistan and then in Iraq. We see, instead, the self-sacrifice of our own citizens as they affirm in and through their own lives the ultimate meaning of the popular sovereign. We continue to distinguish friend from enemy.

Torture and sacrifice are reciprocal images. Moreover, they reside in the very same act. This ambiguity of man's body—tortured and divine—is the imagery of the Cross. If we could always tell the difference between sacrifice and torture, then we would have no trouble distinguishing love from evil. In politics, however, killing and being killed are so inextricably linked that we cannot tell them apart. Our own history of violence appears to us as a sacred history of sacrifice. It does not appear that way to others, who see only the destruction and pain, not the promise of the sacred.

Not surprisingly, political meanings remain entangled in the deepest mythical foundations of the culture. If we would call torture evil, as we must, then we have indeed reached the goal of our inquiry into evil, for evil is located at the source of our own symbolic world. Man is out of place in a world constituted by labor. To find his way out, he must overcome death itself. Just there, in the flight from death, we find the foundation of evil.

CONCLUSION

■ ■ ■ ■

TRAGEDY, COMEDY, AND THE
BANALITY OF EVIL

Every Jewish scholar raised in the postwar period feels a need to write his or her book on the Holocaust. This has been mine. I have done it without raising the Jewish question explicitly, and with no inquiry into the historical origins and context of the Holocaust. Still, much that I have argued bears directly on our understanding of the Holocaust. On my analysis, what was peculiar in Germany was the intersection of two forms of evil. The evil of politics—killing and being killed for the state—but also the evil of slavery—localizing in the other the shame of nature. The Jew was simultaneously the enemy and the shame of nature.[1] He was represented as physically repulsive, as weak and perverse—that is, as shameful in his nature yet still a threat. Hitler spoke of Jews as "apes" and "parasites"; Himmler, as having "slave-like souls."[2] The Aryan race expressed again that prelapsarian man who is an image of God, while the Jews were the "mightiest counterpart."[3] In the peculiar dynamics of Nazi ideology, the competing understandings of nature were expressed in the double perceptions of the Jew as the enemy but also as a threat to the biological stock of the German race. The ideology of slavery under conditions of war easily moves beyond expulsion of the shame of nature to physical destruction. The Nazis began by dreaming of expulsion to Madagascar but ended up at Auschwitz. Out of this combination of evils emerges that distinctly modern phenomenon of genocide.

---

[1] While the Nazis believed that the Jew was the product of a discredited high culture, they also believed that the consequence was a perversion of nature. On the culture/nature distinction, see chapter 4 above.

[2] H. Arendt, *The Origins of Totalitarianism* 457 (1958) (quoting Himmler).

[3] A. Hitler, *Mein Kampf* 300 (R. Manheim, trans. 1971); see also ibid. 302 ("Jewish people . . . without any true culture").

My inquiry has not been one of applied political or moral theory. I have pursued a more elusive issue: not what it was about Germans that allowed the murder of six million Jews but what it is about man that can account for such evil. I do not think we will find the answer to that question by looking outside ourselves, at the circumstances under which groups and individuals act.[4] Of course, circumstances matter, but they matter in the sense that they make socially and politically possible that which is existentially possible. They do not make us other than we are, and what we are includes a vast potential for evil. Whether we act on that potential depends, in part, on our circumstances—personal and political. Until we understand that potential, however, we will always be puzzled by the turn toward evil, no matter how desperate the circumstances. After all, those same circumstances can bring out the very best in man as well. We find saints among the poverty-stricken and pacifists in belligerent times.

The sources of evil are as deep as the sources of love. Both arise out of the intolerable character of our own finitude. We can never be content with the fact that we will die. The difference between evil and love is the difference between flight from, and transcendence of, death. Because of their common origin, these are not always easy to distinguish even for those within the experience. Consider, for example, the way that patriotism can become violently xenophobic, or love intolerant and possessive. In chapter 2, I investigated the way that existing forms of transcendence come to be seen as forms of flight, producing the perceptions of idolatry and Pharisaism. In chapter 3, I investigated the way that love itself can produce the conditions of evil. The transcendence of death through love is so close to death itself that we can turn away in flight, producing the evils of hatred and murder. In chapter 4, I argued that slavery falls directly within this tension of flight and transcendence, for it is belief in the slave's failure to transcend the conditions of the shame of nature—the finite, suffering body—that marks the difference with the master. This is a measure of the other

[4] See, e.g., D. Goldhagen, *Hitler's Willing Executioners: Ordinary Germans and the Holocaust* (1996); D. Horowitz, *The Deadly Ethnic Riot* (2001); E. Staub, *Roots of Evil: The Origins of Genocide and Other Group Violence* (1992).

that easily turns in upon the self, appearing as the master's flight from the conditions of his own finitude: there is no slavery in the West without a guilty conscience. It can also ground a self-hatred among a repressed population—whether slave or colonized. Finally, in chapter 5, I argued that the difference between transcendence and flight in politics can come down to the difference between winning and losing a war. This is not because the difference is merely subjective, a matter of where one stands. Rather, it is because transcendence is a function of faith. When we lose faith, all that is left of the sacrificial act is the maimed and destroyed body. At that point, sacrifice takes on the appearance of torture. Western politics replicates the deepest truths of Western religion: whether Christ and, before him, Isaac are seen as self-sacrificing or as tortured is a matter of faith alone.

As long as Western man has engaged in self-reflection, he has found in himself a potential for terrible actions. Oedipus kills his father and marries his mother; Adam and Eve sin; Cain murders Abel. And so it goes. To understand evil, we have to take seriously the conceptual resources of our tradition. Most especially, we have to take account of the religious origins of much that is still constitutive of the Western way of thought. Evil is not a fact of our nature, as it was produced by a creator, God. It is rather a possibility created by the conceptual structure within which we understand ourselves and our relationship to the world. As that conceptual structure changes, the character of evil also changes. It changes as a matter of self-understanding, that is, of what we are prepared to see in ourselves, but also as a matter of fact in our relationship to the world. There is no subjective and objective in this respect. The world that presents itself as meaningful to us is only the world that our own imaginations make possible. To understand the conceptual structure of the imagination is to understand the possibilities for our being in the world. Those possibilities have been shaped as much by the Judeo-Christian tradition of fall, grace, and redemption as by the Enlightenment tradition of reason and objectivity.

We cannot understand evil without taking into account the nature of the sacred, not because evil is sin or a violation of divine commands but because the sacred presents itself as a distinctive and ultimately important truth apart from which a subject cannot make sense of himself or of his experience of the world. Intuitively we know that evil and the sacred are deeply connected. The Fall is part of the religious myth of creation. For millennia, the symbol of evil was a fallen angel, Satan. Approaching evil, we still feel that we are beyond the boundaries of our ordinary forms of experience and explanation. Evil is not just some deficient form of behavior or a forgetting of the rules. For this reason, the inquiry into evil does not start within the profane and everyday but starts instead with those experiences that touch upon the sacred. Just as pollution is always tied to the sacred for archaic man, evil remains intimately related to the sacred for us.

There are, however, as many ways to represent the sacred as there are forms of experiencing an ultimate meaning. At various points in this inquiry, I have pointed not only to traditional religious forms but to love, to nationalism, and to the infinite potential of language and consciousness. All offer perspectives on the sacred. If we no longer experience a world of the sacred, then we will have little use for a concept of evil. Evil will be just another term for the bad or the disapproved. It may be a form of emphasis—the really bad—but it will no longer point to the problematic character of being itself. It will be a sociological or psychological phenomenon, not a metaphysical problem. My point has not been to deny that bad actions require psychological and sociological explanations—and responses—but rather to open up an exploration of the sense we have that more is at issue in the phenomenon of evil.

Evil, I have argued, arises out of the deepest tension in the soul of man. Despite his participation in the infinite or an ultimate meaning, the subject is bound to a finite body and a particular set of circumstances. For a subject with aspirations for the infinite, this is an intolerable contradiction. We want to identify wholly and completely with the infinite in our nature—with God's love, the nation, or the awe before the ultimate majesty of nature or the moral law. This produces the demand for sacrifice, for sacrifice is an act of transubstantiation by which the body becomes a point of the showing forth of the infinite. When we fail in this movement of transubstantiation—and we all do fail at some point and in some ways—we find only death. At that point we discover the possibility of evil in each of us. Evil is the rage of an infinite soul before the finite conditions of the subject. This contradiction of the infinite and the finite—the tension between transcendence and flight from death—is the phenomenon I have explored here.

I do not claim to have offered a complete account of evil, let alone a complete account of all the bad things that happen to people or that they do to one another. Circumstances and pathology—individual and social—certainly contribute their share to misery. Not all suffering is evil, but all of it is bad. The battlefield may offer an opportunity for self-transcendence, but so does familial love. Even though familial love offers its own opportunities for evil, I would choose love over battle. Still, the choice is not up to me. We inherit the forms of meaning as much as we inherit the forms of technology. My effort has been to illuminate from within one strand of our experience: the existential conditions of evil.

Much contemporary inquiry turns to external circumstances to explain evil. It asks what are the conditions under which individuals or societies commit atrocious actions. These are valuable inquiries. Nevertheless, to make this turn to circumstance is to turn away from the particular insights of Judeo-Christian thought; it is effectively to return to the classical tradition. Oedipus committed evil acts because he was unfortunate in his birth. He was a victim of circumstances, doing that which he would have preferred not to do and that which he would never have chosen to do. He lived in a terrifying world precisely because he could never be sure of the meaning of his own actions. Clever as he was, he could not reason himself to the truth of his own actions. For the Greeks, the understanding of circumstance began with an inquiry into the gods. For us, it begins with an inquiry into history and sociology. These inquiries are not the same, yet they do share a common impulse to explain evil by explaining the context within which behavior makes sense or fails to make sense to the actor. What we do is a product of where we are, rather than an expression of who we are.

Adam and Eve are not the victims of circumstance. They know exactly what they are doing. They have been warned, yet they sin. There is no mistake when Cain murders Abel. To understand evil in the Judeo-Christian tradition, we have to turn inward. For Oedipus, the world was impenetrable to good intentions. His was a world in which reason was never commensurate with its object. But in *Genesis*, man names creation. From the beginning, there is a symmetry between man as subject and his world as object. This man lives in a fully human world because his world is the object of his own creation: first as representation—that is, naming—and, second, as the product of his will. The human world in this tradition is always a product of labor. After the Fall, we know the good and we labor to achieve it. We also know, however, that we are dust and shall return to dust. To live with the knowledge of both is, we might say, superhuman.

To understand evil, we must understand the character of the will: that faculty by which we realize the self in the world and the world in the self. We find a tension between two forms of realization: a moment of identification and a moment of separation, of transcendence and of finitude. We are bound to the world wholly and completely as to an object of infinite concern. Traditionally, this was the appearance of the sacred. In our contemporary world, it is the moment of love. Love grounds our concern about the world. But just as love brought Adam to labor, so are we still condemned to labor for our love. Evil emerges out of the gap between transcendence and labor, that is, between the aspiration for the infinite and the finite character of man. One of the memorable symbols of the Holocaust was the sign at Auschwitz that read "Arbeit Macht Frei." The symbolism here is richer than that of a deliberate falsehood in a camp devoted to extermination. Rather, it is a perversion of the deepest aspects of the Western tradition: no matter how hard man works to achieve the good, he cannot save himself. That freedom which is redemption must come from outside, from the sacred.

The promise of Western religion has been to overcome this gap. One representation of that promise was the law God gave the Jews. That representation is succeeded by the perfect synthesis that is Christ himself: the infinite realized in the finite. Man himself cannot find that synthesis on his own; it is not a matter of realizing the truth of his own being. Instead, what is required is an act of redemptive grace—a showing forth of the sacred—in order to obtain again that Edenic bliss man possessed before the Fall. Western religious forms have never secured a single form of synthesis. Indeed, as I argued in chapter 2, the religious forms of evil are best understood as a family argument over the nature of this synthesis. No synthesis is stable, because it is the tension itself that constitutes our nature. Accordingly, in the religious tradition, evil appears as the "false" synthesis. It is the claim to have realized the infinite in the finite in a manner that appears now to be a rejection of the "truth." Idolatry, for example, is not worship of the wrong god; it is worship of nothing at all. This is not different from the evil of political life: once faith in a political sovereign fails, what had been seen as the realization of ultimate value appears only as the evil of meaningless death and tortured destruction. When faith fails, we not only look foolish to ourselves but we may discover that we have killed and destroyed those we loved—as well as those we hated— for no purpose whatsoever. To those who lacked the faith in the first place, including those with different faiths, all that was ever seen was death and destruction.

My account of the sources and character of evil stands opposed to the most famous of Holocaust books: Hannah Arendt's *Eichmann in Jerusalem*. Her conclusion was that to understand the Holocaust we have to take up the category of "administrative murder." When we do so, we find the "banality of evil." Eichmann was not a disturbingly bad man by our ordinary standards of character. The prosecution tried to paint him as a kind of sadist, but that description just did not hold. He was, instead, a kind of clown—a completely banal person. On Arendt's view, he lacked the capacity to think, meaning he lacked the capacity to use language in a fully human way. He could not pursue a genuine discourse, because he could not take up the other's point of view. He could not imagine the other as a subject; he could not put himself in the place of another. Without this, language is not possible. Instead of discourse, Eichmann's verbal expressions never advanced beyond the repetition of clichés. Unlike the manipulative politician who produces a propaganda machine, Eichmann believed the clichés he mouthed. He lived a life in which the clichés had become regulative ideals.[5]

Eichmann spent his life worrying about complying with the spirit of the law and measuring his own success within the bureaucratic hier-

---

[5] H. Arendt, *Eichmann in Jerusalem: A Report on the Banality of Evil* 48–49 (1964).

archy. That he was killing people simply never—or at least rarely—entered his moral conscience. For Arendt, Eichmann represents a possibility within modernity: evil, she said, has no "roots," by which she meant that it is a surface phenomenon. "The phenomenon of evil deeds," she wrote, "committed on a gigantic scale, could not be traced to any particularity of wickedness, pathology, or ideological conviction in the doer, whose only personal distinction was a perhaps extraordinary shallowness."[6] Germany had become a nation that had somehow lost the capacity to think or, minimally, lacked sufficient thought to resist the turn to genocide led by Hitler and the Nazi party leadership.[7] We cannot explain exactly how and why this happened in Germany but not everywhere in Europe. Some nations resisted the Nazis' effort to pursue the "final solution"; some did not. In some places, resistance was directed by the political leadership; in others, the sense of the moral retained its grip on the general population. In Germany, however, the moral point of view collapsed completely.

Arendt suggests that Nazi Germany realized a state made possible by the conditions of modernity: bureaucratic, technologically proficient, and possessing a surplus population. The possibility of genocide, in her view, remains an aspect of the modern condition. That these conditions made the Third Reich possible, however, does not explain why that possibility was realized. Why these conditions produce genocide in some places and not others is a mystery as deep as the origins of thought itself. Why do people stop thinking? Why is it that killing no longer looks to them like murder? To answer these questions, Arendt, too, would turn from the existential to the social and the historical. It happened in Germany because of the disasters of the First World War and the Weimar Republic, because of the appearance of Hitler and the incompetence of other political elites, because the rest of Europe let it happen—the list of conditions is as long as the historical inquiry itself.

Arendt is right to emphasize the ordinary character of evil. She is also right to emphasize its historical particularity and its unpredictable

[6] H. Arendt "Thinking and Moral Considerations: A Lecture," 38 *Social Research* 417 (1971).

[7] On morality, mores, and thought, see H. Arendt. "Personal Responsibility under Dictatorship," in *The Listener* 205 (Aug. 1964).

character. We cannot say in advance whether extreme conditions will produce heroism or evil. But she is wrong to link the ordinary to the banal. She is wrong to think that Eichmann's failure is one of thought, as if evil resides in a forgetting of the human condition. Her error here is of a piece with her error in thinking that concern with the "social question"—the question of state responsibility for the material conditions of life itself—precludes a genuine politics.[8] Politics and genuine discourse are, for her, one and the same. Anything less is less than human; it is to fall back into the material conditions of our animal nature. It is mere labor. Sacrifice, however, is never the end of a logical argument, although it is the literal end of political discourse. Politics is not "thoughtless" even when it is not discursive. Politics is its own conceptual form, which does not measure itself against the standards of logic or morality.[9] The language of politics is rhetoric, and it is rhetoric that Arendt confuses with banality.

Expanding the scope of the inquiry into the forms of evil reveals there is little that is banal about evil. Banality suggests a flattening of experience, a kind of lack of personal investment. But the inquiry into evil shows us a subject raging at his own mortality. It shows us a character who refuses the conditions of his own finitude, and would overcome those conditions by expelling the shame of nature and turning death into sacrifice. What Arendt sees as the banality of Eichmann's life appears actually to be the penetration of these existential impulses deep into the life of the ordinary citizen. Eichmann's banality is not different in kind from that of the ordinary citizen-soldier. The soldier, too, fails to think, if by that we mean trying to understand the world from the enemy's viewpoint. The soldierly virtues do not include self-reflection and discourse with or about the enemy. He does not engage in a discursive act; he kills, and he dies. He proves to himself and others that he is ready to sacrifice himself for the sake of an idea.

Indeed, Arendt's report on the trial of Eichmann reveals a person whose banality is always reaching toward the dignity of the political. Eichmann may mouth clichés, but they are about sacrifice, about the

---

[8] See H. Arendt, *On Revolution* 22–24, 59–114 (1965).

[9] See P. Kahn, *Putting Liberalism in Its Place* 236–40 (2005). Of course, any individual can measure politics against logic and morality, just as he can measure logic and morality against politics.

need to dedicate himself wholly to an idea, about adherence to a rule, and about the dignity that comes from disregard of his own personal interests. He has no toleration for corruption and wants only to be a purely political being. In his case, politics equates with following the rule of law in the spirit that the lawmaker—Hitler—would demand. This is his oddly modified Kantianism. It means being "hard" in the sense of suppressing whatever ordinary moral impulses he may have had. Eichmann, while not a statesman, shows us something of the meaning behind Goebbel's final remark that they would "go down in history as the greatest statesmen of all time or as the greatest criminals." This is just that intersection of transcendence and evil that I described in chapter 5.

Like Eichmann, soldiers do not just mouth the clichés of patriotism; they believe them. The alternative to thinking in Arendt's sense can be faith, not thoughtlessness. Soldiers do terrible things for the sake of their political faith. If they win, they may be heroes. If they lose, they may be an embarrassment to the progressive development of the nation—just as Eichmann was an embarrassment to postwar Germany. Eichmann feels this when he speaks of sacrificing himself to relieve the guilt of the new generation of Germans. He would be the scapegoat—again a cliché but one that motivates a conception of political sacrifice.

None of this excuses Eichmann's behavior. We are never just political beings; we are never without the capacity for moral judgment. That does not mean that the political is a normative order subordinate to the moral. At times, the political and the moral converge; at other times, the two are in competition with no "correct" outcome.[10] The triumph of the political, however, is not somehow the decline into banality. It is the power of the claim for sacrifice as the means for realizing a kind of immortality. Just here, we find the undeniable attraction in evil. It is the attraction of power: the power to put off death. That attraction, as I have argued, is there from the beginning in the myth of Cain.

In retrospect, the flight from death can always appear banal. To see it that way is already to acknowledge that the claim for transcendence

---

[10] On the competition between the moral and the political, see Kahn, *Putting Liberalism in Its Place* 244–56.

has failed. Evil would put off death by locating it in the other. This strategy is doomed to fail for death is our common fate. There is always something pathetic in evil, not, of course, at the moment that evil rages but when the guilty are put on trial. Viewing Eichmann, we find the pathos that is the failure of the human. It is the pathos of believing that an idol can be sacred or that political sacrifice can transcend death.

I have argued that the faith in redemption is necessary, but also necessarily bound up with its own failure. Man falls. No matter how deep his faith, he cannot escape doubt. When doubt leaves him only with the fact of his death, he turns away in rage. We cannot have the sacred without evil, love without hatred, or politics without enemies. If we must give up the sacred to avoid evil, we are being asked to give up the human. That possibility leads us either to a classical—and Kantian—world of pure reason, in which man is just one possible locus of reason, or to the contemporary ethos of entertainment in which we pursue the satisfaction of our particular interests and make no claim to any truth beyond the experience itself. These are the possibilities of reason and of interest. But between the reason of the Greeks and the interests of the moderns was an experience of the human in and through the faculty of the will. I do not believe we are in a position to reframe the character of our experience, such that love and evil disappear. In truth, we have no choice about the nature of the human. We can turn away from our existential condition as the infinite in the finite only for so long—regardless of whether we turn to reason or to interest.

And so Eichmann is hanged. He goes to his death with just that combination of dignity and banality that so puzzled Arendt. He claims to be a Christlike figure, even as he proclaims that he does not believe in God. He understands himself to be engaging in a kind of redemptive act of sacrifice for the nation, but he cannot express this in any way other than mouthing yet more clichés. Arendt might be right that by 1960 Eichmann appears as little more than a clown to those who would report on his behavior. But if he is a clown, this only repeats one of the oldest lessons of all: tragedy and comedy are not so very different from each other. The unresolvable antinomy in the human subject between the infinite and the finite produces tragedy; every claim to resolve that antinomy can, in the end, be seen as comic. Eichmann is a clown because he believes himself to be Christ, when, in fact, what we see is only a silly man hanging from the gallows. Of this kind of clowning, however, we are all in danger.

INDEX

Abel, 18, 126–27
Abraham, 35, 84n56, 204, 209. *See also* Isaac
action: choice and, 46; discourse and, 40–41; principles and, 46–47; reason and, 57; subjectivity and, 42. *See also* agency
Adam and Eve: and death, 114–16; and discourse, 38–39; fundamentalist interpretation of, 96–97; and love, 106–12; Oedipus versus Adam, 42; as plural being, 38; rationalist interpretation of, 97–98; and sex, 122n28; and shame, 44, 112–14; and sin, 88; and will, 38. *See also* Eve; *Genesis*
agency: evil dependent on, 16; of Oedipus, 25–26. *See also* action
angst, 13–14
antinomies: finite/infinite, 48–49, 51, 68; of nature, 150–54; of will, 51. *See also* dualisms
Apology (Plato), 24
Arendt, Hannah, 7, 10, 172, 217–21
Argentina, 206
Aristophanes, in Plato's *Symposium*, 107–8, 112
Aristotle, 6, 11, 23n11, 37n41, 115, 116, 146, 161
Auden, W. H., 133

Augustine, Saint, 38n, 40n47, 42n52, 88, 89, 110n4, 120n22
Auschwitz, 216

bad, evil versus, 2
banality of evil, 7, 217–19
Bayle, Pierre, 3–4
begetting, creation as, 79–80
beliefs. *See* faith; meaning
Benjamin, Walter, 51
body: Christianity and, 89; love and evil acting on, 140. *See also* sacrifice
Britain, 172n46

Cain, 18–19, 34, 126–27
care: love and, 111, 124, 134–35; pain and, 179
catechism, 35
celibacy, 109n
children: and authority, 121; existential meaning of, 115; innocence of, 120–22, 121n26; parent-child relationship, 120–21, 130–33, 135
choice: action and, 46; death and, 45–46; finitude and, 44–46; and meaning, 43–45; shame and, 47; subjectivity and, 42–47
Christ: and creator-created relationship, 78–80; efficient cause of, as unknown, 81; infinite/finite in,